MEN AND MOTORS OF
'THE AUSTIN'

Austin

"*Most everything worthwhile is born of some dreamer's dream.*"

Sir Herbert Austin (1866–1941) thought enough of the above quotation to keep a framed copy in his office at Longbridge. It originally came from a book he received as a prize for good attendance as a youngster at Sunday school. The image of Herbert Austin comes from the medallion produced by artist Jean Beddow for the 50th anniversary of the Austin Motor Company in 1955.

MEN AND MOTORS OF
'THE AUSTIN'

The inside story of
a century of car making at Longbridge

BARNEY SHARRATT

Haynes Publishing

First published in 2000

A catalogue record for this book is available
from the British Library

ISBN 1 85960 671 7

Library of Congress catalog card no. 00-131888

Published by Haynes Publishing, Sparkford,
Nr Yeovil, Somerset BA22 7JJ, England

Tel. 01963 442030 Fax 01963 440001
Int. tel. +44 1963 442030 Fax +44 1963 440001
E-mail: sales@haynes-manuals.co.uk
Web site: www.haynes.co.uk

Haynes North America, Inc.,
861 Lawrence Drive, Newbury Park,
California 91320, USA

Designed by G&M, Raunds, Northamptonshire
Printed and bound in England by
J. H. Haynes & Co. Ltd, Sparkford

Contents

A dedication to:

Petit George de la Maison Austin

No-one had a more intimate and practical knowledge of Austin motor cars of all eras than George Coates. George, an inspiration to all who knew him, died peacefully at the age of 91 in 1994.

George and I became great friends. What a pleasure it was to hear him recall the many fascinating details of the half century he chalked up at 'The Austin'. The variety of important assignments entrusted to him during those years show that Herbert Austin himself held George in high regard.

From 1924 onwards, George made many trips throughout France while testing Austin prototypes and struck up a friendship with Maurice Charpentier, an Austin agent in Le Mans. Some years ago, when I drove into Maurice's garage in my Austin A35, he looked a little confused when I passed on George's best wishes. Seconds later his eyes lit up, 'Ah mais oui, Petit George de la Maison Austin – un homme sans égal.' Maurice had summed up George perfectly: 'Little George of The Austin – a man without equal'.

George's stories provided the original inspiration for this book.

Introduction and acknowledgements

This story of 'The Austin' has, as far as possible, been presented in the words of the men themselves – words gleaned from numerous 'Men of The Austin' over the last 20 and more years.

Although this book is offered as a complete story in its own right, it is also intended to be something of both a supplement and complement to the splendid efforts of other writers on Austin and related companies. The works of Anders Clausager, Jeff Daniels, Sir Michael Edwardes, Graham Robson, Graham Turner, Dave Whyley, Bob Wyatt and others (see Bibliography) have allowed me the luxury of not having to repeat all the technical data, detailed production figures or political intrigue that they have so successfully provided and portrayed. Omitting such details has often meant steeling myself to the extreme but I have endeavoured to keep in mind the main objective of this book – that of enabling men of 'The Austin' to preserve in their own words the story behind almost a century of car making at Longbridge.

My main concern, having interviewed so many Austin men, right from the shop floor to senior management, is to portray adequately something of the eras in which they lived as well as something of the blood, sweat and tears that led to both successes and failures – and the joys and disappointments of both. In short, to depict life as it was for men of 'The Austin'.

I have tried to present the story in a balanced and non-judgmental fashion. Not an easy task when even those intimately involved regularly come up with very different versions of the one event. This being so, I have worked on the principle that preserving the differing views of many is the only hope of aspiring to anything like historical accuracy.

I do hope that some of the stories recounted herein are not seen as a denigration of great figures of the past. Two men in particular, the dynamic but rough and ready Leonard Lord, and the brilliant but idiosyncratic Alec Issigonis, were deservedly knighted for their services to this country. Great characters like that never fail to leave a wealth of stories in their wake, not all of them complimentary.

It is easy to see now how the British motor industry could have fared a great deal better than it did. But those responsible for its management seem to have been presented with an endless procession of problems to which there was never any such thing as a solution – unless they could have simply started afresh. Few competitors, for example, were saddled with such a complicated history or owned such a hotch-potch of plants as the increasingly chaotic BMC/BMH and British Leyland. No other industry was quite so used and abused, being expected at one time or another to act as this country's economic regulator or as a dispenser of social justice. It is difficult to appreciate the agonies management must have suffered in finding that they could rarely take the course of action that would have been right in the long run because of the serious (and perhaps even terminal) disruptions and hardships that would have immediately ensued.

In my earlier book, *Post War Baby Austins,* I managed to thank by name all 'Men of The Austin' who had so kindly helped me. For this present work I have been aided by so many of them that it would be quite impossible to do so. My thanks are no less sincere. Their names and something of the part they played in the history of 'The Austin' will be revealed as the story unfolds. Many are no longer with us, but my hope is that the generous way in which they helped with my research will continue to be appreciated by future generations after we are all long gone. It gave me enormous pleasure to hear their stories and it is with equal pleasure that I now pass them on.

Many thanks are due to Anders Clausager,

archivist of the British Motor Industry Heritage Trust (BMIHT), for kindly running his experienced eye over the final manuscript and making several helpful suggestions. Most of the production figures quoted in this book, including those tabulated in the appendix, are either the fruits of Anders' own research or have been provided from other BMIHT or Longbridge sources. Many thanks, too, to Karam Ram of the photographic department at BMIHT for his diligence in locating and providing so many of the photographs. I am also greatly indebted to my brother, Michael, and my good friend, Jack Watson, for their invaluable help and support in preparing the manuscript. Finally, to my wife, Cath, who has aided and abetted me in this lengthy project in so many ways over so many years, a very special vote of thanks.

Barney Sharratt,
Selby,
June 2000

Picture acknowledgements

The majority of the photographs and artwork reproduced in this book are the copyright of the British Motor Industry Heritage Trust and must not be reproduced without their permission.

1

A single machine, 1905–1918

"We have one huge machine in which cars are produced from start to finish."

HERBERT AUSTIN

"Who? Herbert Austin? Does he work here?" asked the Longbridge telephonist in doubting tones.

Poor Herbert, after all his efforts, a Longbridge employee that knew him not.

Admittedly this was 1987, by which time Sir Herbert had lain in his grave for some 46 years, but on the other end of that line was Stanley Edge, co-designer with Herbert of the famous Austin Seven. Stanley was not amused. He had only mentioned his association with Sir Herbert in order to establish entitlement to discount when ordering a new Mini but failed to understand how anyone who owed their very livelihood to Herbert Austin could be totally ignorant of this great man; a man who had helped pioneer and champion mechanical road transport in days when 'horseless carriages' were seen by many as the mere playthings of the rich; a man that Stanley revered as 'The father of the British motor industry'.

Born in Buckinghamshire in 1866 and schooled in Yorkshire, Herbert Austin spent his early working life in Australia, initially with an engineering firm managed by his uncle. Whilst in Australia he

Herbert Austin takes the wheel at the start-up of the first Longbridge-built Austin in 1906. This painting, by artist Robert Johnston (see front cover) was produced for a booklet to celebrate Austin's Golden Jubilee in 1955. It was based on an original photograph.

acquired a thorough grounding, not only in mechanical engineering, but also in forge and foundry work and developed a passionate interest in machine-tool design. Even more importantly, as he explained to *The Autocar* in 1929, it was there that his life's greatest ambition, "to motorise the masses", found birth. "It was then that I discovered the urgency of the transport need, for I was able to observe the difficulties and dangers under which the 'out-back' settler was compelled to live and labour. Embedded in my memory, and never likely to be effaced, are journeys through the bush in every kind of conveyance … Families were born and reared hundreds of miles from the nearest medical aid … I made a kind of compact with myself that I would one day, by some means or other, build motor cars that could be used by these lonely but loveable people of the bush … [and so ensure that this 'Never-never land'] … would be robbed of much of its inhumanity, cruelty and terror."

It was the design and development work which Herbert Austin undertook for the Wolseley Sheep Shearing Company of Australia which eventually led to the fulfilment of that pledge. So satisfied was Wolseley with his work that in 1893 he was asked to

Austin's 'Winged-wheel' badge was designed by Herbert Austin himself, with stylised dust 'representing rapid, controlled, wheeled motion'. It was used in catalogues right from 1906 and by 1907 had been registered as a trademark and allotted its position on the radiator of the cars. The radiator cap/mascot was available as an extra in either brass or nickel for 12s 6d (62.5p).

return to England as the manager of their British operations.

Although difficulties with their early sheep-shearing machines led Wolseley to diversify into machine tools and cycle parts, the directors were not initially interested in Herbert's proposal that they should also produce motor cars. There have been conflicting accounts as to exactly what happened next but during 1896 and subsequently during 1897/8, whilst general manager of the Wolseley Sheep Shearing Company's factory in Birmingham, Herbert Austin did manage to build two experimental tri-cars. Having thus gained the interest of the Wolseley directors he then built the first four-wheeled Wolseley in 1899.

The excitement generated during the road testing of those early vehicles had convinced Austin that if cars could be produced cheaply enough then they would be in great demand. But his differences with the Wolseley directors meant that it was a very disillusioned Herbert Austin who wrote to his friend and steel supplier Frank Kayser in 1899 claiming, "… present arrangements won't suit me by any means … As you know I have worked like a slave ever since I came here and have refused several offers at double my salary to go elsewhere, and yet today despite having lived a very quiet retired life I couldn't raise £200 outside my household goods. I have repeatedly paid my expenses out of my own pocket rather than let the company get into difficulties.

"I claim without reservation that the whole of the home trade now amounting to over £10,000 a year has been got together by my personal exertions without assistance from anyone … most of it depends on patents and improvements introduced by me … Do you wonder at my being dissatisfied? … If I had been a drunken waster or an incompetent mechanic then I would expect to be low down but I have got energy still left to make a good bid for something better."

His desire to manage a separate Wolseley car company was realised in 1901 when the Vickers armaments concern financed a new Wolseley Tool & Motor Car Company. Under Herbert Austin's management, Wolseley soon became established as one of the leading car makers in the country. But his dealings with the Wolseley directors were still far from harmonious, so in 1905 he decided to go into car manufacture on his own account.

In later years he spoke with regret at not having done so earlier but to go it alone was not an easy decision. Knowing that he would have to borrow most of the required capital, friends had tried to dissuade him. The future of the fledgeling motor industry was still far from assured and Herbert's decision to set up his factory way out in the countryside, some seven miles from the centre of Birmingham, seemed the height of folly to some.

Herbert knew what he was doing. According to Freddie Henry, who began his Austin apprenticeship in 1926, "When he handed in his resignation at Wolseley he was ready to move into Longbridge and produce a car he had already designed at home with the help of two ex-Wolseley designers, A. J. Hancock and A. V. Davidge."

Hancock, who remained chief designer until shortly after the death of Herbert Austin in 1941, later wrote, "At last came the great day for transference to the works at Longbridge, which journey we made in Lord Austin's 8hp two-cylinder Wolseley car, which was loaded up with our boards and T-squares … we settled down with makeshift desks and got on with the drawings, Lord Austin having his private office next door … The first front axle, being forged, needed a good deal of machining and hand work, and after milling this into a rough H-section, Lord Austin took a hand in chipping out the junctions of the cuts, and was so energetic that he broke the chisel and cut his hand very badly, but contrary to modern first-aid instructions, he soon wrapped a rag round it and went on with his chipping. In due course, the first chassis was finished, a rough seat was lashed on, and Lord Austin drove it

out of the shop amid a cloud of smoke."

Austin's early cars were described very favourably in the motoring press. The Longbridge factory, soon to be known as 'The Austin', rapidly grew into a seemingly disorganised jumble of forge, machine shops and assembly shops. But Herbert took a delight in describing it as 'one single machine' where each shop was geared to provide the necessary flow of components for a steady output of cars. It was a source of great pride to him that his factory was capable of designing and building the complete car. Unlike William Morris, who began car production at Cowley in 1913, he was no mere assembler of bought-in parts. "We have one huge machine in which cars are produced from start to finish."

Other than when speaking of his beloved factory, Herbert seems to have been a man of few words, apparently never uttering more than a "humph" whenever a "humph" would suffice. His men knew he was capable of performing any job in the works because he would readily remove his jacket to demonstrate any particular skill whenever he thought it necessary. Sometimes he was even a little too eager to do so. Taking a file from the hands of Cyril Edwards in the toolroom, he energetically showed him how to use it and then shot off elsewhere. Poor Cyril had been carefully tickling a couple of thou off a gauge and Herbert had completely ruined it!

In *British Automobiles Overseas* of August 1955 R. P. Thompson wrote of Herbert Austin, "A man of plain speech and dress, he did not indulge in alco-

Herbert Austin with the Works fire brigade c1910.

holic beverages, neither did he smoke, and applicants for staff positions were carefully scrutinised for evidence of these vices. Too much colour in the cheeks, or stained fingers, were apt to bring the interview to an abrupt conclusion."

In those he did employ, Austin clearly engendered a loyalty born of great respect. To say that some of his men even revered him would hardly be overstating the case and, as we shall see later, several of his early employees showed a willingness to stand by him through some very lean times. Alf Depper joined Austin as a lad of 14 in 1906 and helped Herbert's brother, Harry, to prepare the first gearbox for machining. Herbert had told Alf's father that although he had no apprenticeship scheme he was prepared to, "Take the lad on and see how he shapes." Alf obviously 'shaped' all right, only retiring in 1966, after 60 years at 'The Austin' and several decades as head of Austin's experimental department.

Bobby Howitt, who was Austin's secretary throughout Herbert's Longbridge days, spoke of Herbert as a prolific inventor and also said of him, "First and foremost he was a worker and expected his staff to be always available, with no eye on the clock. From the commencement, only the best materials, and the highest class of workmanship, were good enough for his new product, and this resulted in a reliability without equal."

Top *Two Austin stalwarts with 109 years of service between them. Alf Depper (standing), 60 years, and George Coates, 49 years. The car is a 1907 four-cylinder 40hp Austin York landaulet.*

Middle *A single-cylinder Austin 7hp of 1910. Only one of these 'old thumpers', as George Coates described them, was actually built at Longbridge before production was transferred to the Swift Cycle company and virtually identical cars were badged as either Swifts or Austins. Priced at £150, the car was described in Austin's catalogue as suitable for beginners and younger members of the family. "We decided it was absolutely necessary to limit seating capacity to two persons. To ensure that this feature is not violated in practice we only sell the car complete with two-seated body, and while the chassis may be amply strong enough for three persons, we only recommend two being carried."*

Bottom *Austin's Town Carriage of 1911 was built on the same chassis as the 15hp light delivery van. The short wheelbase and central position of the driver were said to enable it to be manoeuvred with ease in heavy traffic. It was also claimed to be, "A warm favourite with ladies on account of its trim and smart appearance, and the comfort derived from a cosy interior and quiet running. It can also be used as a high-class taxi cab, and it has proved a great success for this purpose", although there is no evidence to support the latter claim.*

The comfortable Longbridge limousines of 1906 onwards helped Austin acquire recognition as accomplished coach-builders. (Note the 'Austin emergency seat' fitted to this example.)

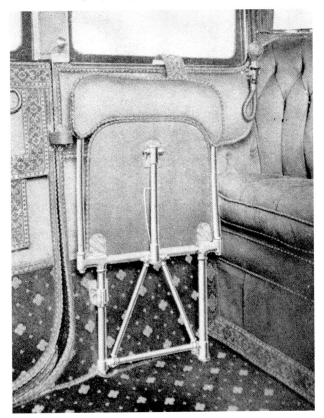

The Longbridge body and trim shop, c1910.

Even the earliest of Austin sales brochures showed a considerable concern for customer satisfaction. In 1906 Austin were offering to: "send our carriage designer to confer with and advise anyone not able to visit the works" and also described the painting of the vehicles as a process, "carried out under exceptionally favourable conditions, as the works are situated on the south-west side of Birmingham, where there is no chance of the dust and smoke from other manufacturers spoiling the finish." Anxious to ease his clients' entry into the new-fangled world of motoring, Austin recommended that, whenever possible, they or their chauffeur should avail themselves of a week's free instruction at the Works.

In their 1907 catalogue, the Austin Motor Company drew particular attention to "the care which we have taken to study the special requirements of motorists who prefer to have a thoroughly reliable and elegant touring vehicle, rather than a high-powered flimsily-built car constructed for record breaking."

These were not mere words. Indeed, it is hard to find fault with Austin historian Bob Wyatt, when he

suggests that if you take a look at the earliest Austins they betray Herbert's lengthy training in heavy engineering and seem to suggest that his principle may well have been, "Never use a quarter-inch bolt where a one and a half-inch one will do!"

Be that as it may, Austin's splendid range of phaetons, limousines and landaulets were soon admired as much for their superior coachwork as their dependability and, in 1912, Herbert took great delight in accepting the presidency of the Institute of Carriage Builders, feeling that this showed his activities were not merely confined to the mechanical phase of motor engineering, but that he was also considered an outstanding figure in the coach-building world.

Coach-built or not, the handbook for the Austin 30hp of 1915 shows that Austin clearly expected his cars to be "go anywhere" vehicles. Detailed suggestions for those proposing to tackle virgin territory read almost as a 'spoof' today.

"It is assumed that the motorist has his car in good order, and the usual equipment of tools. In addition he should provide himself with a large hammer, having not less than a five-pound head, a stout crowbar, about 150ft of ¾in rope, a block and tackle, a shovel, a galvanised iron bucket, a good axe, a blowlamp and soldering outfit, four good Parsons chains, a coil of tough iron wire, such as is known in the colonies as baling wire is the best, as it is very pliable and tough; also a sheet of canvas or any waterproof material large enough to cover the radiator completely and hang a little below: likewise several yards of very strong canvas about 18in wide, a large Stilson wrench about a foot long, a strong piece of board about 12in by 15in and lastly some rubber solution. The large hammer will be found very useful as where there are rocks, tree stumps or other obstacles about, the front axle may get bent and with the aid of the blowlamp and the hammer it can be heated and straightened. A steering rod or other part can be treated in the same manner."

The waterproof material was to protect the electrics by covering the radiator when fording a river and the axe was for chopping down small trees to use as levers in an emergency.

By the advent of war in 1914 the Austin Motor Company was turning out almost a thousand cars a year but the hostilities saw Herbert devote his considerable energies to reorganising the factory in support of the war effort. Lorries, ambulances, armoured cars, aeroplanes, portable generating sets, searchlights, marine engines, shells and the guns to fire them – Longbridge produced them all in profusion.

Herbert's choice of a rural location and the finance that became readily available from the Ministry of Munitions meant his factory was able to expand in almost bomb-burst fashion itself. A new North Works of machine shops and forge was erected in 1916, followed by a West Works munitions plant in 1917, the original factory becoming known as South Works. In 1917, 70 acres of adjacent

Pony Express or early car transporter? An early Austin export stands on the factory weighbridge before the commencement of its journey to New Zealand, c1913.

SE5a aircraft production at Longbridge c1917. At the outbreak of the First World War, aircraft were mainly used for reconnaissance purposes until the means and routines of air-to-air combat were gradually devised. Prior to 1917, bombing was only made by Zeppelin airships.

land were turned into the circular Flying Ground by removing the top of Cofton Hill.

In 1915, Austin built 52 RE7 aircraft for the Royal Flying Corps, then 450 RE8s, partly for the RFC and, after 1918, the remainder for the newly formed RAF. They also built about 1,500 SE5a aircraft – one of the most successful of the war.

Longbridge's war production also included a large order from the Imperial Russian Army for 2–3 ton trucks to be used as mobile workshops, 20hp Austin tourers to be rebodied as ambulances, and 30hp cars to be converted into armoured cars.

Alf Depper thus found himself on an exciting three-year stint in Russia instructing the army in the maintenance of the Austin vehicles during active service. "The roads were very rutted so the springs didn't last long," he later recalled. "On the poor quality Russian petrol the engines had to get very warm before they ran smoothly and in those pre 'anti-freeze' days all the vehicles, including the armoured cars, had to be drained off at night."

An Austin twin-prop shafted low-loader of 1918. Frank Kayser, of Kayser Ellison, supplied much of the capital required in the early days of 'The Austin'. Russia ordered a total of 1,100 2–3 ton lorry chassis but come the revolution, the orders were cancelled and Austin was left with many unwanted vehicles. The radiator was behind the engine in the driver's cab. The differential was mounted on the gearbox with a separate prop shaft to each rear wheel.

By 1917 Alf was working just behind the front lines and could feel the rumblings of revolution. "The Russian troops were treated like cattle and discontent was rising."

Come the 1917 Revolution, the contracts with Austin were immediately cancelled and Alf had to hotfoot it to St Petersburg before making his way home through Finland and Sweden. Watching television in 1967, he could hardly believe his eyes when, in the May Day Parade to mark the 50th Anniversary of the Revolution, he saw one of his 1914 Austin armoured cars trundling through Red Square amidst the might of Russia's modern military hardware!

During the war, Austin's work force multiplied some tenfold to over 20,000. Those coming from far afield found travelling difficult, many having to walk several miles each way. Although Herbert Austin built a fleet of buses and hired special trains, many were still having difficulty, so in 1916 he built

A detachment of Russian troops with twin-turret Austin armoured cars awaits orders near Tookanoff, c1916. Enemy gunners eventually found that by shooting at the joints of the armour plate these vehicles could be 'opened up'.

A group of Longbridge 'Munitionettes' c1917, who did their bit for Britain during the First World War by producing shells for the war effort. That the girls soon outstripped the productivity of the men was put down to the fact they were more nimble of finger!

an 'Austin village' of prefabricated cedar-wood bungalows to the north of the factory.

The 200 bungalows, "of a type provided for the settlers in the bleak expanses of North America", were ordered from the Aladdin Company in Michigan who promised bungalow owners a dollar for every knot they could find in the wood. The houses were erected in a horseshoe arrangement which would have formed an oval, had the full plans been implemented. A second batch of 250 houses was never delivered. Officially, all available shipping capacity was said to have been required for the 'war effort' but this did not stop rumours of how the War Department had supposedly censored news of the final batch being sunk in the Atlantic by enemy submarines.

Twenty-five pairs of brick-built houses were spaced out between the wooden bungalows to act as fire-breaks. With seven people billeted in each bungalow and up to a dozen people in each house, the village housed some 2,000 workers in all, many of them Belgian refugees.

Tom Staples joined Austin as a war munitions volunteer in 1917 and went into one of the first bungalows to be tenanted. In his 94th year, while proudly showing off his bungalow, he recalled, "When people learned where I lived they would say, 'Oh, not in one of those rabbit hutches.'" At which point Tom would ask them, "Have you three bedrooms? Have you central heating? Have you an inside toilet? Have you a bathroom with a lovely white enamel bath?" Even in the 1930s, '40s and '50s, the answer to those questions was usually no, but in 1917 the bungalows had all these facilities, a good kitchen and a 20ft lounge. In 75 years of trying, Tom Staples failed to find a single knot on which to claim a dollar.

Careful tree planting produced a delightfully leafy setting for the avenues of bungalows. Many Austin villagers are now second and third generation residents and Herbert Austin would no doubt be very proud to see the spirit that prevails in his village today. He would be happy too that the Austin Village Preservation Society aims to preserve and cherish this peaceful haven as a living slice of Austin history.

Longbridge's war production totalled more than 2,000 aeroplanes, 2,500 aero engines, 2,000 trucks, 650 guns and 8,000,000 shells. In recognition of that effort, Herbert Austin received a knighthood in 1917. He was also honoured by Belgium as a Commander of the Order of Leopold II in 1919, for housing and employing some 3,000 Belgian refugees.

Indeed, it was the German occupation of Belgium which eventually led to George Coates arriving at Longbridge in 1919 to begin his Austin apprenticeship – the subject of the next chapter.

2

An Austin apprentice

"When I saw those huge shops, all the machinery, all the men, it was amazing."

GEORGE COATES

Men who served an apprenticeship at 'The Austin' were always much sought after in the motor industry because of the thorough grounding they were given in all aspects of motor manufacture, a grounding clearly illustrated by George Coates's account of his own apprenticeship.

George Coates, as he approached his 90th year in 1993, with the tools he used to adjust the carburation of the Austin Sevens in 1923.

Born in 1903 at Chantilly, near Paris, where his father trained horses for Baron Rothschild, George spoke fluent French. Before the First World War the family moved to Liège in Belgium where their stay there came to a sad and abrupt end in 1914.

In George's own words, "We had just started our summer holidays, *les grandes vacances*. At 6 o'clock one morning the gun went off on the fortress at the top of the hill. It was an agreed signal for us, as boy scouts, to assemble there to carry any messages. An officer called me up on to the fortress and handed me his binoculars. In the distance there was a cornfield, all golden corn, but it was rapidly turning a shiny black – the helmets of German infantry – they'd got that far by midday, 4 August 1914. We were told to leave without delay. Father had to stay behind but he and mother shared out their money in 5-franc pieces and we just walked out of the house with a small suitcase. We made for Ostend but there were no boats because of the German submarines so we found a small hotel. We hadn't been there long before there was an awful commotion. People running down the staircase, suitcases were coming out of windows and oh, the queues and arguing and shoving and pushing. It was fear, just fear. We got on the boat for Dover but a tug hailed us to go to Folkestone instead – submarines again. We stayed the night in London and the next day made for Cheltenham."

George never saw his father again but later learned that he had been imprisoned by the Germans at Wittenberg where he died of typhus in 1915.

After fleeing Belgium, George attended Cirencester Grammar School before joining Herbert

The milling section of a machine shop in which George worked during his apprenticeship, c1920. Just imagine all those belts whanging and flapping away!

Austin's first intake of apprentices at Nazareth House on a snowy January morning in 1919. Nazareth House, which stood immediately opposite 'The Austin', had been an orphanage run by nuns before the First World War, but in 1918, Herbert Austin rented the building as an Austin engineering college.

Well into his eighties, George surveyed his entire apprenticeship as though it had happened only yesterday. "My English was still very shaky when I reported to the labour exchange in the front yard. I was handed over to an old foreman. Old Man Richards they called him. He'd got a young man working for him, Bill West, a machine tool fitter. It was about 10 o'clock before I actually got to the job and I remember Bill West pulling out a can of tea and a lump of cake and sharing it with me saying, 'Don't boil water for the tea, just go to the hot tap to make it.' Later on I found that some of the blokes used to make tea on the soldering torch. If Harry Austin copped them he wouldn't say anything, but

just stood there until the can boiled dry. He didn't think they should be using the Works gas to make their own tea.

"I became Bill West's fitter's mate. We alternated between No 1 and No 2 machine shops or anywhere else we were needed. It was a case of 'Hand me this,' or 'hand me that.' I carried his tool kit you see, because that showed his status as a skilled man. I was astonished at the size of the place. I'd only seen fitting shops in garages up until then, but when I saw those huge shops, all the machinery, all the men, it was amazing.

"It wasn't just the machines that impressed me. There was the sawmill where great stacks of wood were seasoning for the bodies. Just further up was the stable with six beautiful shire horses. Honestly they were a picture and the blokes were so proud of them. They were used to shift the machines about. There was an awful lot of that to do when setting up for cars again after the 14–18 war.

"I was taught by Bill West and Old Man Richards how to hold a file, how to keep it flat; and the hacksaw, how to stand with one leg in front and one behind, hold it straight and keep it level, keep a steady pressure but vary your speed with the metal, as fast as you like with brass but with steel to bear hard but take it slowly.

"As for the stamp shop, I'd never seen the like before. Stamping red hot metals to make the flywheels and so on. It used to scare me to see the sparks flying. Bloomin' red hot lumps of steel, you see. You made the blank of say a crown wheel and it would be machined afterwards. The hammer was dropped two or three times on to a hot billet of steel – bump – bump – and you'd oil it so that it wouldn't stick in the die and there'd be smoke and sparks and all – bump – bump – bump – and you'd got a crown wheel.

"In the panel shop the blokes were on mechanical hammers, pushing the steel in and out to make it round or make it thinner and spread it into a shape. Then they'd put it in rollers and roll it backwards and forwards. That was bloomin' hard work believe me, but from a flat piece of steel they could make a complete wing.

"When they thought I knew enough about machine tools I was put on press tools at the other end of the stamp shop. On the Twenty Horse tourer, instead of hammering and rolling the mudguards by hand they started to press them out using a bloomin'

The engine assembly shop in which George was shown how to hand-fit the engine bearings.

big fly press. The flywheel must have been 15ft or more across. Those were our first presses in about 1922, for the Twenty Horse rear mudguards.

"I had a spell in the aluminium and brass foundry too. In fact I had a nasty accident there. We were in a hurry and a funnel on a moulding box tipped over and filled my shoe with molten metal. I dropped to the floor and stuck my leg up in the air and the bloomin' stuff ran down my leg. I managed to get my sock off and douse my foot in sand. It was dirty sand, but I had to cool it with something. They gave me a piggy-back across to the ambulance station and the nurse told me off for putting my foot in the sand but she washed it and made sure it was clean. It was a second-degree burn and I had nine weeks on crutches.

"After that I went into the erecting shop and started on frame members for the Twenty Horse and the Heavy Twelve. We used jigs with dowels to hold the chassis members in position. You drilled through and then put the hot rivets in and hammered them home with nice round heads. The chassis would go further down the line and they'd stick the axles and brake rods on. Further down still they'd stick on the engine and gearbox unit and connect the propshaft and it was ready to roll.

"Then they put me on lighting sets made from

car engines with a platform at the back for the dynamo. We built them for the army and for private houses that had no mains electricity. Although the lighting sets used the same basic engine parts as the cars, they were in cast-iron instead of aluminium. The more weight the better for the lighting sets.

"After that they sent me down to the axle shop where I worked on the Twenty Horse and Heavy Twelve rear axles. We set them by using a felt pad to coat the crown wheel with engineer's blue, a thin blue paste, and then put the pinion in and turned it round until it marked where it was touching. The inspector would then want to see it. The crown wheel and pinion had straight teeth in those days. We used to run them up on a motor and move the pinion or crown wheel in and out if they were noisy. You got to know how it should sound. The Seven Horse axles were easy to adjust because they had slotted shims.

"I worked on engine assembly too. The white metal was poured in to the bearings with an allowance for machining. You fitted the bearings to a

test bar by 'blueing' the bar very thinly and then clamping the big end up and moving it back and forwards. Then we took it to pieces and scraped down any high spots, 'blued' the shaft again and put it back on. You had to get it marking at four spots an inch.

"After that the crank was set up in the bench. If you put a con rod on the crank and it was too loose you would 'face' the two bearing halves and then scrape it in again. You'd get all four con-rods so that they would just about drop under their own weight round the crank. Believe me there was some bloomin' bolting and unbolting to do in order to get a proper fit.

"Things were very tight financially for apprentices but we did get entertainment in the Works, especially at weekends. There was dancing and brass bands and a Works cinema as well for tuppence. Pearl White, Charlie Chaplin and so on. If you weren't keen on drinking that was the best place. You got mixed company and it was warm. It was the food at Nazareth House that shook me. Honestly it was dreadful. After lunch we'd nip over to the canteen at the Works which was in the old spraying shop for the First World War aircraft. You could get a jam roly-poly there for tuppence and that filled things up. Oh you had to top up.

Herbert Austin's office and (inset) George Coates with a bust of Herbert Austin. The inset photograph was taken in the office in 1985, 61 years after George had stood there to be quizzed by Herbert about his fluency in French.

A Longbridge-built Austin tractor, c1920. George Coates began his travels abroad for Austin with a spell at Austin's Liancourt tractor works in 1924.

"After a while Nazareth House closed down and some of us were billeted in West Works canteen. We had a dormitory there, up top, on a balcony and we listened to the band while in the bath. Well, I say bath, we'd found urns of some description to have a bath in and the Works brass band would be playing away down below on the stage where they had the boxing ring. I had a go in the ring one night with Captain Waite, Herbert Austin's son-in-law. Bang – he bloomin' floored me, but at least he picked me up afterwards.

"Towards the end of my apprenticeship, I was working on a lathe bed. It had been an 18-pounder gun lathe during the war, and we were converting these into jigs for machining the circular gearboxes for the Austin tractor. The saddle wouldn't traverse from one end to the other without jamming on the raised name in the casting, so I was chipping away at the letters when a bloke tapped me on the shoulder. It was Old Man Austin. 'What are you doing son?' 'I'm trying to get the saddle to cross over.' 'Well, mind your eyes and put some rags round your hand, and for heaven's sake, hold the hammer the right way.' He showed me how to hold it, pushing his bowler hat backwards so that it didn't fall off as he bent down to have a close look at my hand. The cast-iron chippings were like glass and of course they'd cut my left hand that I was holding the chisel with. 'Put some rags round it,' he said, 'Put some rags round it.'

"I didn't know that he'd cut his own hand while chiselling away on the axle of the first Austin, but now you've told me that, it explains why he was so worried. That wasn't the first time I'd met the old man because he'd signed my indentures when I was taken on, but later on I had quite a bit to do with him.

"It all started because of the Austin tractor. It had been introduced in 1919 and was selling well for a while but production shifted to France about 1921 when Austin bought a factory at Liancourt near Paris to beat the French import tariff.

"One day in 1924, Bobby Howitt, the Old Man's secretary, sent for me and showed me into Sir Herbert's office. Sir Herbert said, 'They tell me you speak French.' I replied, 'Well yes, I do.' He asked, 'Well what's a hammer? What's a chisel?' and so on. I rattled the answers off all right; marteau, burin, tenaille. I wondered how he knew about my French but I think it was through Bobby Howitt being a scoutmaster. He'd been planning to take the scouts to Belgium, so naturally, I'd told him that I used to live there.

"Before I knew it, I was on my way to Liancourt where they wanted me to act as interpreter at the tractor works. The manager had hopped off with about £40,000. The factory had been closed and some of the drawings had gone, so I started translating new layouts and work schedules.

"Anyway, that's how I started my overseas travels for the Austin Motor Company, with my goings on with the tractors in 1924, just at the end of my apprenticeship."

3

The Twenties – the harsh realities of peace

"We nearly went to the wall, there is no doubt about that. 'The Austin' was the largest automobile factory in the country and we were just bursting to make cars, but nobody could afford them."

GEORGE COATES

The armistice of 1918 and the resultant loss of defence contracts left Austin with a singularly useless capacity, the facility to churn out aircraft and armaments that no-one then wanted. A short-lived post-war boom soon turned to deep depression with days of plenty being replaced by much tougher times. Many thousands of workers had to be sacked and Austin had to dig deep into the coffers to re-equip the entire factory for peacetime production. During 1919, large numbers of automatic machines were installed with the aim of applying the knowledge gained in the mass-production of armaments to the mass-production of cars, but supplying an insatiable war machine and persuading an increasingly impecunious public to buy new motor cars were two very different matters.

Before hitting on a strategy that allowed the company to benefit from his newly acquired mass-production techniques, Herbert Austin did rather stumble about a bit. Immediately post-war he had an understandable though ill-founded hope of transferring the experience gained in aircraft manufacture to the production and sale of light aircraft for private use.

Another ill-judged move was his decision to pin the hopes of car production on a Ford-inspired one-model policy. Particularly ill-judged because the model chosen was the rather hefty 3.6-litre Austin Twenty.

"The old man was running a Hudson and it seems the Twenty Horse was virtually based on that. It even said 'gas' on the hand throttle, just like the

The Austin Whippet, introduced in 1918, had wings that folded for easy storage or to enable the aircraft to be towed behind a car. A few Whippets were built but there was insufficient demand to make it a viable project.

Hudson, but the new mono-bloc four-cylinder engine was designed by a chap called Capel" recalled Stanley Edge, who was involved in the design of the engine. "At the end of the war they set up a new drawing office next to Sir Herbert's own office. I went in there in 1918, putting all the limits on Capel's drawings of the Twenty Horse crankshaft. Haefeli was assistant chief engineer under Hancock and Billy Ellcock was in charge of the chassis frame. The Twenty Horse was very robustly built but it was a big clumsy monster and although by 1920 they had begun to churn out quite a few, it didn't really sell very well. Times got very hard indeed and a change in taxation in 1921, which heavily penalised larger-engined cars, nearly put the lid on things."

The company was certainly on the brink of disaster. By 1921 the 21,000 employees of 1917 had dwindled to only 5,000 and it was becoming increasingly difficult to find work for even that number. There were petitions that the company should be wound up and, although Austin did just manage to hold things together, a receiver was brought in to oversee finances and clear out unsold stock.

"We nearly went to the wall," said George Coates, "there is no doubt about that. 'The Austin' was the largest automobile factory in the country and we were just bursting to make cars, but nobody could afford them. You certainly wondered about pay days. At one stage we owed about £2 million which was a lot of money in those days. The shares were almost worthless. Some of those who had been with Herbert Austin from the start told him they didn't mind waiting for their wages. Yes, they thought a lot of him. Things were so bad that they counted out the nuts and bolts to us. They even counted out plain washers. I remember Herbert Austin standing on the canteen steps in the front yard telling the men he'd managed to get two more carburettors or two more magnetos. It might seem daft now but we would have to take a carburettor off a completed car or chassis in order to move the others about. We'd strap the carb on with a big rubber band, take the float out and fill the chamber up with petrol to take the chassis across the road. We did that with the Twenty Horse and the Twelve Horse."

In 1921, Alf Depper was one of that select band of Austin men who happily carried on working without receiving any wages. According to his son Maurice, "It only came out 30 years later that he hadn't got paid when Austin was broke. Not even mother knew because he drew on his savings to give her the housekeeping".

Herbert Austin showed his gratitude by promising the four or five senior men who did likewise, "You have got a job here for just as long as you can stagger through the gates."

Austin advertising for their post First World War 20hp four-cylinder car suggested that one of the 'Pleasures of Peace' would be "seeing the world in an Austin 20 Touring Car." (See colour section.)

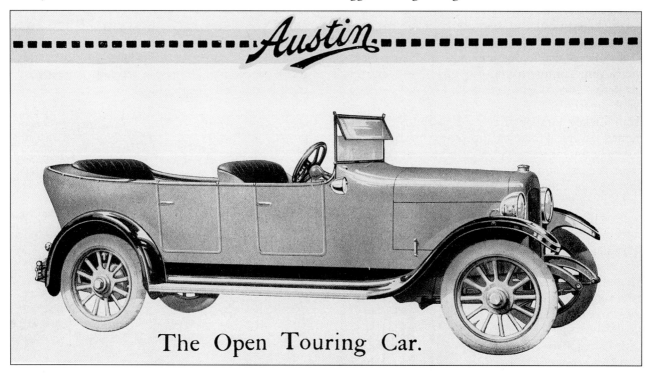

The Open Touring Car.

The Heavy Twelve was launched in 1921 and was "more or less a scaled down Twenty but a thoroughly successful and dependable vehicle" – Stanley Edge.

It did not take Austin long to ditch his one-model policy. According to Stanley Edge, "That's when he decided to produce both the Twelve Horse and Seven Horse. The Twelve was more or less a scaled-down Twenty but was a thoroughly successful and dependable vehicle. Design of the Twelve Horse commenced just before I went to the Grange to do the Seven. It must have been early 1921 because I set some Twelve Horse engine stuff out before I went. In fact, if I wanted to go down to the Works from Lickey Grange they'd often send an experimental Twelve Horse car up to get me. It was still rather heavy for its power output but was certainly a great success and did particularly well for Austin later on as a London cab."

The Seven Horse, introduced in 1922 as Austin's 'Motor for the Millions', was of such crucial importance in getting 'The Austin' back on its feet that the story of its conception and design is recorded in the next chapter. Here, we confine ourselves to the early days of its production but must first mention two men who arrived on the scene in Austin's darkest days of 1921/22: Carl Englebach, who became works director, and Ernest Payton, who took charge of finances. Both men proved to be worth their weight in gold but had been appointed at the behest

of the receiver, not by Herbert Austin. As an extremely able production engineer, Englebach was responsible for several very effective reorganisations of the factory. In later years, Englebach's son, Peter, recalled how his father only took the job on because the banks were searching for somebody to 'salvage'

"It's all our own: no waiting for the menfolk", was a line that would be used in Austin advertising to try to interest women in their new product. Lady Austin may not have been too impressed with her first sight of the car but her daughters Irene and Zeta were interested enough to try out this early example in 1922.

Austin. Initially he refused to do so unless Herbert Austin was banned from the Works but relented after reaching an understanding with the receivers that Austin would not interfere with his plans to reorganise the factory. Although this did not bode well for a happy relationship it seems that when Englebach and Austin got to know each other they became the greatest of friends.

As for the Austin Seven, Alf Depper, who had joined Austin's experimental department on his return from Russia in 1917, recalled how on Easter Saturday evening, 1922, he and Herbert Austin were the first to take the new Seven out for a run, and how Herbert's wife seemed far from impressed. "The Governor and I went up Lickey Road in it and called at Lickey Grange to see Lady Austin. When she came out he said, 'What do you think about this?' She just said it wanted cleaning, so after he'd had a look around the brakes and that, we went down to Wychbold where the wireless station was and that was its first long run;

Here, the first Austin Seven racer (No 3) awaits the start of the Italian Grand Prix in 1923. Captain Waite sits in the car and Alf Depper stands beside it. They won the class for cars of 750cc. Inset, a line from Alf's treasured telegram.

Wychbold and back. No trouble at all."

Both Alf Depper and Arthur Waite were soon involved in racing the Sevens. In later years, Austin's racing cars would be transported in rather smart trailers but for Alf, who acted as chief mechanic and racing partner to Waite, it was a question of setting off early and driving the car to the track. "When we got there all we did was to turn our caps the other way round, put on a pair of goggles, and we were ready to race."

A variety of problems meant it took them almost four days to get to the Seven's first race at Brooklands in 1923, but they were rewarded with a win. Said Alf, "It was a sure thing for the little baby. It was a very proud moment. A fortnight after winning the race at Brooklands we had an invitation to the opening of the Monza track. We had the luck to win that, the Grand Prix of Italy."

Grandson David Depper still proudly retains the medal that Alf won for that Cyclecar Grand Prix at Monza and cherishes the post-race telegram that Alf sent to his wife reading: AUSTIN FIRST – LOVE ALFI. The following year, Waite and Depper came third at Le Mans in the same car.

George Coates found himself road testing some of the earliest Sevens. "After making three circuits of

AUSTIN FIRST + LOVE ALFI

In the pits at Le Mans in 1924 during the Grand Prix des Voiturettes. Car No 8 (the same car that ran at Monza) was brought in to third place by Captain Waite with Alf Depper riding as his mechanic.

the Flying Ground we would set off through Rubery and Marlbrook and we then ascended Rose Hill the long way and past Lickey church, where Herbert Austin now lies buried. We'd try the brakes

The Austin road test department of 1923. George Coates is seated to the immediate right of the name board.

going down the other side of the hill, turn round at the bottom and then ascend the hill in the opposite direction to make our way back to the factory. The cars were properly warmed up by this time so we could check the performance up Rose Hill. You put your foot down from the Bilberry tea rooms and if you were still in top gear as you passed the school gate on the right, then the car was something like standard. You'd expect to be able to hold second gear until you reached the telegraph pole at Lickey church. No Seven would go over the hill in top. You had to drop into first with the very early ones. Later versions got over in second.

George Coates, far left, with others testing Sevens on the cinder track of the Flying Ground in 1923/24.

"In the early days of the Seven we were plagued with 'smokers'. We were trying to turn out a hundred a week but there were so many smokers that numbers were well down for a long while. A smoker would show its colours on the first descent of Rose Hill and continue smoking all the way back to the Works. The trouble was eventually cured with oil control rings and by placing baffles in the base of the cylinders.

"One evening in 1923 there was a string of us out on test in Longbridge Lane, doing overtime because of the smokers. There was a bit of a curve near the old duck pond – it's a main bus route now – and these three girls were walking abreast with their backs to us. Of course, the bloomin' horns were like baa-lambs, not a lot of use, and when the car ahead of me had gone past them, the girls spread out again without looking backwards. I yanked the handbrake on as well as the footbrake and swerved to clear 'em but the front wheels locked up and it rolled over. Apparently they'd tried some extra resin in the brake linings but it just made them grab. The girls

A photograph that reminded George Coates of the evening in 1923 when he swerved to avoid the young girls in Longbridge Lane. It was probably taken in 1925. (Austin Seven Clubs Association)

were shrieking their heads off. George Caldicott who had been in front turned back to help. We pushed the car back on its wheels and you know I just started up the engine and it drove back to the Works as nice as you like.

"I tried to sneak in through the timber yard but Jimmy Wheeler, the Road Test foreman, spotted me. He sent me to Harry Austin, who at that time was superintendent of the Road Test. He wasn't very pleased and I wondered if I'd get kicked off road testing. In the end Wheeler said, 'Fortunately for you, the car isn't really damaged. We'll only have to replace the windscreen stays.' That was the first Seven that had been turned over so naturally they wanted to know how it happened. Of course with me being a young lad they might have thought I was a hothead.

"I suppose I might have been in those days. We used to have a bit of fun up on the Flying Ground in the Seven Horse because there was nobody up there then. The circular track was made with ashes from the boilers. We'd race each other round that track. Three trips round and the winner got ten cigarettes. We'd take the top off the carburettor and put a washer on the float to make it heavier and we would advance the ignition a bit too. They went like the clappers if you did that.

"Of course, we wouldn't have driven like that if Herbert Austin had been around. One day I was told I had to take him to Stratford. Even before we got to Barnt Green he was telling me to sit up straight and hold both hands on the wheel. He said, 'I want you to drive like an electric motor; slowly up through the revs and slowly down. If you keep your hands on the wheel and keep your eyes open you won't have to slam your brakes on.' He said, 'Thirty miles an hour is my speed.' Yes, even on the main roads, that was as fast as he wanted to go."

Frank Fletcher was another who spent almost 50 years at Longbridge. "My first job, at 16 years old in 1924, was making Seven Horse floors in South Works. When you finished you stamped your number on the tunnel to show who had done the job. They weren't doing a hundred a week when I started, nowhere near it. There were about four or five pairs of us building the floors. There wasn't much spot welding in those days so the early floors had thousands of ⅛in rivets in them. When they introduced spot welding in the late Twenties the men thought it wouldn't hold. I remember Bert Challoner, our superintendent, getting a hammer

The West Works body shop in the mid-1920s where Stan Blunn completed his apprenticeship.

and chisel and trying to part the pieces of spot-welded metal but he couldn't. The floors were built ready for the aluminium body to be dropped on. They were all tourers at first. They assembled, painted and trimmed the whole body in our shop. We even built our own spoked wheels and own radiators. There were no tracks. You worked on a stand and carried the body off one stand on to the next."

In the early 1920s, the Heavy Road Test, which catered for the Twenty Horse and Heavy Twelve chassis, also came under Harry Austin's jurisdiction. George Coates described the test routine. "We road-tested the chassis loaded with boxes of sand, 56lb weights or flywheels, anything to weigh them down. There was no windscreen and the front mudguards were just hessian. You had to be careful on the ice with the Twenty Horse chassis or it would spin like a top. It would go round three times quite easily. That's how I lost all my teeth. Not the spinning, no, the cold, the frost, straight in the mouth. I'd had quite a few fillings and they just fell out with the intense cold. We wore full-length rubber capes tied at the neck, but just sat on a box with only a back bar to hang on to. That's how I got my piles! There was also a Finished Road Test after the fully trimmed bodies had been fitted."

After the war, Austin's West Works, with its sawmill, body erecting shop, trim shop and a new paint shop, which saw the introduction of spray painting in 1919, was used entirely for coachwork construction.

Stan Blunn, started as an apprentice in 1922 and completed almost 49 years at 'The Austin', initially building the wooden bodies in West Works body shop. "I had to work three months probation for nothing. Then they'd either kick you out or keep you on. If they kept you on you got 7s 6d a week but had to buy all your own tools. I gradually built up my tools and was very proud of them.

"In 1924/25 I worked on the Mayfair limousines and the landaulets. It was really skilled work. Each body had the customer's name on and you were responsible for it being up to standard. I always worked with a skilled man, with my bench on the off side of the car and his on the other. We built the wooden bodies on a metal framework that was similar to the chassis that the body would eventually go on. We started with the wooden floor with its trap doors to get at the chassis, then built the pillars, the roof and the back panel. After that came the doors

The Austin Motor Company came of age in June 1926. The smaller circle, right, is a running track prepared specially for the day but the larger circuit on which the roundabout stands, was the Works test track.

and the front scuttle. We used to make the aluminium panels for the bodies, but later on we had panel beaters producing panels that were sort of half ready. You just had to clean 'em up a bit and fit them on to the frames. You had to be skilled in both metal and wood, so it was an interesting job but sometimes you'd go in on say a Wednesday and they'd say come back on Thursday or Friday. You were often short in those days."

Times were certainly hard when Bill Chance started in the finishing shop at West Works in 1923. "I was on the big ones, the Ranelaghs, the limousine with a division. I worked on all the show cars so was in work when others were laid off. When I first started you were given enough pins to put a set of door casings on but they were all counted out to you. You only had to get one a bit awkward and it bent, so you had to take it back to the store to show it was bent and even then you had to get a requisition off the foreman, just to get a panel pin. Oh, things were tight. If you didn't get into the gate by two minutes past eight you couldn't get in at all. You would have to report to the personnel department and they would ring and ask the foreman if you were necessary for that day. If not, you were back home. That died out as the unions got stronger but it was awful really because you had paid your fare to get up there and might lose a day's work for half a minute."

In October 1926, Austin launched the six-cylinder Twenty Horse which replaced the four-cylinder model in mid-1929.

Bill also spoke of the first assembly line conveyor being installed about 1925. "What a contraption! A chap used to blow a whistle when it was going to move. You were supposed to jump out of the body while the whole thing shuddered and lurched forward but sometimes you went with it. It was quite something, I tell you."

The coming of age of the Austin Motor Company was celebrated with a gala and sports day in June 1926. As well as track events there were tennis, bowls and boxing tournaments, and a motor parade, gymkhana and fair. For the youngsters there was fancy dress and Punch & Judy – all up on the Flying Ground. You could buy a jam sandwich or an ice cream for a penny, doughnuts being literally two-a-penny and meat pies or ham rolls tuppence. Ale cost seven pence. Sir Herbert Austin himself acted as the referee and director of sports with every shop in the works, such as the 7hp Road Test and the West Paint Shop, supplying a team for a grand tug of war.

Over the years there were many such occasions at 'The Austin'. Freddie Henry was obviously proud of the poster he produced for the 1927 Apprentices'

cabaret and dance, which he recalled in his mid-eighties, with a twinkle in his eye, "After it went up on a board near the Old Man's office, Harold Brack, the apprentices' training manager, called me in and said the Old Man had asked him to congratulate me on my artistry but felt that the high-kicking girls weren't quite appropriate in the main entrance of the Austin Motor Company. I mean it only just showed a bit of leg and a bit of knicker, but that's how he felt about it."

In 1928, George Coates was involved with the French version of the Austin Seven. "I was sent to Boulogne for two days to give the 'low down' on the Austin Seven to a representative of Lucien Rosengart. While there I got instructions to carry on to Rosengart's place in Paris and those two days turned into seven months. Rosengart had negotiated an agreement to build the Austin Seven and sell it under his own name. McNab, the foreman of the stamp shop at Longbridge was there too – a big shot, who at Longbridge had 600 people under him. They used to say that if he walked up the shop at Longbridge and a particular hammer wasn't in use it would go up and down by itself – scared of being told off. But he was a good boss, a real Scot with a good voice. He would say, 'Git me Jodge. Noo, tell 'em Jodge.' He wanted me to sort out the French blokes. There was a dodgy camshaft which they kept trying to push through the engine test department. In the end I put a grindstone to it and broke it in two. Rosengart sent for me and gave me a dressing down, but I wasn't going to let an engine go through with that shaft in. I told him, 'You said you wanted the same quality as Longbridge and that is what you will get.' You had to watch the French blokes, they tried all sorts of things.

"They weren't satisfied with the brakes so increased the length of the brake levers by ⅜in on all four wheels. The brakes were still a little spongy and to investigate the reason they put this bloomin' chassis up on a hoist and drove each wheel with a separate electric motor. After starting up the motors they would put on the brakes and you could see the chassis twisting. They tried strengthening the wishbones but it didn't help, so they decided to add an extra chassis member, parallel to the propshaft, to join the front and rear cross members.

"We were busy with that when Old Man Austin turned up. I was on the floor in my beret and blue overalls and he said, 'Is that you Coates? What are you doing down there?' So I told him about the new

George Coates in the Bois de Boulogne, Paris, with the 16/6 specially prepared for the 1929 shows. Inset is the small ivory nameplate that was affixed to the car's dashboard.

chassis member and he said, 'There's no need for that.' But I told him how they had made the levers longer and how the chassis was twisting. He said, 'It can't do. It can't do.' Then he dashed off and fetched the foreman in charge, a proper Frenchman you know, red cheeks and a moustache, and the Old Man said to me, 'Tell him I want to see this thing working.' Well, he got it going and showed Herbert how it reared up under braking and how the torque-tube was bearing on the rear cross member. He had to accept it in the end.

"Then he said, 'Come on, we are going to see the tractors'. Blimey it was all go you know. I'd been up to Dieppe the previous day to pick up the Seven Horse that the Old Man was going to drive to Liancourt. I'd run out of water when the casting on the side of the block had come loose and the engine seized up for a while. It stopped way out in the country and the ditches were bone dry so I tried to pee in it but gave that up when I slipped. The radiator was too bloody hot for that game! Fortunately a motor bike came along and the chap fetched me some water. By that time it was cool enough to put the water in and when I saw where the water was coming from I tightened things up and got it to Paris in one piece.

"It was a big-doored Top Hat Saloon. I was keeping my fingers crossed that it would behave itself on the way to Liancourt because Austin and Rosengart

The 100,000th Seven outside the works in 1929.

set off in it with Rosengart driving. I was travelling behind with Rosengart's chauffeur in a Renault with the radiator at the back of the scuttle. It was steaming like mad and we just couldn't keep up. When we eventually found them stopped by the roadside the Old Man said, 'Where the dickens have you been? Did you stop for a coffee?' But you know we couldn't get more than about 30mph out of the Renault and of course the bloomin' Seven would keep up 40mph and more. When the chauffeur said he couldn't keep up Old Man Austin laughed like hell."

Although Herbert Austin was irritated by Rosengart's use of that additional chassis member, when Austin introduced coupled brakes on the Seven in June 1930, they also found an extra chassis member essential. Austin even provided a chassis member for retro-fitting to any cars whose owners wished to update with the new coupled brakes.

In 1928, Austin introduced the highly successful 16/6. At the 1929 Paris show, George Coates was demonstrating an example that had been specially prepared in the experimental department. "The cams had been 'stoned' so that all the valves opened at exactly the right moment and the crank and flywheel were fully balanced. They used a cast iron surface table and two stands with perfectly horizontal knife-edge rails on which you put the flywheel and crank to balance it by trial and error. There were no high-tech machines to balance things in those days, but the slow running was magnificent. It ticked over like a sewing machine. The car had Herbert Austin's nameplate on the dash, but it was used as a demonstrator and a taxi to ferry the top brass at the different shows. People wouldn't believe it was running until I lifted the bonnet to let them see the drive for the dynamo."

It was the Seven, however, that was Herbert Austin's greatest joy. In 1929 the 100,000th Seven left the works. When Herbert Austin was interviewed by *The Autocar* that year he said, "I look back on the year 1922 as one that marks an important milestone in my life, for it was then that I introduced the now-famous Seven. The Seven has done more than anything previously accomplished to bring about the realisation of my ambition to motorise the masses."

By the end of the 1920s, thanks largely to the Seven and the Twelve Horse, the Austin Motor Company was back on course with a workforce of 13,500 and an output of some 50,000 cars a year, over half of which were Sevens.

4

A motor for the millions – the Austin Seven

"I was a bit ashamed of it because there was so much leg-pulling, but the family man took to it right away."

STANLEY EDGE

In 1916, Stanley Howard Edge was a 13-year-old pupil at Halesowen Grammar School. His father worked in the cashier's office at Longbridge but had high hopes that young Stanley would take up some sort of academic career. Stanley had other ideas. All his schoolmasters bar one had gone off to war, but he persuaded his headmaster to "rather grudgingly

The Austin AFT3 Osprey, built in the Aero shop at Longbridge where Stanley Edge began his career, about to make its maiden flight at Martlesham Heath in March 1918. Young Stanley, second from left, was happy to keep his feet firmly on the ground. "I certainly wasn't in the front rank begging to go up. They'd engaged a foreman from the Hull Aircraft Company and he took it up. A brave man, I thought."

agree" that he and one of his pals could teach themselves engineering. "We went to Hudson's book shop and got all sorts of books to teach ourselves mechanical drawing."

By 1917, Stanley was quite proud of his drawings and asked his father to show them to the chief draughtsman at Longbridge to see if there might be an opening for him. Somewhat loath, his father hawked the drawings around a dozen different drawing offices at the Works, the car drawing office being out of action due to the war effort. By the time he found his way to the aero experimental shop he had decided he was on a loser so was quite shaken when they asked, "When can he start?" When he explained that Stanley wasn't yet 14 they simply said, "Not to worry, he can start in August", the August of 1917, immediately after Stanley's 14th birthday.

The aero shop where Stanley began work was building an experimental tri-plane, the Austin AFT3 Osprey. Stanley believed the Osprey was being developed to take on Germany's 'Red Baron,' Manfred von Richthofen, famous for the daring flying of his scarlet Fokker Triplane, but who was shot down over the Somme just as the Osprey was about to make its maiden flight.

With the war coming to an end there was little future for such aircraft so Stanley's foreman advised him, "Just look at the shop out there. We've got rows and rows of SE5 fighters. You had better get yourself down to the main car drawing office." On arriving there Stanley found that Herbert Austin's original team had surreptitiously recommenced car design. Said Stanley, "By 1918 they were going hammer and tongs designing the Twenty Horse. I was in that drawing office when the hooter sounded in November 1918 to celebrate the end of the war and we all downed tools and went home."

Drawing office staff began work at 9 o'clock, but Stanley's train from Halesowen got him to the Works by eight. "Consequently I would be there in the office rooting about with nothing particular to do and Herbert Austin would often come in. He was quite a shy man. He'd say, 'Do you know where they keep the so and so?' and I'd say, 'Yes Sir' and lay it in front of him. Sometimes I didn't walk away and he'd look at me as if to say, 'Off you go.' But I'd stay and he'd have to say something, so we got talking about design and it seems I must have impressed him."

Staff were being cut back left, right and centre, so when chief designer Hancock sent for Stanley and said solemnly but very politely, "Sit down Mr Edge," Stanley thought he too was to be shown the door. Imagine his relief when Hancock said, "I don't

Stanley Edge was emphatic that the Austin Seven was not designed on the Lickey Grange billiard table. This standard-sized board and T-square were those used for all his drawings. Note how he had burnt 'S. H. Edge' (Stanley Howard Edge) on the back of the board.

want you to breathe a word of this to anyone, but Sir Herbert wants you to go up to Lickey Grange and be his draughtsman. He wants you to live there so you must go home and ask your father's permission." Although Stanley was more than ready to agree to the proposal, Hancock insisted. "He says you must ask your father."

Stanley merely informed his parents that he was going to Lickey Grange. "I didn't ask them but they didn't object, so I went back and told Joey Hancock that it was all right and Hancock said, 'Go back to your drawing board and Sir Herbert will come to see you himself when he's got time.'"

A day or two later, Sir Herbert came bustling into the office and, as usual, everybody wondered what he wanted. To their "open-mouthed astonishment" he went straight down the row to young Stanley and said, "We can't talk here, but will you come up and see me next Sunday morning?"

Up at Lickey Grange, Stanley learnt that he was to be taken off the payroll at Longbridge and be paid by Herbert Austin himself as the draughtsman/designer on a new small car project. "The Old Man stressed that he didn't want anyone to know what was going on and then took me through the library and into the billiard room where he showed me the sketches that he'd already made. He'd got a Rover Eight all set out, as near as no matter a Rover Eight, he'd virtually copied it. I never saw him put a ruler to a paper all the time I was with him, but the sketch was about as big as the Rover Eight itself, all laid out on the billiard table."

The tale that the Seven was designed on the billiard table, other than perhaps that initial sketch by Sir Herbert Austin, was refuted by Stanley. "You couldn't put a square on the billiard table, but in the billiard room there was a little alcove where I could work on my own drawing board. I did the arrangements and all the details on that board and the first cars were actually made from my drawings.

"We flogged away at this 'Rover' for some time, a horizontally opposed, air-cooled twin. I was only a youngster but I didn't like it. Before I managed to get a few of my own ideas into the project we tried everything, even a radial three-cylinder engine. Some French lunatic had tried that and Herbert Austin was a great admirer of French design. Leading up to Christmas of 1921 we put every possible layout on paper. We even had a diamond arrangement of wheels, with one either side, one in front and one at the back.

"We did eventually get away from the horizontal twin because I'd noticed that most Continental small cars of the day, Amilcars, Grégoires and the like, had four-cylinder engines. Some writer did once take it upon himself to say that I had measured up a Peugeot Quadrilette but that was absolute damn nonsense. I still have a list of the French cars I laid before Sir Herbert, but I didn't see a Peugeot until much later.

"The eventual power unit was entirely my own, but I'll tell you what did influence me. I had a sectional drawing of an FN four-cylinder air-cooled motorcycle of 750cc that used 52mm bores. I wasn't really competent to design a crankshaft mathematically from first principles. But I reckoned that if this FN motorcycle had a two-bearing crank of 1in diameter and a certain length (being air cooled it had to have more space between the cylinders) then

I would be well on the safe side by using a 1⅛in, much shorter crank. It was only a rule of thumb but we had very little trouble with the cranks.

"One week the Old Man was away for three or four days. Being an MP he had to go to Parliament and all the rest of it, so I set out a four-cylinder engine, complete with clutch and gearbox. When he came back I – well – with great nervousness, I told him I'd set this thing out. He only grunted at it. 'Mmmm, Mmm, Mm' and I had to ask, 'Well, what about it? Shall I go ahead?' 'Oh well,' he said, 'you've gone to the trouble of doing it, so you might as well.' It may seem a boast, but to put it quite frankly, I think as a youngster who'd studied engines since leaving school, I was rather more up to date in that department than he was. So that's how it came about, the Seven's four-cylinder engine.

"The Old Man could be stubborn. After we had laid out the engine with a 52mm bore giving 696cc I suggested we should increase the bore to produce 748 or 749cc and thus bring it into the 750cc class already established in the motor industry. He said, 'No, 696cc will be quite enough.' I thought, well they are bound to want it sooner or later so I left a bit of extra material on the cylinder walls and it was quite comfortably bored out from 52 to 54mm within less than a hundred cars. Everybody agreed it would be better if it could be bored out and I pointed out that I had left sufficient material for that to be done.

"The chassis frame was entirely Herbert Austin's idea. Nor could I have made a good job of the steering mechanism or rear axle without Herbert Austin to guide me. Believe me or not, when I went up to the Grange, although I knew all about engines and gearboxes, I had never seen the inside of an Austin rear axle. We were departmentalised, even in those days, into engine section, chassis section and so on. So I used some old axle drawings from pre-war Austins and scaled things down. I must say the Old Man didn't like a lot of it. He'd say, 'Oh no, much too heavy, much too heavy,' and he'd show me how it should be. I also worked from a drawing of the Austin Twenty clutch and gearbox. Of course I knew a bit about that so I didn't have much trouble in designing the gearbox. I knew nothing about bodywork but he indicated what he wanted and I set out the body as well."

During his time designing the Seven, Stanley had his lunch and dinner at the Grange but slept in the lodge. A maid would leave his meals on a table in the library and would poke her head around the billiard room door to let him know when they were served. The library was a source of great pleasure to

Stanley and he recalled telling his father of Sir Herbert's row upon row of leather-bound books. "My father was no lover of Sir Herbert and simply asked, 'Has he ever read any of them?' In later years I found he had bought his library; lock, stock and barrel from Sir Hickman Bacon, Bart, of Thonock Hall, Gainsborough. I often wonder how I found time while I was designing this car, but I read several volumes of Walter Scott. From that day to this I have never taken Scott's *Antiquary* off the shelf, yet I well remember the lines:

They saddled a hundred milk-white steeds,
They saddled a hundred black.
With a chaffron of steel at each horse's head
And a mail-ed knight on his back.

"Believe me, I could go on and I haven't seen that book since 1922 yet those lines remain with me. I was a disappointment to my father, I'm sure I was. If he had had his way I would have been a scholar.

"Herbert Austin was a very serious-minded man but he'd been pretty kindly and patient with me. However, from late February until the Easter of 1922 I found him getting more and more bad tempered as each week went by. You couldn't live with him. He was hellishly bad tempered. I only learnt much later that he was having quite a battle with his directors to get money allocated for the Seven. Anyway, just before the Easter he was granted £1,500 to produce three cars and he said, 'I want you to bring all your drawings to the Works on Tuesday morning'. It was Easter Tuesday and when I got there I found they'd made a walled-in section with an office at the end for me.

"I had produced drawings with proper tolerances on them so they didn't have to alter anything. The first three cars were built between Easter and Whitsuntide 1922. Herbert Austin brought along an old boy called McLellan, a superintendent, and Alf Depper from experimental and two or three fitters and an apprentice. That was the team to build the first three cars. Nobody else was allowed to see them.

"The crankshaft was an interesting job. I knew where to find slabs of KE 805 (Kayser Ellison 805 key steel) out of which they made Woodruff keys, and I purloined it. We drilled the outline of the crank in this slab of steel. I believe the production people had to do without Woodruff keys for a week because I had pinched their steel but in those days it was a case of every man for himself. It wasn't easy because Englebach was employed by the Receiver to see that none of this 'thieving' if you like, went on. Of course we were quite as good at dodging him as he was at preventing it.

"When I rode in the first Seven with Sir Herbert his immediate reaction was, well, he was picking faults. He said, 'We must have a straight screen.' It was only at about ten degrees, but he thought a sloping screen would damage people's eyes. Of course, after making the screen upright we had to change the hood irons.

"In about July or early August 1922, Hancock and Sir Herbert came into my little office. It was quite amusing. They didn't speak to me. They spoke

A 1923 Seven Horse 'family model' being put to the very use its designers Herbert Austin and Stanley Edge had intended.

Advertising suggested you could motor in comfort for "no more than the cost of a tram ticket" in your Austin Seven.

about me. Hancock said, 'Don't you think, Sir Herbert, that now the cars have been designed it would be quicker if Mr Edge came back into the drawing office and used the facilities there to lick the drawings into final shape and put them on standard sheets?' Sir Herbert wouldn't say yes and he wouldn't say no. I like to think he was saying to himself, 'well, young Edge hasn't done badly so far, so let him just keep on a bit longer'. Anyway, Joey Hancock could see he wasn't getting anywhere, he

wasn't going to have his way, so he said, 'Alternatively, Sir Herbert, we could send somebody up to assist Mr Edge.' Sir Herbert said yes to that."

Did Herbert Austin ever compliment Stanley on the work he did on the Seven?

"No, he never said, 'Well done', definitely not. My father asked me, 'Now you've done all this work for him, has he offered you any more money?' I said he hadn't so he said, 'Well tackle him.' So with

What would Stanley have made of this? An early Seven (c1925) four-up yet still expected to pull a Rice Folding Caravan – with balding tyres too, photographed c1930.

great daring one day I said, 'Now this job is well on the way, can I have an increase in salary?' Do you know what he said? One word. 'Why?' I said, 'Well, I want to get on.' He said, 'We all want to get on, don't we?' That's how he talked you see but a rise did come through. Quite a generous increase for those days."

Longbridge weekly staff records show that Stanley was indeed suspended from the official payroll in October 1921 when his salary was £2 5s (£2.25) a week. When replaced on the Longbridge payroll in April 1922 he received £3 per week – an increase of 33⅓ per cent.

Because Herbert Austin himself had patented a lot of the ideas that were used in the Seven he personally received a two-guinea royalty on each car built. As Stanley Edge good-humouredly put it, "Aye, he did, by God. Many of those patents were for my ideas too. Whether he engaged me because I was under 21 or not I don't know, but in those days being under 21 meant you had no rights at all. They wouldn't take my money at the bank. Lloyds wouldn't take me on at all in 1923 when I was 20 years old. After much persuasion the London Joint City & Midland Bank Ltd, – it became the Midland Bank later on – did take me on but wrote 'Minor' on my bank book. So I couldn't have patented anything myself. Whether that entered his head I don't know, but he was pretty shrewd.

"Of course there was a good deal of ridicule of the original Seven. When I went to work in Lincoln in 1925 I was a bit ashamed of it because there was so much leg-pulling but the family man took to it right away.

"I have to avoid offending Seven owners today [1988]. Some of them have made pretty weird modifications and they take me on one side and say, 'Look I've done this and I've done that.' And I say, 'Oh, very good, very good.' I have to refrain from saying, 'Well, bloody silly, you should have left it alone and enjoyed it as it was.' Of course, once they have paid their money you can't stop 'em putting a double decker body on it, if they want to, can you?"

Continuing in this merry vein Stanley's eyes lit up as he asked, "Have you heard the record sung by old Clarkson Rose about the Austin Seven?" Without waiting for an answer Stanley burst into a jolly imitation of Rose singing, "Funny little Austin Seven" – "and on the other side," said Stanley, "was the Austin Unity Song written by Collie Knox." With a deep intake of breath, his arms conducting a non-existent orchestra, and his cheeks getting rosier by the minute, Stanley broke into song once more, "All stand united, with Austin as our aim, Our path

Stanley was still driving this Longbridge-built Mini in 1987, his 85th year. It was while purchasing this car that he was asked by a Longbridge telephonist, "Herbert Austin, does he work here?"

is lighted with progress for the flame, no shirkers, all workers, all playing the game." "Oh dear," said Stanley, "Herbert Austin made a present of that record to all the dealers at their annual dinner in the Connaught Rooms in 1928. The dealers don't seem to have been too pleased with it because apparently many of the records were left in the gents. Anyway, the little Austin Seven must have made them a bob or two. After all they sold nearly 300,000 of them, didn't they?"

Stanley died in his 87th year in 1990 but will always be remembered as one who, despite his tender years, made a considerable contribution to the success of Herbert Austin's most remarkable creation, the diminutive Austin Seven.

A favourite saying of this charming man was, "Good-enough is just not good enough." The meticulous care taken in the design of the Austin Seven is surely testimony enough that Stanley Howard Edge practised what he preached.

5

The Thirties – turbulent times

"Those new presses were the old man's pride and joy. It was quite something to see the whole side of a car being pressed out instead of blokes having to hammer day and night with different tools."

GEORGE COATES

Herbert Austin faced the 1930s believing the improved conditions of 1929/30 would continue to bring an increased demand for larger cars, the Austin range then consisting of the Twenty Horse, Sixteen and Twelve as well as the diminutive Seven. But as things turned out, it was Herbert's yet-to-be-launched 10hp car that became the star of the decade.

Austin styling from the late 1920s onwards was undertaken by Ricardo Burzi. Originally employed by Lancia, Burzi became *persona non grata* in Italy after an Italian paper commissioned his artistic abilities to lampoon Mussolini. Having to leave Italy in a hurry, Burzi was fortunate that a recommendation from Vincenzo Lancia saw him taken under Herbert Austin's wing. A man of considerable charm, Burzi

The Light Twelve Six was launched in 1931 and the Light Twelve Four in 1932. Here we see both models being assembled at Longbridge.

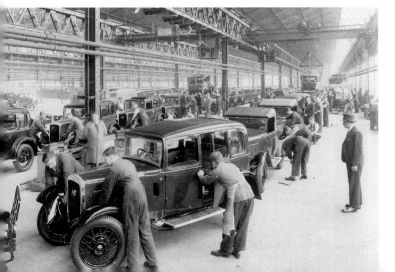

was soon known as Dick throughout the Longbridge works.

His arrival saw George Parker, Austin's chief body designer since 1909, somewhat side-lined. Stanley Edge remembered Parker as, "a genuine old body builder who had served his apprenticeship with a carriage builder in Hereford. He was a countryman from Grosmont, born in 1885, and as he walked round the shop he looked just like the farmers of those days. He liked his beer but there is little wonder he worked up a thirst because every week-end, from 1909 to 1928, he cycled the 68 miles each way to his home in Grosmont."

Arthur West who worked for Parker in body design recalled, "Parker always seemed to get to know through the grapevine if Herbert Austin was on the move in our direction and would come out of his office to make sure everyone was hard at it before Herbert arrived. This obviously annoyed Herbert so he would occasionally warn the gateman of the exact time of his arrival the following day, saying, 'Have the gates open for me, but if I find out that anybody knows about it you'll be looking for a job.' His car could then sweep straight through the Works with Herbert keeping a sharp look out for any slackers."

Parker did not actually retire until 1950 but Jack Clare, who started in 'body experimental' at the age of 15 in 1932, recalled. "I worked on the prototype of the new Westminster, launched in 1933. By that time it was certainly Dick Burzi and Herbert Austin who would design the bodies between them." Sketches still in existence show that Herbert Austin

The Austin 10/4 of May 1932 plugged the gap in Austin's range between the Seven and Twelve.

was often personally involved in designs, even down to the minutest of details.

The Light 12/6, with its new all-steel body, was launched in 1931 but contrary to Herbert Austin's earlier expectations, the depression of 1930/31 saw an increase in demand for cars towards the lower end of the range, particularly for cars of around 10hp, about the only size not catered for by Austin. Herbert had no choice but to plug the gap between his Seven and Twelve with the Austin 10/4, announced in May 1932.

Chief Designer Hancock later recalled how they first chewed things over in Sir Herbert's office. "Could we make a 10hp car that was roomy and good and weighed not more than 15cwt?" Their discussions convinced Herbert Austin that merely

increasing the size of the Seven would not produce the family car they sought so he embarked on the design of a car intermediate in size and price between the Seven and the 12/6 in order that the Austin range would then include every size of car on the market.

Austin emphasised that his new Ten-Four was a model quite distinct from the Seven and Twelve. "A glance at the chassis or complete vehicle will immediately confirm that this car is not the hybrid offspring of preceding types, nor an old model in a new guise. Every new Austin is designed in detail, assembly by assembly, to meet a definite demand and we have not departed from this policy in evolving the Ten. The motoring public can have complete confidence that this new car will do the

Austin's top-of-the-range six-cylinder chassis being assembled in North Works chassis erecting shop c1932.

"The Austin Seven – a big car reduced in scale but not in completeness." In a 1933 brochure entitled When a Woman Buys a Car, *Austin advertising exhorted "Madam take the wheel", going on to claim, "Today there are thousands, tens of thousands, of women who own their own cars, driving them everywhere, and experiencing the tremendously wider life which the ownership of a car gives."*

They also opined: "You can go out in your Ten-Four, on a doubtful day, dressed in your loveliest."

work of a Ten in typical Austin fashion, while being as economical to run as any car of its size. It will uphold the Austin tradition of dependability and sterling value. In short it will meet a vital need of today in providing economical motoring for the average British family."

He was right, too. By 1933 the Ten was outselling even the Seven.

The importance Herbert Austin attached to small details is clearly illustrated by George Coates's account of Herbert's arrival at the Paris show in 1932. "I was in m'blue overalls and m'berry, setting up the stand but as soon as he came in it was a case of, 'C'mon Coates let's go. What have you seen that's new?' I hadn't time to put on my cow gown or anything. I just had to march off with him. Of course they were all babbling away in French and he wanted to know, 'What does he say? What does he want?' Then it was a question of, 'Ask him this,' or 'ask him that.' He always made sure that our cars

The Grand Palais, Paris, 1932. George Coates (at the rear of the 10/4 chassis) chats to the Panama-hatted Gootieris, a San Sebastian Austin agent.

had been polished and dusted. He'd take a good look at the interior to see there were no marks on the carpets or anything. There was coconut matting in all the alleyways at Paris and just sand underneath so the dust carried everywhere. He would ask for the bonnet to be opened and he'd have a look to see if there was any dust on the engine or chassis. There hadn't to be any finger marks anywhere. He once noticed a few water spots from washing the car that had gone rusty on the cast iron fan-belt pulley. 'Oh,' he said, 'you haven't been round here.' Then he opened the rear door of the limousine and found a bit of dust on the Austin sign near the running board. Oh boy, he didn't miss much."

October 1932 saw the launch of a new Light 12/4, which was a much greater success than the 12/6, and by 1934, when Sir Herbert Austin was elected president of the Society of Motor Manufacturers and Traders, Austin were offering 44 separate models on nine different chassis from a factory that had expanded to some 100 acres.

Although the Austin Motor Company's notepaper of the 1930s exhorted one to "Buy British goods and help to reduce unemployment", Austin

Note the Austin badges on the berets of the four drivers who took the Sevens around Denmark in 1932. George Coates is second from left.

was determined to increase his exports too. George Coates recalled a promotional trip to Denmark in 1932. "The idea was to establish dealerships throughout Denmark. I was left on the quay at Hull with four Sevens. When I got to Copenhagen the main agent provided three other drivers. First I had to show them how to handle the clutch because it was a bit all-or-nothing, and then we started our little promenade round Denmark. We stayed in each town for an hour or two, demonstrating the cars in the market places. The Danes liked the Seven but some of the blokes were so big that they just couldn't get in. Most of them had to wrap their knees around the steering wheel. We'd got 'em parked up in one town and I popped off to get a

Proving you can get a quart into a pint pot. George Coates was only 5ft 6in tall but this Dane was obviously 7ft and more. Note the barber in his white coat.

haircut. When I returned there was this big bloke looking at the cars, a seven footer, and people started pulling my leg about the car not being able to take him. I said, 'Not at all, the seats are adjustable. If the gentleman will come with me I will show him that it will take him perfectly well.' Of course the crowd waited for us to return and laughed like anything, but they were surprised when this chap told them that we had been up to 50kph. By that time even the hairdresser had come out in his white coat to see what all the laughter was about. After that we repeated the exercise in Holland, Belgium and Switzerland."

In early 1933, George took a Light 12/4 prototype for a 5,000-mile test to Portugal. "I was just told, 'Go and do 5,000 miles but keep it away from the agents.' I wasn't given a route and I had no back-up or spares. I was just given the car and the car's tool kit, a standard tool kit that any owner would have. Of course it was a real tool kit in those days. A whole set of spanners, pliers and screwdrivers. There was a set of feelers for the spark plugs and distributor. I had to send Herbert a report every day. The car had a new chassis with a cross-braced frame and Armstrong friction shock absorbers that you could adjust with a wing nut. The Portuguese roads were dreadful and by the time I got home the inner cruciform part of the frame, which was riveted to the main frame, had all come loose. They wanted to know if I had taken it across ploughed fields."

Meanwhile, Austin and Englebach had been constantly striving to keep the Longbridge factory abreast of the latest mass-production techniques. Alfred Ash, an apprentice from 1927 to 1931, was in the West Works body planning office. "The first big job I worked on was a brand new conveyorised paint plant in about 1934. We had to design the slings, the conveyors, booths, ovens, the entire plant. After that we went on to install a new heavy press shop for the all-steel bodies in about 1935. A bay was built on the side of the factory to move all the small presses into so that we could install the big presses in the main shop."

According to George Coates, "Those new presses were the Old Man's pride and joy. It was quite something to see the whole side of a car being pressed out instead of blokes having to hammer day and night with different tools."

That Herbert Austin cared greatly about every aspect of the business can be seen from the briefing he gave George Coates in 1936. "He sent for me to give me instructions about taking a special limousine to the Paris show. He said, 'Whatever you do, get it hoisted aboard on a platform. On no account

In 1934 there was, for Austin, a radical change in the styling of the Seven, to produce the Ruby with its smoothly cowled radiator grille.

The new style was extended to the rest of the Austin range for 1935. Here we see the 10/4 Lichfield saloon.

must you allow them to lift it in slings and cushions or they will bend the wings.'"

"At Folkestone," said George, "it took them half an hour to get the platform out – bloomin' big thing it was – and it stayed with the car on the boat, so at Boulogne I told them to keep it handy until I came back. I tipped them half-a-crown (12½p) between about six blokes. When I got back to the Works and filled out my expenses the Old Man said, 'What's this?' He wouldn't have it. He said, 'I don't go round giving the blokes sixpence with their pay packet. If you want to be a big shot then pay it yourself.' Oh no, he didn't believe in tipping. There were no raised platforms then on the French railways and when Herbert came along with his big suitcases the porters had to hitch them up into the carriage and then on to the racks. He did sometimes think about tipping them because you would see him fiddling with a silver threepenny bit which he then put back in his waistcoat pocket!"

It seems Herbert Austin did not believe in the need for unions either and actively discouraged union membership. A few union members were always employed at Longbridge but only because of the difficulty of finding non-union craftsmen in some trades. The great influx of labour during the First World War did see union membership flourish for a while but by 1925 management had seen to it that the shop stewards organisation had been severely weakened. What were seen as unacceptable management decisions would still regularly produce men who were prepared to stand up for better treatment but as most were neither shop stewards nor even union members they would, more often than not, soon find themselves out of a job.

With such a low level of union representation it was the rate fixers who often had to take the brunt of worker discontent. Bill Chance started as a rate fixer in the trim shop in 1936. "As a rate fixer you had to skin anything or anybody for a farthing – experiment with everything to try and get a farthing off the job. One of the girls on trimming once turned to me and said, 'Why don't you stick a broom up me arse and make me sweep the shop at the same time.' I was drained!"

Unions or no unions, the majority of Longbridge employees undoubtedly had a great respect for Herbert Austin. In the 1936 Honours List he was created a Baron and became Lord Austin of Longbridge but the men continued to refer to him simply but affectionately as the Old Man or Old Man Austin.

Things were certainly going well at this time and 1936 saw the launch of the Cambridge 10hp, Ascot

12hp and Goodwood 14hp. The Cambridge in particular helped Austin achieve a production of 90,000 cars in 1936/37, a figure not to be beaten until after the Second World War.

Not that everyone was laughing all the way to the bank. Bill Manning started in the pattern shop as a boy of 14 in April 1939. "I had passed the eleven-plus but times were very hard so my parents couldn't send me on to secondary school. There were four of us and dad was unemployed. One Christmas we had nothing at all, well, some apples and oranges and mother made a plum pudding but there were no presents. I'm not pleading poverty because we were all very poor in the Thirties. I started work in second-hand shoes and trousers which they sent to London for; blue, thick serge trousers which cost five bob (25p). My wage was ten shillings and tuppence, that's 51p a week for 48 hours. I lived at Stoke Prior about ten miles away and the return bus fare was one shilling (5p) a day. That took six shillings out of my 10s 2d, so I had two bob pocket money and my mother had 2s 2d to keep me, so she soon made sure I had a bike. The 'tea money' brought me more than my wage. I used to fill 24 cans on a lunch time and I got threepence a week off each man. That was the going rate although I got sixpence off some. So that gave me over six shillings.

"The tea money went on buying my tools. You were on a bench with a senior man. He'd lend you his tools but it was expected that when you'd got the money you bought your own. We always had to wear a collar and tie and you had a smock or cow gown as we called it. If your tie was dangling down he'd get a chisel and chop it off; that's how you learnt. You might be working across the bench and if you weren't doing it right you'd get a rap straight across the fingers with a steel rule. It didn't do us any harm. To me it was a wonderful life, a challenge from start to finish. One night I took home the little pattern I was making to show my mum. It was only a little bracket of some sort but I was so proud. 'The Austin' was my life. We haven't a lot now but Austin gave us everything we have."

Although the war was about to see the Longbridge factory turned almost inside out, there were to be considerable ructions even before that with the arrival of one Leonard Percy Lord in early 1938.

Crude, coarse, belligerent, ruthless and inhuman; at one time or another, Leonard Lord has been described as all of those. But whatever his faults, Lord was a shrewd and capable man who had already more than proved his worth, under William Morris, as a devastatingly effective production engineer. So effective in fact that he felt grossly under-rewarded

In 1936, the smoother style was further developed with the introduction of the Cambridge 10, Ascot 12 and Goodwood 14, the sloping tails producing the first Austin models with a rear luggage compartment.

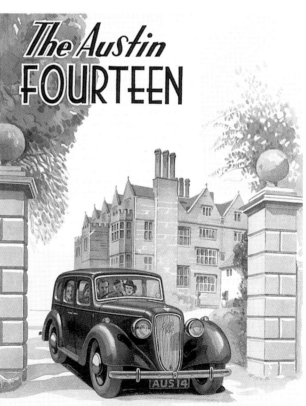

Leonard Lord's new 8, 10 and 12hp cars of 1939 saw Austins becoming quite up-to-date in style. This is the 12hp saloon which retained a separate chassis.

for his efforts. A plea to Morris for a reasonable share in the profits found the two men at loggerheads. A bitter clash ended with Lord's resignation.

When Austin heard that Lord might be available he instructed Englebach to invite him to Sunday lunch, in order to discuss the possibility of him coming to Longbridge but with strict instructions to inspect his table manners! How Englebach, whose eyesight was failing so badly that he required guiding around the factory, could be entrusted with the latter task is hard to say, but both he and Herbert Austin were apparently satisfied that Lord would be just the man to take over Englebach's duties. Perhaps there was also some truth in Austin historian Bob Wyatt's suggestion that Austin wanted

Lord not only "for his undoubted organising and engineering ability, but also because he knew that Lord would do everything in his power to beat Nuffield as a car maker."

When Lord arrived at Longbridge in 1938 he must have found it a very conservative place. Although Herbert Austin was about ready to give up the reins, the ideals he had engendered in his men, conscien-

The 8 and 10hp used a platform chassis seen here – a step in the direction of unitary construction.

The winter of 1938/39 saw Austin introduce their overhead-valve-engined Bedford-inspired trucks, seen here in the chassis erecting shop.

tious workmanship along with sober and gentle-manly conduct, were part and parcel of the scene.

As Lord made his first rounds of the various shops in the Works, whispers preceded him, labelling this new powder keg of a gaffer as 'a bloke from Morris' – a poor recommendation to Austin men if ever there was one!

"When he took over as Works Director," said Stanley Edge, "it was as if a whirlwind had hit the place. Talk about a new broom. He was seen as a tyrant, a man who started turning the place upside down before he'd been there five minutes. He immediately tangled with Payton, Austin's second in command, and upset Haefeli, a senior designer, who found Lord giving orders to the men before he even knew who Lord was."

Many of the men, however, were surprised to find they quite liked him. They admired his direct-ness and his obvious knowledge of the work they were doing. Frank Fletcher remembered his leniency. "Lord was very good to the men. Herbert Austin never allowed anyone to smoke so men would sneak out maybe a dozen times a day to smoke in the toilets. The doors in the toilets had little square holes so that the Works coppers could see if anyone was smoking. You would hang your cow gown over the hole but they'd push it aside to see what was going on. If you were caught you'd either get a warning or be suspended for a couple of days. That all finished with the arrival of Lord. He allowed you to smoke on the job if it was safe. He got more output that way than ever before."

Herbert Austin, although far from happy about the men being allowed to smoke, allowed Len Lord to have his head and as Lord could make mincemeat of any other would-be adversaries, he soon had the place a hive of new activity.

Within 18 months he had launched his own range of 8, 10 and 12hp cars and brought Austin back into the commercial vehicle field by launching trucks of 2–5 ton capacity in the winter of 1938/39. In order to achieve such rapid progress Lord was not averse to utilising other people's ideas. Just as his Morris Eight of 1934 had owed a great deal to Ford's Y-Type, his 1939 Austin truck was undoubtedly a dead ringer of the contemporary Bedford.

Having launched his new cars and trucks, Leonard Lord still had further plans up his sleeve for the considerable reorganisation and expansion of 'The Austin'. But Adolf Hitler had his plans too.

Swastikas everywhere as Hitler makes his appearance on the Austin stand in Spring 1939 at the Berlin Motor Show.

6

At war again,
1939–1945

"During the war it was easy money. All our contracts were on a 'cost plus' basis. We couldn't go wrong."

BILL ROWKINS OF THE LONGBRIDGE COST OFFICE

"The girls in the sewing room did a roaring trade in gas mask cases. Your gas mask came in a cardboard box with a piece of string to go round your neck but the girls were soon turning out lovely leather ones in green, brown or black at a shilling a go. I was one of the kids in the store and if they wanted someone to take something up to George Bidell, who looked after the machines in the sewing room, we all used to disappear. When you went up there mate, it was full of girls and women and by the time you had got halfway down you were ready to run for your bloody life. They would have your trousers off as soon as look at you. You no sooner got in the door than the cat calls started, very suggestive ones too."

A 12hp Austin Aero Works fire tender 1938.

When Peter Lowe recounted the above tale he also spoke of the war-time spirit within the works. "Sometimes it was just like a street market. The blokes from Bromsgrove, we called them the Bromsgrove Swedes, brought in their produce and displayed it like a flower show. Even little pigs in pokes and chickens and God knows what else. The money went towards the Spitfire fund."

Longbridge men and women are justifiably proud of their contribution to the production of aircraft and armaments during the Second World War. Over 3,000 aircraft and 60,000 Mercury and Pegasus engines or engine sets; 359 Horsa glider fuselages, used for both the Normandy landings and the ill-fated Arnhem drop; all churned out in a frenzy of activity along with a full range of army vehicles including 13,000 of the famous K2 ambulances and over 36,000 four-wheel-

Stirling bomber aircraft production at Longbridge.

drive trucks. Nor did car production cease entirely, the War Office placing orders for both 8 and 10hp utility cars. It meant a grand total of some 120,000 vehicles, along with massive quantities of ammunition, pressings for over half a million jerrycans and some two million tin hats.

Although Herbert Austin gradually took less and less part in this war-time activity he had certainly led the way. With the inevitability of war he was made chairman of a Government-sponsored Shadow Factory Scheme for aircraft production. Having bought the adjoining Parsonage Farm, he was awarded a contract to build an aero factory which, by the outbreak of war, was already producing the Fairey Battle.

Longbridge liaison officer, Geoff Cooper recalled, "We managed the 'Aero' as we called it, throughout the war and built about 1,200 Fairey Battles, all of which flew off from Longbridge. They winched the planes up a ramp from the flight shed to the Flying Ground. From 1940, we built the first four-engined RAF bomber, the Stirling. We built over 600 at the rate of one a day. Then we took on the Lancaster and got that up to one a day and did about 300 or so of those. The Stirlings and Lancasters were too big to take off from Longbridge so they took the fuselage and wings over to Elmdon (now Birmingham Airport) to be assembled and flew them out from

Sections of a total of 359 troop-carrying Horsa glider fuselages built in West Works 1941/44. These gliders could carry 29 fully equipped troops and were towed behind bombers.

there. We also had a short period producing Hurricane Mk II tank-busters for the North Africa campaign and the flight shed was also used to repair and refurbish any Spitfires that could manage to fly in."

Austin's sawmill was very busy during the war, providing timber for the Miles Master training planes and Horsa gliders as well as wooden structures for Hurricanes and Mosquitoes.

Prior to the war, mining engineers had dug tunnels under the Flying Ground which could accommodate 15,000 people. They were roofed in arched steelwork and all the seven or eight entrances were protected with blast doors. Apart from being used as air raid shelters some of the tunnels also doubled up as assembly shops for the Mercury and Pegasus engines.

What stuck in Alfred Ash's mind was the way they ripped out the existing plant at the beginning of the war. "All our beautiful new paint shop, all the conveyors in the finishing shop, they didn't unbolt them, they burnt them out with a welding torch and dumped them. It was an awful shame to see it."

"They thought Longbridge would be bombed out of existence," said George Coates, "so they made a

Aero engine assembly in the Longbridge tunnels that also doubled as air-raid shelters.

model of the works and the Air Ministry camouflaged it by putting numbers on the roof just like a kid's painting book. There were 120 acres of roof to camouflage and it was done in three days. It was so well done that if you went up the Lickey Hills and looked down you couldn't see the Works. It just looked like a field."

George was one of many employees who volunteered for the Home Guard. "I was given a pickaxe handle to look after a tunnel entrance in case any parachutists came to sabotage it. Yes, a pickaxe handle. Eventually we got some uniforms and First World War Lee Enfield rifles. In the end, I had four armoured cars and 40 blokes under me. We had one armoured car on the Flying Ground and patrolled the local roads with the others. We used to collect five rounds of ammunition each and turn it in with the rifle when we came off duty."

Ben Benbow was one of 200 or so Longbridge workers trained for the Auxiliary Fire Service by the Birmingham Fire Brigade. "We had two Austin Twelve trucks in the Auxiliary Fire Service with 300-gallon trailer pumps and four men with each vehicle. As we approached Pebble Mill one night, down the Bristol Road, there was a huge crater. We couldn't pass but the crater had filled up from a burst main so we pumped water from there. We had a relay of about five pumps pumping water about

two miles – in the big Blitz – flames everywhere, tracer bullets and shrapnel flying around. The Salvation Army always stayed out with us during the raids. I'll never forgot the night a woman shouted from behind her garden wall, 'When those bastards have finished dropping their bombs I'll give you lads a cup of tea.' She never did. Her house disappeared and she went with it.

Ray Avery was in West Works body shop. "All the fighting vehicles were done in our experimental shop in West Works. Everything from the 8hp Tilleys to the 3-ton trucks. We did fire pumps, 4x4 armoured carriers, fire engines, ambulances and troop carriers. You name it, we built it. About 500 vehicles a week were coming out of that shop."

Peter Lowe worked on the modification of vehicles for the Normandy landings. "About six weeks

These Austin War Department models illustrate something of Longbridge's war-time production. From left to right: 8hp utility tourer, 10hp utility pick-up, 2-ton ambulance, 6-wheeled version of Austin 3-ton general service lorry, 3-ton 6-wheeled recovery vehicle, and 3-ton 4-wheeled gun portee. Inset: Peter Lowe worked on these Lancaster bomber fuel tanks in South Works press shop. "They were made in two halves and if one started rocking you could guess what was going on inside. Some of the love-birds found them ideal – much safer than in a cinema in those days."

before D-day there was a flap on. Lorries were coming back from all over the place. It was a case of head off, sump off, pistons out and minus 30 or 40 thou pistons in. If an engine was hot when a wagon came off the landing craft into the water the engine seized up. We did hundreds of them, 24 hours a day, seven days a week. All they wanted was a lorry that could get off the beach."

It was the jerrycans that tickled George Coates. "They were made from a sketch of a German one sent from North Africa. We did 25,000 a week. It was a clever design because you could have a string of men carrying them, a can in each hand, side by side. You could join the bits with edge welding, exactly the same as the German ones."

Ben Benbow spoke of using another design of foreign origin. "At the fall of France the Swiss drawings were brought from France for the Oerlikon gun. Len Lord brought them up to the office and I was asked to design a magazine that could be made cheaply from pressings. Haefeli helped me translate the specifications because he was Swiss and also fluent in French. Our magazines were rubbish compared to the precision watchmaker's job of the original, but the idea was to use the magazines a few times and throw them away. They were dirt cheap to make. We turned out 110,000 magazines for the Oerlikon."

From tin hats … to jerrycans … to Oerlikon and Bren gun magazines … Longbridge produced them all by the hundreds of thousands.

Fred Smith played a part in perfecting magazines for the Bren gun. "They had awful trouble with the magazines jamming and Harry Austin came spluttering down to me one day. 'C, c, come, here. We've got a problem,' he said. He always stuttered when he was upset. He said, 'It's jamming and we want 4,000 a week. We are producing the parts but they won't pass them.' I went up to the assembly shop and found a line of girls filing the slots where the bullets dropped through. Well, you can never file exactly straight, certainly the girls couldn't. They aren't 'coloured' are women when it comes to filing, not suited to it. So I looked at this thing and I thought we shall have to try and machine it. Harry Austin said, 'You can't machine 20 gauge metal', but I said, 'Well, let's try.' I mean he wanted them – like yesterday. So I got them to make a jig and we rigged up a cutter and you know they were all fine. No more jamming."

Fred also worked on an anti-tank armour-piercing shell. "It was about 7 inches long and 2½ inches in diameter. On the nose there was a vanadium steel cap but as soon as it hit a tank or whatever the cap just fell off. They were in a bit of a fix over that. Harry Williams, the foreman, said to me, 'I've got a problem here. Have you got any ideas mate?' I thought, what do *I* know about a thing like that but going back to my experience in car radiator making, I thought well, why can't we solder the bloody things on. I thought if we pre-heated the body and put some solder on the nose and dropped the cap on and then put it through a fusing oven, perhaps that would work. Do you know, it was no problem at all. After a test-firing they all came down wondering how the hell I had done it. They automated the process and made Harry Williams a superintendent after that – as a result of my ideas!"

Herbert Austin's choice of a rural location for the factory must have been at least partially instrumental in allowing it to go through the war almost unscathed.

Only one aircraft bombed Longbridge, a lone daylight raider in November 1940. Bob Grice was on duty that day with the Royal Observer Corps in the look-out tower at Frankley. "From there we could drop the switch for the warning lights all over the factory."

Ron Savage, of the South Works press shop explained the system. "I was only a kid of 16 so it was all a bit of a novelty to me. Each part of the factory was allotted its own tunnel. At the beginning of the war, you only had to have one aircraft that had perhaps flown as far as Leamington for the alarm to go off and then everybody would stream into the tunnels. One aircraft miles away could stop the place. So they decided to install lights in the shops. You'd be working away and suddenly see yellow lights flashing. That was the early warning to indicate aircraft in the vicinity. If it looked as though they were getting too close they would flash to red and everybody disappeared. They also cut down on who actually went to the tunnels. In the South press we used to go down into the steel stores underneath so there was a concrete floor above us. When the green lights flashed you'd go back to work. The stoppages were minimised from say a couple of hours to about 20 minutes but people got so used to it they tended to carry on anyway. I suppose it was considered patriotic to carry on working."

Stan Blunn brings us back to the lone raid. "I was working on Beaufighters in Trentham building when the red warning lights went on. By the time I had changed my shoes everyone had gone! They called out the Home Guard under Gerry Knight who gave them rifles and ammunition. They stood in the front yard all firing at this plane several thousand feet up. As the plane circled there were shouts of, 'We've turned him, we've turned him,' but then the bombs dropped."

Peter Lowe was in that Home Guard. "When the air raid sounded I went up on the Flying Ground with an Oerlikon. We were building and testing the magazines for the Oerlikons by that stage so we had plenty of ammunition. The plane came round, pop, pop, pop, shooting the barrage balloons down. God he was way up in the air but everyone was banging away with rifles and Oerlikons and each and everyone thought they had hit it. Somebody shouted, 'We've hit it.' They thought there were bits coming off but when they stopped twiddling we saw they were bombs. I can still see those bombs coming down now and they caught the engineer's shop and about three were killed and several injured. You could feel the blast under your tin hat."

Ben Benbow remembered hearing the next morning that the plane had been shot down near Hereford. "It may just have been government propaganda – you know – 'Don't worry, he might have killed some of your mates but we got him' – sort of thing."

According to Freddie Henry, it was that bombing which led indirectly to illness and death for Herbert Austin, then in his 75th year. "Following that daytime air raid on the Longbridge plant, Lord Austin attended the funeral of those killed. He caught double pneumonia from which he never recovered and a few months later, on 23 May 1941,

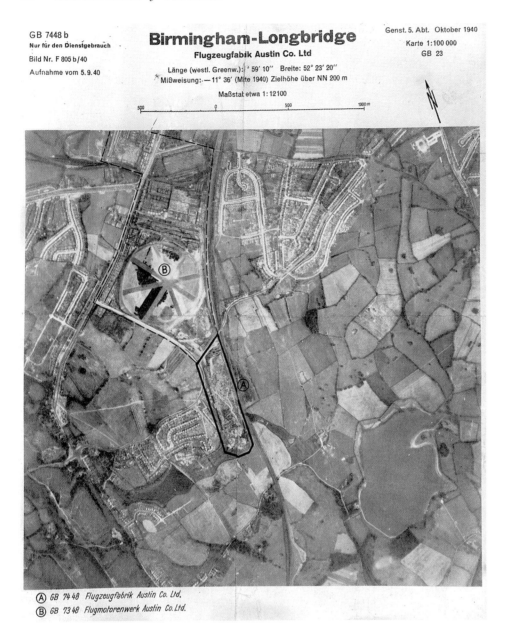

GB 7448 b
Nur für den Dienstgebrauch
Bild Nr. F 805 b/40
Aufnahme vom 5.9.40

Birmingham-Longbridge
Flugzeugfabrik Austin Co. Ltd

Länge (westl. Greenw.): ° 59' 10''   Breite: 52° 23' 20''
Mißweisung:—11° 36' (Mitte 1940) Zielhöhe über NN 200 m

Maßstab etwa 1:12100

500   0   500   1000 m

Genst. 5. Abt. Oktober 1940
Karte 1:100 000
GB 23

Ⓐ GB 74 48 Flugzeugfabrik Austin Co. Ltd.
Ⓑ GB 73 48 Flugmotorenwerk Austin Co. Ltd.

This Luftwaffe aerial view of Longbridge, taken the month before the sole bombing raid, makes it hard to understand how it was not the target of more attacks, except that Herbert Austin's choice of location left it somewhat isolated from the other heavy industries of the region. Area A is denoted correctly as the Austin aircraft factory. Area B, made up of South, North and West Works, is denoted as the Austin aero engine factory, but they also produced the whole range of war materials described. The runways of the circular flying field are clearly visible.

he died following a sudden heart attack at his home."

As a youngster, John Cleaver had the pleasure of working for Herbert Austin in his final days. "I was taken on at Longbridge at the age of 14 in 1940 and spent three months in the Works post office, lugging the mail around in big leather satchels. Then Lord Austin wanted an office boy and when I was sent to him he said to me, 'Your first job every morning is to take my used blotting paper and the contents of my paper basket and burn them.' People have said to me since, 'I bet you got hold of some interesting sketches.' Of course, there were sketches galore, which would be quite valuable now but I did what I was told. Anything in that basket had to be burned.

"He appreciated a job well done, even by an office boy. When he sent for me one day, I found him sat at his desk looking over his half glasses. He said, 'I want you to go to the bank in Northfield and get me a hundred pounds in five pound notes.' Well I'd never owned even a pound note. I don't think I'd ever seen a fiver. My eleven shillings a week went straight to my mother and I had sixpence back. When I came out of the bank I felt as though I was carrying half a million quid. I put it in my pocket but still kept hold of it. When I got back he just dropped the money into a drawer and shut it. I said, 'Aren't you going to count it, sir?' He said, 'There's no need to son.' I felt ten feet tall – fantastic."

John, who was still Herbert's office boy at the time of his death, recalled how the whole factory turned out to pay their last respects; the funeral procession making its way past the Works and slowly up Rose Hill to nearby Lickey churchyard. "I was very upset, as you can imagine. His personal staff, Miss Parker, Bobby Howitt and I, rode in the cortege to the churchyard. I still visit his grave when I go through, brush the leaves off and sit in contemplation."

The death of Herbert Austin saw Leonard Lord become deputy chairman to Ernest Payton and a few months later, Stanley Edge was staggered to hear that Lord had sacked chief designer A. J. Hancock. "It was shameful. Joe was a real gentleman and most courteous. When Lord had sent for Hancock one day Joe intimated that he would be up as quick as he could but that at that very moment he'd got a traveller with him. When Hancock went up Lord said, 'When I send for anyone I want them right away. You don't seem to like that so we'd better part.' Joe, of course, having been with Herbert Austin from the very beginning, was one of those who had stood by Herbert when he was broke and Herbert had said he was never to be dismissed, so Lord said, 'Go home and don't come back. I'll send your salary.'"

Hancock's dismissal saw Haefeli appointed as chief designer. In 1942, after Lord had become joint managing director and deputy chairman to Payton, he took on H. N. (Hubert Noel) Charles from MG and briefed him to set up a development department, a department with one eye on the post-war scene.

Charles is remembered as a brilliant engineer and, according to Gil Jones, who later became chief experimental engineer for BMC, "Charles was one of the first to bring proper scientific principles of design to Longbridge." Initially, Charles worked on any modifications that were required to the tank and truck engines being produced at Longbridge, but it was not long before his development department began work on the overhead-valve engines and independent front suspensions that would be used in the post-war Austin cars.

In early 1943, Lord was asked by the War Department if he had a suitable engine for a proposed British version of the Willys Jeep, an idea to avoid the losses suffered by submarine attacks as the Jeeps were brought across the Atlantic. Lord, in typical fashion, told the military that he had just the thing and then went home and asked his designers to provide him with one in double-quick time. The result was a new four-cylinder overhead-valve 16hp engine using the same cylinder centres as the six-cylinder OHV 3½-litre truck engine.

An enclosed trolley on castors was built to house the components of the engine and the whole lot was shipped down to London for inspection by the Ministry. The Jeep (which, by a tortuous route, eventually became the Rolls-Royce-engined Austin Champ of 1952) never made it into war-time production but after the war the engine was used for Austin's first OHV-engined car, the BS1 16hp. Somewhat ironically, only a civilian version of the Champ used the Austin engine.

Eric Bareham, who would eventually become chief designer of power trains for BMC and the leading light of Austin's superbly successful A and B-Series engines, did many of the layouts for the 16hp engine under Johnnie Rix. Eric recalled, "John Bishop's anti-surge cam profile was first used on the 16hp engine and H. N. Charles also did some work on the valve gear."

Bernard Johnson, who would later head BMC's experimental department, mentioned what turned out to be a prototype of the post-war 16hp car. "They put the new 16hp engine into an old pre-war Austin 12hp car and Lord ran that about during the later stages of the war."

Lord also set up a further post-war planning department under Frank Griffiths. Alfred Ash was in that department. "Mad Frank, we called him. We thought he was stark staring crazy, but he was really way ahead of his time. He was a vegetarian, very unusual in those days, and very keen on mountaineering. He would come into the office on a Monday morning in his mountaineering kit – straight off the hills. He lived in an old farmhouse, always had three heaps of compost going, and grew the most wonderful organic stuff, the benefits of which are only now becoming fully appreciated. Well, that type of outlook translated into his planning. Believe me, Frank had all sorts of things on the brew ready for post war production."

Also on the brew during the war were the makings of a much less compliant workforce. Labour was brought in from all over. Apparently some of the most self-assertive newcomers were women. Les Farmer started on the shop floor in the West Works body shop in 1939 building the new 8 and 10hp models but the onset of war brought a new direction to his career. "They had hundreds of women making parts for the Beaufighter and my gaffer said, 'Les, there are 50 women out there who are worse than 50 Bengal Tigers. Can you fix up their piecework prices and look after them?' It was a baptism of fire. I was only 16 and that was how I got into rate fixing."

The opening of the Austin Aero Factory sparked off a rapid growth in union activity and to cater for the meetings of the 30 or so shop stewards, an ex-

Dick Burzi with a Plasticine model in the 'Holy of Holies' towards the end of the war.

army hut was erected by union volunteers on land adjacent to the factory. Known simply as 'The Hut', this became the traditional meeting place from 1944 onwards. Ironically, this 'escape' from company property came to an end later when the company leased the land for expansion.

Towards the end of the war 'Brother (Dick) Etheridge' became convenor and chief shop steward. Up until that time it was said that to get a meeting with management you had to call a strike, the management resisting with all its power the formation of a union works committee.

Ken Taylor recalled how designs for the proposed post-war cars also began to get underway during the later stages of the war. "Dick Burzi, being registered as an Italian subject, was interned on the Isle of Man after Italy entered the war. Lord made every possible effort to have him released and he was eventually permitted to come back to Longbridge under certain restrictions. He wasn't allowed to visit the drawing offices as before so he spent his time in a place next to Lord's office and that enabled him and Lord to dabble together."

Barry Kelkin's second year at Longbridge was in 1943 and as a youngster he was sent on errands to a place they called the 'Holy of Holies', in which they were working on the design of the Sheerline and

A40s. Barry, clearly remembered seeing Dick Burzi, working away on a Plasticine model of the Sheerline. "I was only a trainee draughtsman but I got seconded into there and they were working on the Sheerline in secrecy because war work was still going on. Most of the Sheerline styling was done on the board. Percy Webb was the leading light. He was an engineering draughtsman but not a stylist. The only stylist was Dick Burzi but Percy Webb had a big hand in it because Dick was just beginning to get involved again. Later on they made a timber model of it and further shaping took place."

Even the embryonic stages of the A90 Atlantic took place during the war. John Cleaver began his apprenticeship in 1941 and did the customary stints in various shops. "In 1943, while I was in the pattern shop, Dick Burzi came in and saw Frank Ross who was governor of the shop. He wanted someone to make plaster casts from an oval clay plaque he had made. On the plaque was a raised profile of what eventually became the A90 Atlantic. He wanted the castings so he could paint them in different colours. He said, 'Do them in a corner so that no-one sees it.' I made half a dozen and when the Atlantic eventually came out I remember thinking that I saw that thing during the war when it was only a piece of Plasticine."

It might only have been a piece of Plasticine but with the war still raging Lord was clearly moulding the shape of Austin's post-war future.

7

Post-war horizons – the world is our blueprint

"Get the stuff in by hook or by crook – any way you like – wagons, trains, planes, just get it in."

LEONARD LORD

Crash, bang, wallop! Whether you loved him or hated him, and there were those who seemingly managed to do both, no-one would deny that Leonard Lord was a man of enormous drive. The end of the Second World War saw him about to lead Austin through the most adventurous period in its history.

With the retirement of Ernest Payton in 1945, Lord assumed the roles of chairman and managing director. Being 'top dog' suited him down to the ground.

These finishing lines show 10hp cars were already in production by early July 1945. In the background are War Department K2 ambulances and trucks still in production.

His immediate priority was to get the pre-war 8, 10 and 12hp cars back into production along with the new overhead-valve 16hp that used the same body and chassis as the 12hp. By getting them all on stream by August 1945 Lord was setting the pace for the whole of the motor industry.

At the same time, Herbert Austin's son-in-law, Colonel Waite, as managing director of the newly formed Austin Export Corporation, was proclaiming, "The world is our blueprint" and vowing that Austin was now to become "an even greater force in world trade." The demand for Austin cars and trucks was indeed worldwide and to help satisfy that demand the vast wartime flight shed was converted into a packing station for all the CKD (completely

knocked down) vehicles that were exported for assembly overseas.

Although it was a seller's market, and Austin had orders stretching well into the future, dire shortages of steel, coal and other materials meant that output was annoyingly below capacity for some time. Determined to feed his machines, Lord provided the purchasing department with a great battery of telephones along with instructions to, "Get the stuff in by hook or by crook – any way you like – wagons, trains, planes, just get it in."

Shortage of materials was not the only factor determining output. When Bill Chance tried to fix the post-war piecework rates for the 8 and 10hp cars he found himself in immediate difficulty. "The chassis shop downed tools over that. I had priced the ten horse and half of them wouldn't have it. It was a serious business because we needed all the cars we could get. We all congregated in the office of Works Manager, Joe Edwards. Harry Austin was there as superintendent of the chassis shop and one

"Get those so-and-so presses working". It was not only shortage of materials that restricted early post-war ouput. Industrial disputes took their toll too.

bloke came out with all this bull about how I was flogging them to death. In the end, Harriman [Lord's deputy] said, 'Look, the pricing is down there, anybody who wants a job, back to work. The rest can go to personnel and will be paid up immediately.' They all went back to work."

Trouble was not always so easily averted. "A lot of the aggravation was simply a product of the times," recalled Les Farmer. "There were chaps on the shop floor who had fought in North Africa and elsewhere and they weren't going to be pushed around. They were prepared to fight again for what they thought was right. I mean, without the unions, wages would have remained very low."

Les vividly described a typical union/management dispute of those days. "We had a strike in the press shop and Joe Edwards sent for myself and Johnnie Moore, the 'super' of the press shop. Edwards listened to our explanation, but I can picture him now, slowly pulling on his Crombie overcoat, then carefully fitting a pair of yellow pigskin gloves to his fingers before saying, 'Well gentleman, I'm now going into the city. I shall be back about two this afternoon. Get those so and so presses working.' The implication was that if we didn't, that was our lot.

"Joe was steeped in production, and quite a hard-case. He had to be to get the output we wanted. He wasn't too interested in the details. I was fairly close to the shop floor and knew that, having been out a day or two, the men were already arguing between themselves so I said, 'Let's get them in the office and give them a bollocking and see if it works.' Well, we threatened and cajoled them, ate a bit of humble pie at the same time, and they agreed to go back if we'd then talk about price. We got the presses rolling about half past one. Joe Edwards came back to find everything in full production, but he didn't even ask how we had settled it. Actually, we had done a bit of horse trading. We'd offered to improve the price a little on the next run but had managed to squash any chain reaction. That's what you had to guard against."

Life in many of the shops at Longbridge was certainly no picnic. "The noise was all-enveloping, really horrendous, and there were great clouds of smoke as the men added oil to the dies and great flashes of light as they hammered the hot metal", recalled Ossie Clossick, who spent 41 years in the forge. "You would have bits of sacking on your arms for the hot oil splashes. I've seen lads working on say a con rod, where to make one forging you might have about 20 blows. You had to fuller the thing down, roll it, bend the forging out, put it in the mould, put it in

"A car without a chassis – ha, ha, ha!" Cars like the chassisless A30 of 1951 were what Lord had in mind when he asked his designers to come up with a state-of-the-art car assembly building (CAB 1) just after the Second World War.

the finisher – bang, bang, bang – finished. These fellas would carry on with their arm protectors burning fiercely. They'd carry on quite happily until the forging was finished. They were as hard as nails, they really were. Most of the men in the forge were from the Black Country. Trying to understand them in the street was bad enough but in the forge it was impossible. The buses that used to bring them over from the Black Country carried several cases of beer for the lads going back off shift. If you worked in the forge you were a top fella – you could handle your beer. By the time they got home they had swigged quite a few pints but it was thirsty work.

"The place was fraught with dangers," continued Ossie, "particularly during that mad post-war dash for output at all costs. A couple of fellows were killed when I was still quite a young bloke. The first chap died when a corner broke off a die and flew out and hit him in the chest. That was him done for, simple as that.

"Another time a sliver of metal was sliced off a punch and caught a fellow in an artery. He was pumping out blood and, knowing that something

pretty dramatic had happened, he did the worst thing possible – made a dash for the ambulance department. He tried to get down there himself but only got halfway and dropped down dead. The assistant superintendent just sat down and wept his heart out."

From the point of view of both safety and efficiency, Longbridge undoubtedly required urgent modernisation, as Barry Brecknell confirmed. "Just after the war the Longbridge machine shops still had hundreds of overhead pulleys up in the rafters with great belts whanging and flapping right down to the men and machines at bench level.

Joe Edwards agreed. "Yes, some of that belt-driven plant was a legacy from the First World War so we set about motorising it all. It was a massive job and cost a fortune."

Getting rid of those belts was only the beginning. Determined that the post-war Austin would be competitive in world markets, Lord embarked on a thorough modernisation of all Longbridge facilities. His finest achievement, a state-of-the-art car assembly building, was the envy of other manufacturers for many years.

John Cleaver saw its beginnings. "I was in the plant layout department under Frank Griffiths – a factory-planning think tank really. Leonard Lord gathered us together and said, 'We are going to build cars like they've never been built before. I don't want any of you blokes going into the present erecting shop or chassis shop because the new cars will have no chassis.' We laughed – a car without a chassis? – ha, ha, ha. But he carried on, 'Forget what we've done in the past. I want a building with a completely clear floor and a hole in the floor for the engine to pop up. A bit further along the axles can pop up and then the body will come along. Bear in mind there will be all different types of bodies, two doors, four doors, all different colours, left and right hand drive, different engine specs and axle ratios and it's all got to be synchronised.'

"We didn't have a chassisless car to work with but we took a Devon to bits and marked everything with masking tape and code numbers and gradually worked out all the different stations on the track, how many people were needed per station and how to marshal the components. That's how CAB 1 (Car Assembly Building 1) eventually came to fruition in 1951."

The new building speeded up assembly enormously and allowed for easy and accurate stock control. A Hollerith punched card system controlled the intricate sequencing operations that allowed any combination of different models to flow down each assembly track. There were four tracks, giving a potential output of one vehicle every 45 seconds.

Duncan Brown was responsible for planning the new building, but the task of installing the vast range of new equipment and conveyor systems fell to Bill Davis, the superintendent engineer of the day. When Bill spoke of Len Lord's part in the planning he rated him as, "a production engineer second

'Austin of England' and proud of it; the Longbridge reception hall of the mid-1950s.

to none. He was also a remarkably good draughtsman."

Dick Perry, an Austin ex-apprentice and one-time managing director of Rolls-Royce, commented, "Len Lord could look at an assembly drawing and cost it just like that. If we looked at a particular plan and there was say a door missing or whatever, Len Lord would be the first to spot it."

Joe Edwards spoke of the efforts to update not only car assembly but also the machining of the component parts. "We called in Alfred Herbert which was then the blue ribbon company of the British machine tool business. We had all their directors in and told them what we wanted. They came back two days later and said they didn't want to do it but would be happy to sell us their milling machines and lathes. I couldn't believe it. Determined not to be beaten we designed and built our own automatic transfer machines. It cost us a fortune because we made a lot of mistakes along the way but no other bugger would do it. With that sort of attitude to progress there is no wonder that Herbert and Company don't exist any more."

In its ability to handle all the intricate processes of design, pattern making, casting, forging and machining that were required to produce those tailor-made automatic transfer machines, Herbert Austin's "Single machine" was clearly demonstrating its true worth. If "other buggers" were not prepared to do it, then Longbridge would not only build the complete motor car, they would design and build the machines to build the cars as well. The Austin-designed multi-station in-line machines would accept the rough casting for say a cylinder block or cylinder head and automatically mill any required smooth surfaces, drill, ream and tap as many holes as were necessary, and blow out any swarf after each stage. The cylinder block was handled by a transfer machine that was over 100ft long and performed 160 operations at its 32 stations. Only two operators were required, one to set a rough casting on its way and another to unload the finished block, 64 seconds later.

But Lord's plans did not stop at providing the means of efficient production. The whole of the old Flying Ground was then developed to provide the factory with a completely new image. In the early 1950s you knew you had arrived at 'Austin of England' by the impressive script high above the imposing curved façade of the new reception building. On your right you could not fail to notice the massive 'Flying A' on the end of the new car assembly building, the rest of the building stretching way into the distance. Immediately opposite the car

Impressive 'Flying As' adorned each end of the new assembly building which stretched right across Austin's former Flying Ground.

assembly building was the fine new administrative block, very soon to be known as the 'Kremlin', where commissionaire Dennis Bush would receive visitors in his immaculate morning suit. The overall impression was that both management and workers alike were proud to belong to 'The Austin'.

Before turning attention to Austin's totally new post-war cars it must be recorded that 1946 saw the whole workforce proudly signing a 16hp saloon painted matt cream which was chosen to represent Austin's one millionth car since production began.

The 16hp was a fine enough car for its day. Its 2.2-litre overhead-valve engine gave it a top speed of 75mph and you could enjoy such speed in armchair comfort. Alf Dolphin explained how those exceptionally comfortable front seats came into being. "When we trimmed the 16hp Bert Challoner asked for the seats to be as wide as possible. Roland Smith, our chargehand, reckoned they were as wide as cinema seats and had the idea of putting the same sort of arm rests at each side. He took his tape with him to the 'flicks' that night and found our seats were a lot wider so we devised the folding armrests. When Bert Challoner saw them he said, 'Those are no use. You can scrap that lot.' A day or two later Len Lord came round and said, 'Oh what a novel idea, I think those ought to be developed.' They turned out to be one of the attractions of the car. In those days I took *The Vehicle Builder's Journal* and

found out that the seats had been patented in the name of Bert Challoner – the very guy who had told us to scrap the idea."

Lord's export drive could only really start in earnest with the launch of his totally new post-war range of cars. For those he was determined to oversee even the minutest of detail.

A new era demanded a thrusting new image and it was the 'Winged B' of Lord's own Bentley which

Signed by the workforce, then sealed in clear cellulose, but not delivered – this 1946 16hp saloon, Austin's 1,000,000th car, was retained as a showpiece for the company and is now with the Heritage Motor Centre, Gaydon. Many of the names included in this book can be found on her bodywork.

The 16hp saloon, Austin's first OHV-engined car, offered armchair comfort inspired by the seats in the local cinema. The same seats were also fitted in the post-war 12hp car.

spawned a similar bonnet motive for Austin. Handing Dick Burzi the Bentley's radiator cap one morning he said, "That's what we need, something like that." A quick Burzi sketch was turned into a plywood model by Jack Clare and Burzi covered it in aluminium foil. Lord had his 'Flying A', the post-war symbol of 'Austin of England', the same day as he suggested it.

An 'Austin of England' script would also grace the cars. Ron Dovey told of how Dick Gallimore, who then headed the experimental body shop, handed him the design. "He said, 'Get some brass and cut that out for me.' It was so delicate I said, 'I'm not a jeweller', but he said, 'Just get on with it.' It took me a fortnight of cutting and filing. My fingers were so sore I had to give it to some of the other lads to have a go at as well."

John Cleaver was involved in the choice of colours for Austin's new post-war livery. "George Harriman, Lord's deputy, had asked for ideas so we did all sorts of schemes in just about every possible colour, but there was a Board meeting and word filtered down that Chris Buckley, Austin's sales manager, who was a director of Aston Villa, had said 'Claret and blue are the 'Villa' colours so why not use those?' So that's what we used along with a beige colour as a background. Appropriately enough, Startins at Aston were the first distributors to use the Aston Villa colours."

Everything was happening apace. Roger Lewis,

then building prototypes of the early A40 engines, recalled how everything was wanted in a hurry. "Easter break or not, it made no difference. You were expected to give your life to the job. Lord himself would be round to see us regularly and if a man was offered a cigarette by Lord, well, quite honestly, that was better than a pay rise."

Max Oliver was on similar work. "Many a time we'd work all night. Sunday too, and on into Monday morning. We were proud of the job and never even thought of overtime. If the gaffer said work all night we just got on and did it."

Although Lord claimed that if cars were any good they sold themselves, he was not averse to spending considerable sums on publicity. The various stunts organised by his early post-war publicity man, Alan Hess, must have cost a fortune, but did keep Austin cars in the limelight during the late 1940s and early '50s.

Sam Haynes, from Morris Commercial, was appointed advertising manager in 1948. "When Lord interviewed me he said, 'I didn't think I'd ever want anyone from Morris (although Lord himself had come from Morris) but you seem all right to me.' After the interview he said, "I want the job done properly. I don't want you telling me you've saved a couple of thousand quid by skimping on something.' That was a good start for me. My advertising budget was £2–3 million even in 1950/51. I'd produce the budget and take it to LPL and that was that – no other meetings or anything. We had four men doing nothing else but showing people round the factory, about 8,000 folk a year, and gave them all a good lunch. We reckoned it was good publicity."

Although the whole world was crying out for motor cars, in the aftermath of war it was essential to repay our war debts by earning U.S. dollars. The question was whether British cars would sell on the American market in sufficient numbers to make operations there viable. Len Lord was at least determined to find out. His declared strategy was to aim at those parts of the American market not catered for by the Americans themselves. There was room he thought for both a well-finished larger car of distinctive appearance and a small, economical car of lively performance. With the launch of the Sheerline and A40 in 1947, he felt confident he had the cars that were required.

The 'Flying A' in the 'Big Apple'. In 1952, Austin of England controlled their North American operations from these premises just off Fifth Avenue in New York. Nine cars could be displayed in the showroom at street level (inset), spares could be stored in the basement and the upper floors housed a staff of 50.

8

The ships are waiting – the Devon, Dorset, Somerset, Hampshire and Hereford

"One mile free in every three.
If you are a real smart guy,
Austin is the car to buy."

Corny maybe, but that was the jingle used on American commercial radio to announce Austin's new A40. It continued, "Don't forget folks, when you buy that Austin your savings have just begun because at 30 miles to the gallon you save 30 cents on every dollar you'd normally spend on fuel."

Hoping to use the A40 Devon and Dorset to open up the vast potential of the North American market, Leonard Lord unveiled the prototypes to American dealers in August 1947, proclaiming, "The two cars are of identical design … True the Devon has four doors while the Dorset has two, but they have the same wheelbase and the same type of frame … The only difference being that the Dorset is four inches narrower than the Devon. Both models have exactly the same engine and transmission."

The original intention had been to introduce a narrower Dorset as an A35 by using a 1,000cc version of the Devon's 1,200cc OHV engine. As it turned out, the narrow-bodied, smaller-engined car never went into production so the Dorset name was used for a two-door version of the Devon.

"Colour comes back into motoring", proclaimed Austin, when the Devon and Dorset replaced Austin's 8, 10 and 12hp cars in the autumn of 1947. They were certainly a great advance on their predecessors but it was not just the new pastel shades or even the smooth, curvy lines and built-in headlamps. They also came with independent front suspension and a very lively and efficient 1,200cc OHV engine.

Taking a closer look, one might have wondered if amongst all this progress, Austin had also taken a giant step backwards. What on earth was the car doing with a separate chassis? Surely a logical progression from the platform chassis of the pre-war 8 and 10hp design would be further moves to a fully integrated structure?

Austin had its reasons. The platform-type chassis of the 8 and 10hp cars had not been entirely satisfactory. Not only that, independent front suspension was new to the Austin range and the prospect of attaching it to either a platform chassis or an integrated bodyshell did not appeal. There were enough problems in perfecting the system itself.

An even more compelling reason was that some overseas countries charged lower import duty on unassembled or CKD chassis in order to support their own body-building industry. A separate chassis meant they could also mount their own van, pickup and, in the case of Australia, convertible bodies, using local labour.

In order to attract worldwide publicity for the new A40s, George Eyston, who had taken the World Land Speed Record to 350mph in 1937, was invited to take part in the testing of the prototypes. After tests in the Swiss Alps in June 1947 a gramophone record was produced on which Eyston proclaimed the A40's virtues.

Naturally, in describing these "arduous tests covering some of the most gruelling roads in the world", he brought out all the strong points of the cars, including the "ample urge of the new engine." He described the gradients encountered as "so long that one may have to cover 15 miles in a stretch in the lower gears and on descending from the snows to the deep valleys beyond, off and on, the brakes are applied for 17 or 18 miles.

"Never once did this magnificent engine show the slightest signs of overheating. But, of course, under such conditions the brakes are almost of more importance than the engine – especially when the road winds along the edge of a 1,000ft precipice … The hydraulic/mechanical brake operation gave the driver every confidence in these conditions and there was no sign of brake fading … The road holding and steering were as sure footed as a mountain goat."

Reality, of course, is never quite the same as the advertising blurb. On that test of prototypes were two 1,200cc Devons and two 1,000cc narrow-bodied Dorsets. It is perfectly true that all the cars coped well with the mountains, performing well, yet with water temperatures remaining well below boiling point. However, all the cars rattled and shuddered on rough roads and the front wings vibrated particularly badly. Bonnets soon got out of line and became difficult to open. On one car the bonnet opened at speed and broke the windscreen.

After returning home, two cars, one of each engine size, undertook 7,000 miles of continuous day-and-night running. On a merry-go-round to the Welsh coast and back, they worked three shifts in a 24-hour day with only 15 minutes being allowed for refuelling and crew changeover. By the beginning of July 1947, HOE 313, a narrow version with a 1,000cc engine, had covered nearly 5,000 miles at an average running speed of 39mph, returning 31.6mpg. Its running mate, HOE 315, with a 1,200cc engine and standard Devon chassis, had covered 4,600 miles at 39mph and 29.7mpg.

Under this high-speed testing the tyres scrubbed badly and only lasted 3,000 miles. The problem was accentuated because wear in the steering joints would cause the 'toe-in' to vary. The well-known A40 front-end-float on undulating roads, the nearest thing you can get to riding a horse, became more noticeable as the tests proceeded and as the dampers lost their effectiveness.

The rush to get the A40 into production saw the smaller, 1,000cc version deemed an unnecessary complication. It was not proving to be that much more economical and the larger-engined car seemed more suited to most export markets.

According to George Coates, people would not have wanted the narrower version anyway. "Even the Devons were too narrow across the seats because of that sweep in the doors. When you worked at the steering you were all elbows; the bloomin' doors were always in the way."

In August 1947, a 1,200cc Devon, JOC 238, did 3,000 miles of endurance testing in Belgium to see if

Devons and Dorsets on test in Switzerland in June 1947. George Coates is on the extreme left, George Harriman stands at the driver's door of HOE 315 and George Eyston at the driver's door of HOE 313. HOE 312 and HOE 313 were narrow-bodied Dorset prototypes. HOE 314 and 315 were Devon prototypes. Note the additional dummy grilles that never made it into production.

the chassis would withstand the notorious Belgian pavé. This was the only A40 whose chassis frame had not fractured on a previous test in Norway, but after a further 2,000 miles in Belgium the chassis broke. The car was then fitted with the curved-arm dampers that would be used for the production cars. As the mileage increased the car began to wander in cross winds. Hammering and rattling developed in the steering and the front suspension became too weak for the rough roads. The hydro-mechanical brakes gave trouble too. The car was hardly ready to go into production but Len Lord could wait no longer.

Liaison officer Geoff Cooper explained: "People will always ask why didn't you get this or that better before launching a car. But you design continuously. You are always altering and improving things. We had been working on the Devon a long time. I know the front suspension brackets kept breaking off but you can do all the testing you like and you won't match what the public will do. We knew that if you got tarry gravel on the brake cross-shaft it could be dodgy. Rix had already designed a completely new system but Lord came along and asked bluntly, 'Does the present system work?' Rix said, 'Yes' and Lord said, 'Issue it.'"

The decision to go into production at that stage is said to have cost £750,000 in warranty claims.

George Coates was with the teams doing rectification work for Emil Frey in Switzerland and Stokvis & Zonen in the Netherlands. "We had teams all over the world working on the Devons and Dorsets. The prototypes were hand-built. We should have tested some built by production methods, but we'd been all of a rush to get them on the market. There was cracking of the chassis and the suspension bump stops. We had to strengthen everything."

Joh Jansen, then technical manager at Stokvis & Zonen, spoke of a Friesland Ford dealer seizing the opportunity to embarrass Austin by putting an A40 in his showroom window. Both front wheels had been removed to reveal the chassis problems. Joh

June 1949 – A40s and an A90 Atlantic about to leave Longbridge for the docks. Mr G. R. Straus, the Minister of Supply (on ladder) talks to George Coates in the Atlantic on the transporter. Stan Yeal, who was in charge of Austin apprentices, looks on. 'Austins for dollars?' Yes, but at a price, Leonard Lord claiming he was earning dollars for Britain by selling the cars in the USA at less than the cost of production.

also spoke of a number of Devons with broken crankshafts. "I was sent to Longbridge to see Charles Rowley, Austin's service manager, about them. His answer was, 'On the Devon? No, never.' But I'd noticed a broken Devon crank propping open his office door, so I said, 'What about that one?' He looked at it for a minute, smiled, and said, 'Shall we have lunch?' I settled for that because he kept his own pigs and was friendly with a baker so we had an unbelievable meal for just after the war. In any case, the Devon was probably the easiest Austin of all to sell."

Feeling that the Americans would need educating in order to get the best out of the Devon, Austin produced a booklet entitled *Exciting to Drive*, which described how the best pulling power would be attained at several hundred rpm higher than for most American engines and that the gears had to be used to maintain the revs. The A40 engine was very tractable by English standards but quite a buzz box to those used to loping lazily along with several litres of V8 burbling idly away.

The Americans obviously had difficulty in getting in and out of the A40 because owners were very soon writing to newspapers explaining the best ways of accomplishing this 'difficult' task. It seems Americans expected to walk into their car and then take their seats but early owners were advising them to enter 'fanny-first' with legs following.

Austin's thrust into America, although a brave one, did not prove very profitable. In 1949 Lord pointed out that in reality they were buying dollars for the rest of Britain by selling cars in the USA at less than the cost of production. Figures from Anders Clausager show that sales of the A40 in the USA peaked at 11,740 in 1948. Canada proved a better outlet, taking more than 23,000 in 1950, while the USA took only 4,800 that year. Australia was a good market too, buying nearly 18,000 A40s in 1951.

Perhaps the signs to be seen outside numerous car washing facilities in America which declared 'Car Wash 60 cents – Austins 50 cents' were the most visible evidence that the A40 had at least made its mark there.

Figures issued by the Ministry of Food in 1949 showed that a 10hp car sold in Canada enabled Britain to buy 163 tons of wheat, while one sold in Australia would purchase 114 tons of wheat or 53 tons of meat, or 14 tons of butter. Using these figures, Austin calculated that during the six days ending 18 December 1949 it had contributed to the National larder no less than 35,045 tons of Canadian wheat or 14,363 tons of meat from

'The ships are waiting' proclaimed a billboard in CAB 1. Production records were being broken almost daily but presumably the poster was meant to spur the men on to even greater efforts.

Late 1947. Very early A40s being readied for export, their chrome covered in a protective finish. The chrome on these examples seems to have been very neatly coated but George Harriman would provide a distemper brush saying, 'Don't worry about getting a bit on the paintwork. Get on round and let's have 'em off.'

Australia. The latter was the equivalent of nearly 37 million domestic meat rations for the week. By the end of 1950, A40s were being turned out at 2,250 a week, or 450 per working day. Production records were being broken almost daily.

In those days, senior management would stride purposefully about the works urging all and sundry to keep things moving. Massive posters in the car assembly building reminded the men that 'The ships are waiting'. Cars for export had their chrome painted with preservative. When George Harriman caught a man spending ages with a one-inch paint brush to coat a lamp rim he gave him a distemper brush saying, "Don't worry about getting a bit on the paintwork. Get on round and let's have 'em off."

Even the CKD shop cat got caught up in the rush. Having nodded off in a crate it ended up in South

Africa, somewhat slimmer by all accounts.

Of course, this mad panic to turn out cars did not help the quality of the finished article. Unable to do the impossible, men would sometimes shrug their shoulders and say, "If they want 'em bad they can have 'em bad," because they found that as long as they kept the tracks moving they kept the management happy too.

When the A40 Somerset arrived on the scene in 1952, Austin had produced 273,958 Devons but only 15,939 Dorsets, the latter having ceased production in the late summer of 1949. More than 75 per cent of the A40s went for export, earning £88,000,000 for Britain.

Why were Dorset sales so poor? Those in the car trade were of the opinion that, for the most part, the only reason a two-door car of those days sold at all was because some customers could not afford or did not wish to pay the extra for a four-door one. The majority of A40 purchasers were obviously quite happy to pay the relatively small extra amount being asked for the four-door Devon. In the USA there was only a difference of $55 between the two cars. The Devon sold at $1,350 and the Dorset for $1,295.

For the Devon's replacement, Len Lord commissioned the international industrial design consultant Raymond Loewy to produce some models. Loewy put Tucker Madawick, a stylist from his London office, on to the job. Of his work for Austin, Tucker

recalled, "As design consultants, we were the bad guys. We were intruders. We were brought in by topside. Not by marketing, not by the engineers, but by the top brass. Brought in to shake 'em up, wake 'em up, and enhance the sales."

Tucker's view of Len Lord? "He was a very aggressive business man and obviously wanted to wake up sleepy Austin. After we had had the Austin account about 14 months Lord called me and said, 'You know Mr Madawick, we've never met your Mr Loewy. Does he really exist or is he just a myth? I must meet this man Loewy.' He had a point too, because I would send a monthly packet of sketches to Loewy and the New York office would run a critique on them and then charge Austin a lot of money. There was this great use of the Loewy name in the States, but 3,000 miles away they were asking, 'Is there really a Mr Loewy?' I called Raymond Loewy and he agreed to come over."

The visit went well enough but Leonard Lord did not always see eye-to-eye with Loewy's men because he was not keen to have quite as much of an American flavour to the cars as they proposed.

Ken Taylor, a Longbridge layout engineer at the time Tucker Madawick was working on the Somerset, recalled, "When Loewy's men left Longbridge for London each Friday afternoon, Lord would be down into the modelling shop before they had even reached the station. He immediately had everyone, including Burzi and all his modellers, working flat out until Loewy's men returned on Monday lunchtime. I remember someone saying that he had had the head-lamps everywhere but on the roof. It was obvious he had no intention of using any style other than his own

A helping hand from Uncle Sam. Tucker Madawick, one of Raymond Loewy's stylists, produced these quarter scale clay models at their London office for a proposed Austin Devon replacement – the A40 Somerset of 1952.

This full-size clay model of the Somerset was produced at Longbridge in something of an Anglo-American contest. Note the dividing line running up the grille and over the bonnet and screen. Tucker Madawick's quarter scale clay model stands sheeted over on the table behind.

and I must say I think the final design of the Somerset was one of the best since the war.

"Up to that time the full-size models at Longbridge had always been produced in wood but the Americans brought a special clay. They set up a large sheet of aluminium, polished on both sides, mounted vertically on the centre line of the floor-mounted surface table. While Raymond Loewy's team worked on their half model on one side of the sheet, Lord and Burzi worked on the other side. The polished aluminium provided a reflection so that the visual impression was of a whole car when viewed from either side. We engineers were very

It was proposed that the wings and bonnet of this hand-built Somerset prototype would tilt forward in one piece. Len Lord's chalked shape eventually decided the size and position of the bonnet opening for the production cars.

curious to see what was going on and made various excuses to visit the shop. One comment I overheard was that the exercise had made Lord realise just how good a stylist Dick Burzi was."

Tucker Madawick obviously found Dick Burzi something of an enigma. "We couldn't get him into the city. We thought if we could get him to London we could buy him a lunch and get to the inside of things. But he was a man of excuses. We were not that compatible with Austin. Whatever we brought to the fountain, they seemed to have little sympathy for it. Although the Somerset was a combination of us and Burzi, Austin mainly went 'in house' rather than use much of our stuff."

Basically the Somerset was a rebodied Devon but the engine was slightly uprated to 42bhp by employing the same cylinder head as the A40 Sports.

Barry Wood, in body experimental, recounted a happening during the building of a prototype Somerset. "We were trying to make the whole of the Somerset's bonnet and wings tip forward in one piece but we were having so much bother with it shuddering as it closed that Len Lord told all those gathered round to clear off. He then chalked on the shape of the Somerset bonnet and that was it. Its position and shape was determined by Len Lord's chalk mark."

Roger Lewis was in the team that took a Somerset prototype to Spain in 1951, a journey he could hardly forget in a hurry. "We were on our way to Madrid from Gibraltar, going through this village in convoy, when a woman came out of a shop. She seemed to be watching the cars that had already passed and walked straight in front of me in the Somerset. I caught her with the side light on the left hand wing. She wasn't badly hurt but the police were on the job in no time. They put us in an hotel under house arrest and next morning took us down to the clink to make a statement. Eventually they must have been satisfied because they let us go. Georgie Coates was a great help because they understood his French and he stayed with me to help explain matters. I had been driving with Harry Broome but he had managed to bugger off!" What Roger had not realised at the time was that he was only released after Longbridge had agreed to put up a £30,000 bail bond.

One could hardly argue with Austin's claim that the Somerset was a worthy successor to the Devon. Although it did not sell in quite the same numbers, it did earn many a dollar for Britain. By 1952, of course, it was up against much stiffer competition as other manufacturers got their act together.

A Somerset had the distinction of being proclaimed the Company's 2,000,000th car in 1953, only seven years after that 16hp had clocked up the first million. In its day, the Somerset was a very desirable family car, the more rounded body panels exuding an air of solidity and quality.

The A70 Hampshire, launched in September 1948, as the replacement for Austin's 16hp saloon, evolved in typical Len Lord fashion. According to Bernard Johnson, "Sir John Black of Standard had announced the Vanguard ages before he could make it. Len Lord went over to see Black who showed him the Vanguard and they compared notes about what they were doing for their new models; Lord on the A40 and Black the Vanguard. Leonard Lord came straight back from Standard and into our shop and said, 'I want you to put the 16hp engine into the Devon chassis to compete with the Vanguard.' Of course it was not as simple as that. We had to split an A40 chassis right down the middle, widen it by three of four inches and then cut the front off because we needed a slightly longer wheelbase and engine bay for mounting the 2.2-litre engine. It was absolutely fascinating. We built three of those cars and the guys over in West Works made the bodies in Gallimore's shop. Everything was determined by Lou Kings in

Road Test using those three cars; ride, suspension, back axle ratios, performance figures, the lot.

"When they came to put the car into production, Billy Ellcock produced a bigger, better and stronger chassis. There is no doubt that it needed it but you know when they put that production version down the line, as the A70 Hampshire, it was hopeless. The ride was no good because they had made a much stiffer structure which didn't flex. There was a great panic because we still had the original three running as sweet as anything but the new cars were rough – no good at all. To put them right we had to completely change the spring rates and alter the damping."

In the rush to produce the complete range of post-war models Jules Haefeli, who had succeeded Hancock as Austin's chief designer, was continuously subjected to great pressure. Lord would either be breathing down his neck or disregarding him completely. Harry Wall who looked after the Austin bodies made by Pressed Steel, described how Lord went about getting the A40 Devon body widened to produce the A70 Hampshire: "Without consulting Haefeli, he took me to see Dick Gallimore in body experimental and told me, 'Tie in with Dick here, but don't mention it to Stanfield (his chief body designer) if you happen to bump into him.'"

When the three widened and lengthened A40s were first fitted with the 16hp engine they used A40 running gear. Not unnaturally, the brakes were prone to fade. During a demonstration run in

In his eagerness to compete with Standard's Vanguard, Lord decided to produce an Austin 16 replacement by simply widening the Devon and adding the 16hp engine. It did not quite work out like that but here we see one of the 1947 Hampshire prototypes that was produced using Devon panels.

The styling of the production Hampshire was developed on several prototypes, as was its chassis. This prototype, JOC 237, is seen here on a Continental test in late 1947 after being fitted with a 'Designs Department' chassis frame which gave a much poorer ride than the modified A40 chassis which this car had originally.

On a lengthy Continental tour that included Norway, Denmark and Sweden, this A70 Hampshire got its wheel stuck in a gulley. George Eyston is adding his weight to the opposite side of the car while George Coates inspects the trapped wheel. "We tried everything", said George, "but after a while a couple of big Swedes came along and lifted it out for us – as easy as you like!"

October 1947 Haefeli said to Lord, "I don't like this car at all. It is against all engineering principles." A day or two later Haefeli told his

The A70 Hereford of 1950, seen here alongside a BOAC Lockheed Constellation, was styled in the same vein and simultaneously with the Somerset, the cars using the same door pressings. The Hampshire's lack of rear leg room had been attended to by increasing the wheelbase.

colleagues, "I'm leaving. I shall not be back."

Although you tangled with Lord at your peril, it would be wrong to suggest that Haefeli's criticism of the A70 was the sole reason for his dismissal; the mechanical difficulties experienced with the A40s and the problems experienced with the Sheerline must have weighed heavily against him too.

The Hampshire's main assets were its six-seater

body (albeit with very little leg-room to the rear) and a lively performance from the reliable engine. With the Hampshire, however, it was the condition of the dampers which determined whether the available performance was usable without resort to sea-sickness tablets.

The A70 Hereford of 1950 was styled in the same vein and at the same time as the Somerset, both cars using the same doors. The Hampshire's lack of rear leg-room had been attended to by increasing the wheelbase.

Jack Clare recalled a time when they were thinking of altering the front of the A70 Hereford. "I suggested to Dick Burzi that the easiest way was to get a production front end and make our alterations on that. I sent some clay down to the paint shop to get the panel colour matched up. We'd had a memo round from Dick that the Duke of Edinburgh was coming so would we make sure everyone was busy. I was working on the grille aperture when in walked Len Lord and the Duke. I'd matched the clay and paint so well that it fooled Len Lord. He said to the Duke, "It's hard to believe it's all clay, isn't it?' – as, of course, it normally would be. The Duke tapped it and said, 'It doesn't sound like clay to me.' Whereupon Lord turned away and left me to explain things. It wasn't difficult because the Duke was very interested."

Jack also spoke of Len Lord suggesting they could produce a full range of cars from one single design by simply adding to the width or length as required. "We made a wooden model with bits to drop in but

So, A40 Somerset, A70 Hereford … and to complete his set of toby jugs Lord encouraged this 1952 Sheerline-replacement proposal that used basically the same doors. Fortunately the idea was abandoned.

it didn't work out as expected. Aesthetically it wasn't good. The original style might suit a small model but not a large one. The greater the size the more scope there is for style."

The nearest Lord got to implementing his idea was the use of identical doors on the Somerset and Hereford and attempts in 1951 and '52 to use the same doors for an update of the A125 Sheerline. Mercifully the latter projects were abandoned, otherwise Austin's look-alike line-up of A30, Somerset, Hereford and the proposed Sheerline would have caused even more mirth in America. The A30, A40 and A70 were already seen as something akin to a set of toby jugs of ever increasing size. They just could not see the point of having a range of cars with only some 3 inches between them in width. To them, they were all small cars. Pointing to the A30, the Americans had asked Johnnie Rix, who succeeded Haefeli as chief designer, "What's this narrow one for? Is it for narrow people?"

Lord had obviously heeded the exhortations of the President of the Board of Trade, Sir Stafford Cripps, to concentrate on exports. He had to if he wanted to safeguard his steel allocation. Perhaps he should also have considered more carefully Cripps's suggestion that motor manufacturers should concentrate their efforts on far fewer models and thus gain the full benefits of mass-production. To design, engineer, prove and tool-up for Lord's 1950 range of A135 Princess, A125 Sheerline, A90 Atlantic, A40 Devon, A40 Sports, A70 Hampshire, FX3 Taxi and all the variants of each, must not only have cost a fortune but must have left his engineers very little time to perfect each model. The logistics and costs of trying to ensure that such a plethora of models could be given an adequate worldwide back-up service hardly bear thinking about.

9

Carriages fit for the gentry – the Austin Sheerline and Vanden Plas Princess

"The best-trimmed trucks in the business."

UNKNOWN CYNIC

Leonard Lord quite fancied himself as a driver and was not happy with the kid-glove way in which George Coates was treating his Bentley one day in the early 1940s.

"He must have been watching my feet, old Leonard", said George. "I'd double declutched all my life, but he said, 'There's synchro on this I've paid a fortune for. Pull up and I'll show you how to go on.' Well, he was changing gear at 80 and 90 on very ordinary roads."

Just as the 'Winged B' of that car had inspired Austin's post-war 'Flying A', the car itself seems to have given Lord the idea that his new top-of-the-range model should be 'a poor man's Bentley'. To that end he decreed the car should have a traditional British look: vertical grille, large and impressive headlights, distinctive knife-edge styling with separate but flowing wings and traditionally mounted side lights. The interior had to be in keeping too: walnut veneer, leather upholstery and luxurious carpets.

Although teething troubles meant it took quite some time to get the Sheerline into full production, it was actually launched before the Devon and Dorset. Jules Haefeli was then still Austin's chief designer. Ben Benbow described Haefeli, a man of Swiss descent, in a manner that only a designer could. "He had the most Teutonic napper (head) you ever saw – six inches straight up the back; $\frac{3}{32}$in radius; dead flat across the top; then another $\frac{3}{32}$in radius – a square!" Both Haefeli and the Sheerline were obviously built on similar lines – rather razor edged.

In 1946, Lord disclosed that Austin would be building two six-cylinder cars with "a choice of two

modern bodies, one by the Austin Motor Company, and the other, which we are calling a Princess, by our recently acquired subsidiary, Vanden Plas of London." He was hoping, he said, "that the distinctive appearance and finish of the Sheerline and Princess would bestow them with a social appeal that could command a premium above that of the highest priced American models."

Although the Sheerline and Princess were the first production Austins to have independent front suspension, Bernard Johnson had helped H. N. Charles of Austin's development department to fit coil-sprung independent front suspension on a 16hp saloon in early 1946. "It worked very well but the designs office wouldn't have anything to do with it. They wouldn't even take a ride in it. Charles had come from MG and it was a case of not-invented-here."

Gil Jones was in agreement. "Charles was brought in by Lord because he wanted someone with new ideas. At Austin, Haefeli and Rix were the old school of design and operated something of a closed shop. They were certainly jealous of Charles."

Developing the front suspension for the Sheerline caused many a headache. Much of the pre-production testing was undertaken by George Coates. "We were three years doing the Sheerline. We'd only got three cars to work with. There was LPL 888 and HOE 316 as well as a 'Strawberry' one that we were hoping to send to America. It just wasn't good enough to go – not for two years anyway. They insisted on using coil springs but torsion bars would have made more sense. We put torsion bars on a Sheerline prototype but they weren't really given a chance to prove their worth."

George did like the lights. "Talk about search lights. They were Lucas P100s with 48-watt bulbs but the frontal area of the lights was about three square feet and we found that if we turned them sideways we could get an extra 4mph."

Anyone who experienced the winter of 1946/47 will hardly have to be reminded of those many months of deep snow. It was certainly no picnic for those road-testing the Sheerlines. "It was far from ideal for any form of motoring, let alone brake testing," said George Coates. "On the snow and ice in the mountains it was very tricky. Imagine – 2½ tons, including the spares, wanting to take charge and you couldn't do a thing about it. We managed to get to Wales in late January and found that whenever the brakes were heavily used they would overheat and fade, and the pedal would go spongy. We would do four stops from 70mph and perhaps some from 90mph. Even after coming back from Droitwich, that's nine miles, the hubs still hadn't cooled down. We lifted the car up and the wheels wouldn't even turn. Slackening the adjusters made no difference because the heat had got to the ball races. We had a Bentley in the shop and if you gave the wheel a good heave round it would run for 3¼ minutes. If you did that to the Sheerline it would go round three quarters of a turn. I demonstrated it several

An early Sheerline with its wheels clear of the ground using the built-in hydraulic jacking system. The intention was for this to assist with maintenance and tyre changing, but one bright spark of an apprentice had an even better idea!

Known then as the 25hp project – this full-size wooden model of the Sheerline stands in South Works experimental shop in February 1946.

times but was told we couldn't afford to spend any more on wheel bearings."

Dennis Harold designed the Sheerline's electrical layout. "Prior to the Sheerline we didn't have many services on a car. No radio, clock or heater. With the Sheerline we even had a hydraulic jacking system which allowed all four wheels to be raised off the ground without the driver leaving his seat. In fact a

lady in Worcester wanted to know why one of our big cars pulled into the lane by her house every morning and the engine was left running hour after hour until the car eventually drove off. It transpired that we were using apprentices to help get some miles on the prototypes and one bright spark was parking in this lane, operating the jacks and leaving the car in gear with the engine running to put his miles on. There was a hell of a row about that."

Both the Sheerline and Princess were launched at the Geneva show in March 1947, with 3,460cc engines as the A110 Sheerline and A120 Princess. The A110 and A120 tags indicated their approximate brake horsepower. It was claimed that, "In every detail they are planned for motoring excellence … have powerful hydraulic braking on all wheels and light, finger-tip steering." Those in the thick of testing could have told you otherwise. After the glitter of the show, there were still many problems to be solved.

Two prototype Sheerlines were taken to Switzerland in June 1947. Dodgy brakes or not, the party spent Friday, 13 June driving the Furka,

Austin's stand at the Geneva Motor Show in March 1947. Behind the A120 Princess the AUS 110 numberplate of the Austin Sheerline can just be seen. Note the one-piece bonnet half of this Princess prototype. Production cars had separate side-panels.

Grimsel and Susten passes! As George Coates explained, "George Eyston was with us and he was satisfied with the power but not the effort to drive it. In the end he let me drive. 'It's too much like hard work,' he said. The steering was heavy at slow speeds and it vibrated on rough roads. When you finished a day's driving, believe me, your arms ached. With 2½ tons at 50–60mph you couldn't possibly brake on the loose stuff. You would have gone straight down the mountain side. We climbed the Italian side of the Gotthard in third gear, 2½ tons of motor car, but it would pull all the time even on the hairpin bends. Yes, the power was all right."

The average petrol consumption for the whole trip was 15.2mpg. In the mountains it dropped to between 12 and 13mpg. In September 1947, HOE 316 was given a new 4-litre engine which gave 13.5mpg on its initial test.

George Coates talked of problems with petrol vaporisation. "Every time we stopped, the petrol in the carburettor boiled. It was right over the exhaust and so the petrol vaporised. It happened in the mountains during the Geneva show. Lord was there and laughed like hell when I took a little bottle of petrol out of my pocket and removed the top of the carb to pour it in. He said, 'You cunning bugger, you're up to all the tricks aren't you?'" The vaporisation problems were eventually cured by insulating parts of the fuel line and using a thicker joint washer

between the petrol pump and engine block.

Although launched as the 110bhp Sheerline and 120bhp Princess, only some 12 of the former and 34 of the latter were built. The specification was almost immediately changed to A125 and A135 respectively, when the capacity of the six-cylinder overhead-valve engine was increased from 3.5 to 4 litres (3,460cc to 3,995cc). The engine was a high-speed version of the contemporary truck engine and, as such, had a Weslake-designed cylinder head. The Sheerline had a single Stromberg carburettor. Eric Bareham, who produced some of the arrangement drawings for the engine, described how the Princess's extra brake

horse power was obtained. "We put three SU carburettors on the Princess. One 'up' and two 'down'. It was a horrible thing, but I couldn't do it any other way. We had to dodge things like steering boxes and what have you."

It was the size of the Sheerline gearbox that surprised George Coates. "It was a devil to change it. You needed a couple of blokes inside the car with ropes round their necks and round the gearbox, straining like anything to get it into line, and another bloke below with a lever. Oh dear. The gears were big enough for a bloomin' lorry."

No doubt it was this Herbert Austin-like over-engineering and the Sheerline's lorry-derived engine which led some wag or other to dream up that 'best-trimmed truck' tag.

Paddy O'Reilly, the superintendent of Austin's heavy press shop, recalled the Sheerline having the biggest roof in the country to be made in one piece and emphasised that the press tools had to be kept in immaculate condition because the lines on the Sheerline were so sharp. Tom Finch, the senior foreman in the press tool room spoke of the press tool required to make the roof panel. "It weighed 35 tons – the whole draw tool – made up of the ring and the punch and the die. It was the biggest tool I

The faired-in headlights of this Sheerline limousine prototype of August 1949 were rejected by Len Lord, the original and more imposing Lucas P100s being reinstated.

made as a young toolmaker and it was as much as you could do to reach across to file it up."

Frank Fletcher was regularly called upon to rectify Sheerline headlights that had been damaged during final assembly. "If anyone dropped the corner of the bonnet on to the big P100 headlamps it would dent them. Quite a lot got dented like that because they were in brass, you see. They were easily rectified by taking a screwdriver handle and pulling it against the inside. The foreman said that every one I did saved him £25."

The Sheerline's £1,000 price tag looked quite attractive before the addition of £278 10s 6d purchase tax. In July 1947 things could have been even worse when 'double purchase tax' of 66⅔ per cent was levied on all cars selling at £1,000 or over, but Austin side-stepped that one by reducing the basic price to £999.

A limousine version of the Sheerline was shown at Earl's Court in 1949. Twelve and a half inches had been added to the wheelbase and a partition behind the driver held two occasional seats. Alf Dolphin remembered the prototype. "When they were modifying the Sheerline into a limousine it was standing in our shop. Len Lord came in and used the vernacular, which I don't use, but to the effect that somebody had made a big mistake! The lamps had been faired into the wings and it made them look insignificant. He had them changed back to the more majestic Sheerline lamps."

In his *Complete Catalogue of Austin Cars Since 1945*, Anders Clausager gives the production figures as approximately 8,000 Sheerline saloons, 700 Sheerline limousines and an additional 300 chassis for the builders of ambulances and hearses.

There was also one very special Sheerline. Motoring pundits of the late 1940s were regularly proclaiming the turbine car as the thing of the future, offering all the advantages of automatic transmission, a huge reduction in wearing parts, and the ability to use a whole range of fuels. Rover and others were certainly looking into the possibilities and Len Lord at Longbridge did not intend to be left out. In the East Works research & development department a team under Dr John Weaving was engaged in what, for the sake of secrecy, was known as the Fluid Flywheel Project.

Peter McNally, then an engineering apprentice under 'Doc' Weaving, recalled how work started in early 1949 when they took over part of the old aero engine test house in East Works where Mercury and Pegasus engines were tested during the war.

"Part of East Works was stacked from floor to ceiling with live shells," recalled Ray Avery, who worked on the project. "Imagine – a central ordnance depot for the Admiralty and there we were playing about with our turbines. In starting up a turbine, if there was excess fuel and the igniters didn't fire properly and you suddenly got a surge there would be a big rush of fire out of the exhaust. We exhausted up to the roof which was 44ft from the ground but we had it on fire once. Nobody noticed for a while and then people started sniffing and wondering what the smell was."

Braden Roberts thought the compressors for their first turbines were from a Spitfire's Merlin engine. Peter McNally agreed. "Yes, we used to go down to a breaker's yard at Aylesbury and bring back a

The louvred bonnet, extended nose and faired-in headlights were the major external differences between TUR 1 and a standard Sheerline. The motive power was a different matter altogether!

Chris Chance (left) and Peter McNally (right) enjoying a trip out in the Sheerline Turbine. It was on this trip that Peter stood squirting a fire extinguisher from the sunshine roof at the flames coming through the bonnet as they drove back to the Works.

complete Merlin engine, take the compressors off for the purposes of developing our own, and then take the rest of the engine back. We only paid for the difference in weight. To light the turbines in our initial experiments we simply lit an oily rag on the end of a long pole. It was really basic stuff. We frightened one or two of the management to death with that one."

On one occasion Len Lord happened to be there when the burning rag procedure took place and is said to have exclaimed, "If they are going to play tricks like that I'm buggering off."

Dave Rickman was in charge of the gas turbine drawing office. "The Sheerline was the only car suitable for the 120hp turbine but even that required alterations." According to sheet metal worker Ray Avery the bonnet was extended to cover the air-intake silencer. "It had to have a silencer on the front because the intake of air is what causes the jet-aircraft-like noise. When you get moving you do get a rushing sound from the exhaust gases but the scream is the intake. The louvres in the bonnet let excess heat away. The air coming in at the front was compressed, passed through the heat exchanger and then the fuel sprayed in was ignited with a Lucas igniter system. The hot gases drove the power turbine which was coupled to a Hobbs gearbox. A shortened propshaft was connected to the normal differential. The exhaust gases were passed over the

heat exchanger before discharge. It was like an automatic drive. At 600 revs she would stay put, just like an automatic car, but if you put your foot down she started to move. Of course, you had to move nearly two tons of metal."

Officially registered as TUR 1, the car was ready for road testing by August 1954. It developed a maximum of 125hp at 23,000rpm and was designed to run on diesel fuel as opposed to paraffin because diesel was both road-legal and available at most filling stations.

Don Hawley of the development department recollects that driving the gas turbine was a hazardous business. "Judging the response time was a bit tricky, particularly in a herd of cows! The noise wasn't too noticeable in the car but pretty noticeable outside. At slower speeds you controlled the road speed by the brake more than the throttle. If you wanted to reduce the time lag when accelerating out of a corner you had to put your throttle down whilst still killing off road speed with the brakes."

Peter McNally recalled a couple of pretty hilarious trips in the car. "Once, as we drove along, we got behind a double-decker bus and the conductor was hanging out from the rear platform scanning the sky to see where the jet aircraft was. We were right up his tail. It would go quite fast provided you had time to build up speed. I don't remember exactly what the maximum speed was but I would think almost 70mph. It caught fire once or twice because of oil and fuel leaks. It happened one day as we climbed Hopwood Hill between Alvechurch and Kings Norton, so we opened the sunshine roof and I stood on the passenger seat squirting a fire extinguisher through the grilles on the bonnet each time it flared up. When we got back to the Works we sorted the leaks."

Ben Benbow reckoned that the pick-up lag was so great that even people on bicycles left the Sheerline standing at traffic lights. Peter McNally concurred. "There was certainly a very slow response to the accelerator. You just had to wait until the power built up. 'T' junctions were quite exciting. You had to hold it on the brake and put your foot hard down to build up the power and then let go and hope. We had a lot of fun with it. Mind you, it was a thirsty beast."

Bernard Johnson knew exactly how thirsty. "We went over to the airfield at Honeybourne and checked the fuel consumption at various speeds. It did something like 4½ miles to the gallon."

Ray Avery remembered Len Lord's reluctance to ride in it. "We did speed tests at Honeybourne and Leonard Lord came one day for a demonstration.

Doc Weaving was driving but Len Lord said, 'You are not getting me in there with that ruddy thing. I'll stand and watch.' He eventually had a ride in the back but he would not sit in the front. Oh no, not with that turbine whizzing round."

When John Hitchman started as an apprentice gas-turbine fitter under Doc Weaving in 1958, the Sheerline had already been scrapped. "The car was well and truly cut up. I'm positive of that, but the engine lay in the department until 1962."

After some ten years of development Doc Weaving had to acknowledge that turbines had failed to make the conquest on land that they had done in the air. The main problems were noise, high fuel consumption, lack of engine braking and the comparatively slow pick-up under acceleration. This led to Longbridge concentrating on the building of turbines for more appropriate uses such as emergency power generators; considerable numbers of Austin 250hp turbines being sold all over the world, several of which are still in service.

A diversion from the main project occurred in 1953 when the Ministry of Supply asked for a 30bhp vehicle turbine. Doc Weaving and his men successfully developed one that produced its 30bhp at about 56,000rpm but an attempt to install it in an A30 failed when they just could not find room for the heat exchangers. Perhaps it was just as well. Imagine, 60,000 revs in an A30 – now that would be exciting.

Leonard Lord (left) and Dr John Weaving with the turbine-powered Sheerline at Honeybourne in 1954. There was no way that Lord was going to ride in that front seat!

During the gestation period of the standard production Sheerline, Vanden Plas, a firm long-associated with the finest of coachwork, became part of the Austin Motor Company. Roland Fox, who on the death of his father in 1954, became managing director of Vanden Plas, described how the merger came about. "After the war we were looking round for new work and it was Fred Connolly who brought us our new direction, a merger with Austin. Fred had been talking to Leonard Lord about the trimming of the Sheerline. Lord said he wanted the Austin range to extend right up to the top limousines to compete with Rolls and Daimler. Fred Connolly told us of Leonard Lord's interest and suggested we give him a ring. Actually we wrote, and Lord replied with an invitation to go up and see him. When father and I went up to Longbridge and talked the matter over he said, 'Think about it. You can join up with us or you can carry on on your own and we'll give you a contract.' He showed us the Sheerline prototype and we suggested that the first thing to do was to produce one of our own. The scale of his proposal was too big for us to handle. There were only the two of us as directors of the company so we decided it would be better to join up with Austin as their first subsidiary in June 1946. They bought us out and we went away to design the Princess."

Did Lord brief them as to what he wanted? "Oh no, he saw us as the experts and left us to it. Our coachbuilt prototype body incorporated all the latest techniques and was accepted without alteration. John Bradley and I designed it. John was the

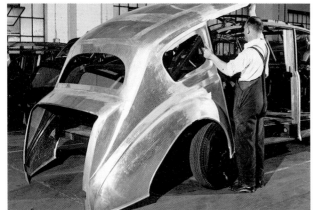

Craftsmen at the Vanden Plas works at Kingsbury working on Princess II bodies and interiors.

technical manager and looked after the drawing office and the technical side of the construction."

The Princess was built on the short wheelbase Sheerline chassis. Its coachbuilt body had timber framework panelled in aluminium. To aid front end rigidity the bonnet and front wings were in steel. The wooden frame was treated with special preservative so the cars could be exported to any country in the world regardless of climate.

Roland Fox described how the Princess name was coined. "Before announcing the car at Geneva we had been considering appropriate names. One morning I thought of the name Princess. Princess Elizabeth and Princess Margaret were in the news almost every day and it seemed an ideal name to lift the product to the top. When I went up to see Leonard Lord about it his eyes sparkled. He shouted to his personal secretary, Miss Bailey, to see what she thought about it. She said she liked it and so he said, "OK. That's what we'll have."

The Princess was launched in 1947 at £1,500 plus

The well-appointed interior of a Princess II short-wheelbase saloon.

£417 8s 4d purchase tax. The headache of the later introduction of double purchase tax was ameliorated by paring the basic price to £1,350 which attracted £751 10s in tax instead of a tax of £1,000 – the basic price of the Sheerline! It was not easy to plan new models when the stroke of a pen in Whitehall could produce a new world overnight.

Roland Fox got on well with Len Lord. "We worked very closely together. We understood each other. He was a former drawing office man and so was I, so we could more or less design things on the desk. We tried to modernise the Princess from time to time. We were never really satisfied with the front end. We made improvements by way of Princess II, III and finally IV with a modified chassis and an entirely new body which incorporated power steering and the Rolls-Royce automatic 'box. It was then that the Austin name was dropped and we began assembling the chassis at our Kingsbury works."

Princesses I, II and III, including those with divisions that were known as Touring Limousines, were built on the Sheerline's short-wheelbase chassis. The long-wheelbase Princess limousine only came into being in 1952. "A couple of years after Austin had produced their own Sheerline limousine," said Roland Fox, "Leonard Lord rang me up and said, 'This bloody limousine of ours, we can't sell it. I'd

The very successful DM4 long-wheelbase Austin Princess/Vanden Plas Princess limousine of 1952/68 was designed at Kingsbury after Len Lord told Roland Fox, "You'd better make the damn thing yourself." Eight of them in all, including the first two and the last two went to Buckingham Palace. NGN 1 and NGN 2 are still owned by HM The Queen. NGN 2 is shown here on display at the Heritage Motor Centre at Gaydon. All the Royal Princesses, were registered as NGN 1 and NGN 2, these registration numbers being transferred to each successive pair of cars.

like you to come up and give us your thoughts on it.' When I got to Longbridge he said, 'Come on let's go down to the garage.' He'd got a private garage underneath his office in the 'Kremlin' and he said, 'There it is. What are we going to do with the damn thing?' I told him that it needed a saw cut through the screen pillars, centre pillars and through the back and the whole roof lifting up about 2½in to allow ease of entry for limousine work. He seemed a bit disgusted and said, 'You would wreck the bloody thing,' and made to walk away but he came back and said, 'Well you'd better make the damn thing yourself.' When I got back to the Kingsbury works I told John Bradley not to worry about fitting in with the pressings for the Sheerline. I said, 'You know all the correct dimensions for a limousine. Stick to those. We've built enough Rolls and Daimlers and so on to know exactly what is necessary. Do that first and

then fit in with any panels that are suitable but don't compromise.' As a result, we introduced our long-wheelbase limousine at Earl's Court in 1952 and it went like a bomb. The Royal household ordered two at the show so the first two were delivered to Buckingham Palace. My father was very ill at the time and died not too long after, but that order gave him great pleasure. That double order from the Palace was repeated three times during the model's life which undoubtedly helped to promote its sale to heads of state and ambassadors throughout the world."

When BMC joined with Jaguar, Vanden Plas took over the new Daimler DS420 limousine, so in 1968, after a life of 17 years, the Princess limousine was phased out, the Queen taking the last two produced.

From Anders Clausager's *Complete Catalogue of Austin Cars Since 1945*, we can see that some 2,110 short-wheelbase Princesses were produced, along with 3,344 long-wheelbase limousines.

Whether or not Herbert Austin would have approved of the Sheerline and Princess is difficult to say. Although very proud of his Seven he was equally concerned that Austin should produce 'carriages fit for the gentry'. As stylish and imposing vehicles, the Sheerline and Princess were undoubtedly superb value for money but were appreciated much less in America than in the more traditional Austin markets of the Commonwealth countries.

10

Going topless –
the A90 Atlantic and A40 Sports

"Quite the most striking thing ever to come out of Longbridge."

HAROLD HASTINGS ON THE ATLANTIC

"I designed the A40 Sports and the Jensen Interceptor at the same time."

ERIC NEALE

"I couldn't resist telling the lads I had worked on it. I'm sure they thought I was a line-shooter but I still remember a great feeling of pride."

Barry Kelkin, who spent many years in body design at Longbridge, was speaking of the time he and his RAF pals came across the Governor of Malta's A90 Atlantic in Valletta in 1949. How pleasant to hear of someone who was 'proud' of the Atlantic, a much-maligned car if ever there was one.

Classic car scribes have likened the poor Atlantic to a pregnant hamster or clockwork mouse. One even deemed it monumentally vulgar. Barry Kelkin would not go along with that. "Yes, it was different," he said, "but we thought it way ahead at the time. Most of the thinking behind the car was Leonard Lord's. He sort of struck out alone on that one."

Your feelings towards such a controversial car must partly depend on the era in which it first came to your attention. The author can at least claim to have been in at the beginning. As a young lad, I

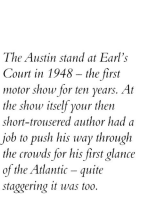

The Austin stand at Earl's Court in 1948 – the first motor show for ten years. At the show itself your then short-trousered author had a job to push his way through the crowds for his first glance of the Atlantic – quite staggering it was too.

remember fighting my way through the crowds which surrounded Austin's new turntable at the 1948 Earl's Court Motor Show. I could not quite believe my eyes as the Atlantic revolved in front of me. Damn it all, I was just getting used to the idea that a British car might have its headlights built into the wings and be bereft of running boards, when along came this kid's dream of a car.

Leonard Lord could hardly be classified as a dreamer, but in this case he does seem to have let fantasy overrule reality. The Atlantic was billed as 'a car for those wanting sports car performance with saloon car comfort' and a car that could be 'open or closed at the touch of a switch'. The latter may have been true, although many owners did have problems with the automatic hood mechanism. But it certainly was not a sports car and the saloon car

comfort did not extend to rear seat passengers. There may have been many who would have liked an Atlantic as a plaything, but very few who could persuade themselves that it was a practical car to own.

Praise or blame, Leonard Lord was obviously man enough to take it. In January 1952 he allowed the Austin magazine to portray him as the main initiator behind all the cars that Austin produced. "In all instances, Mr Lord, Chairman of the Company, makes preliminary roughs."

Even though he would normally have mountains of paper at his disposal there seemed to be some merit in claiming that Lord's 'roughs' might sometimes be 'on the back of an old envelope or any scrap of paper at hand'. After all, didn't Herbert Austin's maid have to exercise extreme caution when disposing of his serviettes at Lickey Grange during the gestation period of the Seven? If Lord wished to be thought a genius, then perhaps he ought to act like one.

In the case of the Atlantic, he was said to have sketched out his original ideas on the back of an old catalogue and passed this on to Dick Burzi "for further development".

An aid in the design process was a Pinin Farina Alfa Romeo which Lord craftily got his hands on in Geneva in 1946. Farina thought he had sold the car to a Mr Cucioli of Milan but it surfaced at Longbridge shortly afterwards.

An 'intermediate' sketch made during the development of the Atlantic bears more resemblance to this Alfa than Len Lord's 'original' sketch, particularly in terms of bonnet details and the shape of the screen, bonnet and headlamps. Features that were carried through from Farina's Alfa to the production Atlantic include the shape of the bonnet and the brightwork around its edge.

Doug Adams helped produce the first wooden model for the Atlantic. "Lord wanted it in double quick time, so we bypassed the softwood models and went straight into hardwood. He spent so much time with us that we made him a stool to sit on."

Phil Stanworth remembers chasing the 'Flying A' into the door leather of an Atlantic prototype. "We covered the doors in a thinner type of 'piping hide' under which we placed a cardboard 'Flying A'. Its shape was burnished in by rubbing the leather with a piece of bone."

The large doors were meant to provide ease of entry to American standards but they weakened the car considerably. On a test drive in an early prototype, George Harriman experienced scuttle shake at quite low speeds. "Just look at that screen," he

What was said to be Leonard Lord's 'original' sketch for the A90 Atlantic (top) is unsurprisingly similar to the final design, but what was said to be an 'intermediate' sketch (bottom) for the Atlantic shows the introduction of the split screen, bonnet features and headlamp shape of Farina's Alfa Romeo.

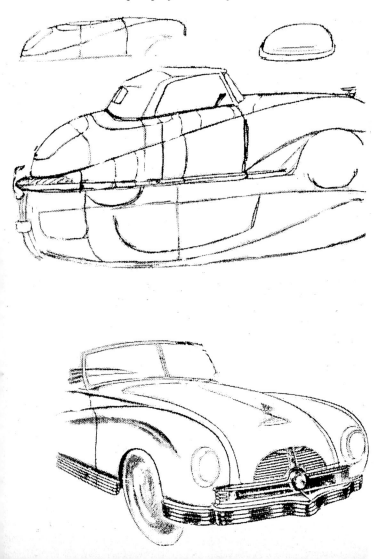

The Pinin Farina Alfa Romeo Cabriolet of 1946 was an influence in the design process for the Atlantic. Note the chrome edging to the bonnet surround which would be translated into chrome beading on the Atlantic's bonnet edge.

shouted. Gil Jones confirmed the screen "shook like mad" and remembered his boss, John Weaving, suggesting that heads might roll if they did not find a cure.

Ken Taylor, who laid out the front end of the body, found himself in the hot seat. "We had been instructed to use the A70 chassis and only found at a very late stage that the torsional rigidity was hopeless for an open-topped car. Chief body engineer Jim Stanfield doubled up on the body mounting brackets but with minimal improvement. Lord had already announced the vehicle in the States so you can imagine the panic involved."

Ken Garrett, who had come to Austin to work on the proposed A30, eventually saved the day. "The vibration of the dash was so violent that they were going to have to scrap it," he said. "They couldn't have put it on the market like that. I had a look and came to the conclusion that the principles we applied to aircraft would apply to the chassis frame. I proposed a sheet of metal above and below to make what we knew in the aircraft industry as a torsion box. Much to their surprise that fixed it. We took British and American patents on it and Austin paid me £5 a year for 15 years until the patent ran out."

It is hardly surprising there were problems with the chassis. The topless A90 was built on an A70 chassis which had started life as the chassis of an A40 saloon that had been cut up and widened. Not exactly bespoke tailoring!

Most of the running gear also came from the A70. The 4⅜in stroke of the A70's engine was retained but the cylinders were bored out to 3⁷⁄₁₆in, giving a capacity of 2,660cc. Twin SU carbs and a compression ratio of 7.5:1 allowed it to develop 88bhp at 4,000rpm and 140lb/ft of torque at 2,500rpm. A rear axle ratio of 3.67:1 gave the 25cwt car a top speed of

March 1948. This hand-built Atlantic prototype was known at the time as a 16hp sports drophead. Note not only the split screen but also the provision of foot pedals to open the doors.

July 1948. George Coates in the driving seat of a pre-production Atlantic prototype in Honefoss, Norway. To the left of the car stand Eric Winter, Austin's Norwegian distributor, and Alan Hess. This was the car with the troublesome one-piece perspex screen.

approximately 95mph. The column gear change and pistol grip handbrake may not have been everyone's cup of tea, but did allow three to be seated up front.

Wesley Hunt was working on a drawing of the Atlantic when along came Len Lord. "We were already having difficulty in finding room for the air cleaner, but Lord insisted he wanted the bonnet lower. Eric Bareham was saying, 'Well I can't see how we are going to do it, sir.' 'Give me a pencil,' said Lord, and he just drew his own line. 'That's what I want,' he said, and walked off. We didn't know what the hell to do. In the end we got the air cleaner people to make a completely new one, a bullet-shaped thing that went alongside the engine instead of above it. That was also why we used SU carbs, instead of the down-draught Zeniths, the intake for the SU being on the side. Lord's bonnet line was almost 4in lower than the original. Believe me, that was a lot."

In July 1948, a light blue pre-production prototype, the only one then built, had covered a mere 251 miles. Along with a prototype A70 Hampshire it then set off on an extensive test through France, Belgium, Holland, Germany and Scandinavia. More than 5,000 miles were covered in three weeks. George Coates remembered that trip. "It was hard on the eyes. There was no curved glass to be had so the prototype had a Perspex screen. It was raining like blazes in Norway and the blowing sands of Holland had scratched the screen quite badly. We had to polish it with pumice powder every morning just to be able to see through it."

Back at home, Ben James was testing the brakes: "MIRA's (Motor Industry Research Association) test track wasn't in operation then so we tested on ordinary roads. We used the side of Rose Hill that runs

A 1950 Atlantic Sports saloon.

down towards Bromsgrove. There weren't many houses there then, so we could open up and get six stops from 60mph before we got to the bottom. The brakes held up very well. As for speed, the best we could do was 98 mph on a good straight of just over a mile. We never quite managed the hundred. It was a little bouncy but the scuttle shake had been pretty well cured."

The hard-top Atlantic, or Sports saloon, did not appear until the 1949 Earl's Court Motor Show. The fixed head allowed for slightly more room in the rear seat and the central section of the rear window could be wound down for ventilation. An excellent idea, but this too had its problems. When Joe Bache of the Austin Export Corporation returned from a Continental trip with Dick Burzi, customs officers wanted to completely remove the window and investigate the cavity. Joe eventually persuaded them not to bother but Dick Burzi was very concerned lest other folk might suffer the same inconvenience.

To be a success in the States the Atlantic would need all the publicity it could get. Alan Hess, who worked on the premise that "you don't record the news, you go out and make it", hatched a plan to show the Americans that the car's four-cylinder engine was perfectly capable of covering great distances at high speed.

In a brave effort they attacked a whole host of American stock car records at the Indianapolis Speedway. After some initial problems the car broke records galore. The Americans still weren't impressed, not even after the price had been slashed to almost give-away proportions. In terms of its projected market the car was a flop.

Of the 7,981 Atlantics built between 1948 and 1952, about half were dropheads. Only 350 went to the States. Australians looked more kindly upon it, and imported 821.

In 1948 Harold Hastings of *The Motor* described the car as "quite the most striking thing that has ever come out of Longbridge." But 'striking' was the adjective Hastings habitually used for designs that some might fancy but that he, personally, did not rate too highly. Many years later he did acknowledge that the Atlantic was deserving of more credit than it had received.

Ultimately, of course, the car was a poor seller. Although Lord had named the majority of his post-war Austins after English counties to 'denote their essentially English origin', the Atlantic was named with the North American market in mind. Lord saw it as a car that the Americans would not be able to resist. U.S. servicemen 'over here' had given the impression there must be thousands of brash young

This fine scraperboard drawing by Aubrey Edwards of Austin's publicity department was used in a supplement to the Austin Magazine *which celebrated the A90's success at Indianapolis. Aubrey was brought back from his honeymoon by Lord in order to produce the booklet, but that cannot have done any lasting damage – Aubrey and his wife Jean celebrated their golden wedding in April 1999.*

Americans, with money burning holes in their pockets, ready to succumb to a flashy, lady-killing, open-topped car. There were, but those brash young Americans were looking in other directions, at Jaguar's fabulous XK120, for example.

Raymond Loewy's men did design Lord a very advanced sports coupé that could well have replaced the Atlantic. But it was not to be. Why not? At the Earl's Court show of 1952, Donald Healey launched his Healey 100 which used many A90 mechanical parts.

Ivor Greening was on the Austin stand at that show. "The show opened on the Wednesday. Healey had been to the Works asking for A90 engines and gearboxes and by show-time he had one car at Jabekke doing a high speed run and the other at Earl's Court as the Healey 100. The Americans were placing orders of 500 and more and wanted to know when they could have them. Healey was saying, 'well I've got this one and another in Belgium' sort of thing. We had our hospitality room upstairs where all the dealers popped in and suddenly there was a big kerfuffle. Donald Healey was saying that our own dealers were asking for the car in large numbers too, so Len Lord turned to Harriman and

Above: This Kenneth Howes' clay model of an advanced sports coupé, which he produced from a sketch by Bob Koto, was offered by the Raymond Loewy Studios as a possible replacement for the Atlantic. Kenneth Howes later designed the Sunbeam Alpine of 1959.

Below: At Earl's Court in 1952, Leonard Lord agreed that Longbridge would produce Donald Healey's sensational Healey 100 (which used many A90 mechanical parts), as the Austin-Healey 100. Here we see Healey outside the 'Kremlin' in an early car being greeted by Lord, in March 1953.

Joe Edwards and said, 'We'll make the bloody thing at Longbridge then. But we'll have to change the name to Austin-Healey 100.' He turned to Jim Bramley and said, 'Jim, alter his stand for him.' So he phoned Clements Brothers who did our stands and they came down that night. I spent most of the night there with Jim and by the next morning the stand had been completely refurbished. That is the only car ever, as far as I know, that changed its name at the Motor Show. We even had a new badge put on it."

In the Austin-Healey, Lord had backed a winner. The Americans loved it.

The Austin-Healey was not the only Austin sports model that came about because an independent manufacturer wanted to use Austin parts. Eric Neale of Jensen described the origins of the Austin A40 Sports launched in 1950. "I went to Longbridge with Richard Jensen hoping to persuade Len Lord to let us have the A70 chassis and Sheerline engine for our Interceptor sports car. Lord loved wheeling and dealing and said he would agree provided we designed him a sports car too. So I designed the Interceptor and A40 Sports at one and the same time.

"When Dick Jensen took the drawings for the A40 Sports to Longbridge, Lord just said, 'Make one.' We made ten prototypes and got an order for 3,200. I didn't build any models. I just used my own method of line development to produce the differ-

This A40 Sports prototype, seen here at the Jensen works, has the shorter bonnet and plain grille of the pre-production cars.

ent sections and handed those out to the panel makers in the experimental shop. The prototypes were all made by hand.

"The assembly of the production A40 Sports was all done at Jensen. We made jigs to argon arc weld the aluminium panels together. The motorised chassis came from Longbridge and we mounted the bodies, painted, trimmed and finished them. The bonnet was in steel but the external body panels,

The A40 Sports as agreed for production in 1950.

including the boot lid, were in aluminium."

Producing an aluminium body not only suited Jensen's capabilities, it also resulted in a lighter car and helped eke out Lord's quota of steel.

Barry Brecknell spent some of his apprenticeship as a pattern maker in the Kirksite foundry in South Works. "From the wooden patterns we cast the press tools for the A40 Sports in Kirksite alloy, instead of steel, so that is a fair indication that it was never intended to be built in any great numbers. All the panels were produced on the rubber press."

Ron Savage recalled that press. "Billy Bedford, who was then superintendent of all press work at Longbridge was very proud of his 'rubber press'. It had produced a phenomenal number of aircraft pressings during the war. The table of the press was 8ft by 4ft. The required punch or several small punches were placed on the table and a big rubber pad about 12in thick pressed the metal into the shape of the punches. We not only did all the panels for the A40 sports but also some for the big Healey and the Vanden Plas Princess."

John Barnett's first job in the development department was tweaking the 1,200cc A40 engine to

The A40 Sports and Bernard Johnson, complete with pith helmet, are greeted by the inhabitants of an East African village.

suit its new role in the A40 Sports. "Johnnie Rix wanted a bit more power than for the A40 saloon so changing to twin SU carbs from a single down-draught Zenith was the obvious first stage. With that and larger inlet valves we upped the power from 42 to 46bhp."

Bernard Johnson spoke of testing one of the first A40 Sports in East Africa in 1950. "We took two A70s, two A40s and one A40 Sports, plus an A40 van full of spares. KLM flew us from London Airport to Nairobi in DC-4s. Heathrow was just a scratch affair at the time. We drove there overnight and to our incredulity we found they had no loading arrangements. The two aircraft were parked way out on the field and they said, 'We'll have to fork lift the cars up on a platform and push them in.' We said, 'OK' but didn't realise they meant we had to do it ourselves. It was a scream. We'd been up all night and there we were bouncing and manoeuvring these cars through a hole in the side of an aircraft – three into one aeroplane and three into the other. Then they bolted some seats in for us. My enthusiasm for flying was soon dispelled because the DC-4 only lumbered along, so the flight to Africa via Rome and Cairo was a story in itself with hour after hour of dreadful turbulence.

"We were interested to see how the dampers and

the suspension would stand up to African conditions. After the first day we knew the dampers on the saloons just weren't good enough. They faded out pretty quickly and the cars then floated but the A40 Sports had cast iron Girling dampers which suffered a lot less from fade than the mazak Armstrong dampers. I suppose the metal expanded less in the heat.

"I had to tape the doors shut on the A40 Sports. They would have fallen off if I hadn't because the car had very little to hold it together. All our running was on dirt roads which regularly degenerated into a corrugated surface with about a 4ft pitch. You picked a speed where you skipped along the top and turned the wheel early for the corners to allow for the time the wheel wasn't touching the ground. Mechanically it was fine. We must have done four or five thousand miles. Sometimes 400 miles in a day. It depended where the townships were. One night we didn't make it to anywhere and we were put up in grass huts. We slept on the floor and a native boy cooked us meals. I never grumbled about the conditions on any road test after that.

How about this for a road? The A40 Sports, said to be playing its part in the Festival of Britain, blasts towards Baghdad on its round-the-world trip in 1951.

"Halfway through the trip we'd only got two cars which were still wholesome. The A40 Sports and an A70 with oversize tyres. One A40 had its sump plug ripped out, lost the oil and ran the bearings. Another had its petrol tank ripped right open and had to run on a rig-up from a jerrycan. For the second half of the journey we just limped along. On the next cars we sank all the plugs so they didn't stick out anymore."

The A40 Sports was launched in 1950 at the Earl's Court Motor Show and in 1951 played a minor part in the Festival of Britain. Alan Hess and Leonard Lord had somehow managed to get officially appointed as goodwill ambassadors for the Festival on the basis of "taking Britain to the peoples of the world who couldn't themselves visit Britain." They had worked out a ruse whereby Lord would publicly bet Hess 'half a dollar' (12½p) that he could not take an A40 Sports around the world in 30 days.

George Coates was one of three who were to accompany Alan Hess on the stunt. To reflect the sun's heat a car was specially finished in matt cream and a white hood. After running-in, the engine was dismantled, checked out and rebuilt. "They wanted to take a spare gearbox but I took the car's 'box to pieces and carefully rebuilt it instead. After all, we

wanted to keep the spares and tools to a minimum. We had two spare wheels, two jerrycans (one for water and one for petrol) and a car-to-aircraft radio-telephone link – all behind the front seats – as well as an extra petrol tank. There wasn't a lot of room for much else!"

A car-to-aircraft radio? Yes, that's right. KLM had put a specially adapted DC-4 Skymaster at their disposal. It would carry half a dozen representatives of the world's press, as well as the two off-duty drivers on each stage.

They left London on 1 July 1951, Alan Hess pairing with Ronald Jeavons and George Coates with Ralph Sleigh. George Coates's memories centred on two of his most difficult stints of driving, from Baghdad to Basra and El Allahabad to Calcutta. "We left Baghdad for Basra at midnight and followed the Tigris all the way. It was a hard clay road full of ruts and oh boy, when you hit that lot, your eyes would bat shut and your bloomin' head nearly came off. I almost lost my rattlers a few times – my false teeth. It was dreadful. We left El Allahabad at midday, drove on through the night and got to Calcutta the following midday. We kept meeting these decorated lorries. Lorries-cum-ferry, cum-bus, cum-every-thing, on a narrow concrete road with a big drop each side. You could blow the horn, flash your lights, do what you liked but it didn't make any

difference, they drove straight at you." Their only 'breakdown' came on this section when a nail from a bullock's shoe punctured a rear tyre.

From Heathrow back to Heathrow only took them 21 days, well within the allotted time, so Leonard Lord showed much public delight in losing his 'half dollar'. Although the press gave the escapade a good write-up they were not really that impressed. According to Norman Milne of the Longbridge publicity department. "Harold Hastings went up to LPL on the tarmac and asked him what the car was doing with only 8,500 miles on the clock if it had been round the world. Lord was a trifle flustered to say the least. When Harold told me the story he said he felt somewhat guilty at having pointed it out but the realisation of how few miles the car had done took the shine off it for him. I think the papers did use a figure of 10,000 miles but Harold said the speedo read just over 8,500 – and Harold was very meticulous. I think that undid Hess's credibility with Len Lord. It wasn't seen as the severe test that a true round the world trip would normally have meant."

Although the A40 Sports was not a terribly fast car, rally driver Angela Phipps certainly knew how to get her 1952 example singing along. "We used to drive everywhere flat out but of course there was little traffic about in those days. The A40 Sports would do 80mph and we aimed to do 80 every-where."

For the 1956 RAC Rally Angela enlisted the help of Pauline Pither, one of Leonard Lord's three daughters, as navigator. As private individuals they were up against the Works entries of Ford, BMC and others. It was the year in which the MGA made its RAC debut, so all sorts of publicity and hype surrounded Pat Moss and her Works car. Undaunted, the girls in the A40 Sports gave it everything they had and, almost unbelievably, soon found themselves leading the ladies championship.

Angela described how they made a navigational error on the very last night and Pat Moss went into the lead. "We thought we hadn't a hope in hell because there was only the final seafront driving test left. Then someone came running in saying, 'You won't believe this but Pat's loused up the test.' She'd simply gone the wrong way but it meant I could just troll along and make sure I didn't make any mistakes. It was bad luck for Pat but we deserved the win with only one mistake in 2,000 miles."

Pauline Pither phoned her father and told him her exciting news along the lines of, "Daddy, daddy, we've won, we've won." Understandably, Leonard Lord's fatherly pleasure in his daughter's success

Back home again – was it all worth it? George Coates, left, looks on as Lord publicly settles his supposed bet with Alan Hess by handing him a cheque for 2s 6d (12.5p)!

was counter-balanced by the fact that one of his four-year-old and obsolete cars had beaten the MGA, their very latest offering. It was not quite what he had planned.

If Eric Neale had had his way there would have been a Jensen-built replacement for the A40 Sports. "For the Motor Show of 1952 I'd got a new Austin sports job almost ready but the suppliers were late with some of the parts. At the show Dick Jensen brought us the news that Leonard Lord had already settled a deal with Healey to make the Healey 100. I said to him, 'All right, if we've missed out, tell Lord that we'll make the bodies for him at anything up to 150 a week.' Dick then asked me if I wouldn't mind going back to the Works to finish our own car. As soon as it was finished I drove it to the Kremlin with Dick and Alan Jensen following behind in an Interceptor. Leonard Lord came out and sat in it. He obviously liked it but he looked at me and said, 'I'm afraid it was born in the vestry this one. It's just too late.' Anyway, they went into a huddle, Dick, Alan and Len Lord and after a while, Dick came back and said, 'We've got it. We've got the contract for the Healey.' My car, JEA 504, became BMC property and they had it down at MG and altered the front end. In my opinion, they spoiled it, but that car may well have influenced the styling of the MGA."

If Eric Neale had had his way there would have been a Jensen-built replacement for the A40 Sports along the lines of his rendering below. The car was built, but because of Lord's deal with Healey, he told Eric Neale, "I'm afraid it was born in the vestry this one. Just too late."

A successful trio. Aileen Gervis, Angela Palfrey (now Phipps) and Pauline Pither, Leonard Lord's daughter. In winning the ladies' trophy in the 1956 RAC Rally their four-year-old obsolete A40 Sports had taken the crown that Lord had hoped would be awarded to one of BMC's latest offerings, the recently launched MGA with Pat Moss at the wheel.

11

A tale of two Metropolitans – the colourful Nash and the Black Cab

"They came in to eye-ball the thing. Yeah, floor traffic we called it."

GEORGE ROMNEY ON THE NASH METROPOLITAN

"It is clearly something the world enjoys when it comes to visit Britain and should be maintained at all reasonable costs."

ANDREW OVERTON ON THE LONDON CAB

By the late 1940s, George Mason, President of Nash Kelvinator, was battling for Nash's survival against the might of 'the big three', General Motors, Ford and Chrysler. His only hope, he figured, was to pioneer a breed of smaller cars aimed at the ever-increasing numbers of multiple car families.

The concept of a Metropolitan-like car was put to him by an independent designer, William Flajole.

Working to a brief from Mason, which stipulated that any design should echo the 'Airflyte' styling of the contemporary Nash, Flajole came up with a Fiat-engined prototype, NXI. NXI, standing for Nash Experimental International.

During 1950, when that prototype was exhibited throughout the USA, the 250,000 people who inspected it were asked to fill in a questionnaire

Did America want an economy car? To try to answer that question a prototype designated NXI (Nash Experimental International) was exhibited throughout the USA during 1950. The 'non-handed' panels had done nothing for the looks of the car so only the 'non-handed' door skins made it into production.

entitled, "Does America Want an Economy Car?"

It was, said Nash, a request for their frank opinions. Many who filled in the questionaire were clearly interested in a smaller car, but their responses showed that the car they had in mind was slightly larger than that on view. They required a car that would take four passengers, more the size of Nash's 100in wheelbase Rambler which, unknown to them, was just about to be announced.

Knowing he already had that sector covered, Mason decided that the Metropolitan should stick to an 85in wheelbase. He would produce it as both a hard-top and convertible with a front seat which was just about able to take three people abreast, and a rear seat fit for limited use by children.

To prepare the ground, Nash's publicity material began questioning the vast amounts of irreplaceable wealth that were being consumed by unnecessarily large vehicles. Many American cars, they argued, were almost exceeding the bounds of good taste in their "wasteful pretentiousness" and they also declared, "you don't need a Queen Mary to cross the Delaware, nor a two-ton car to go shopping for hairpins." A survey had shown that 36 per cent of American families owned two or more cars and the average car held only the driver for over 80 per cent of the time and one passenger for 15 per cent of the time. Only in the remaining 5 per cent of the time were the rear seats in action.

Nash launched their 'compact' Rambler in 1950. The following year, delighted to find that the Rambler accounted for 30 per cent of their output, they decided to go ahead with the even smaller Metropolitan as a 'sub-compact' offering.

The NXI prototype had been designed to incur minimal tooling costs, the pressing for each front wing being used as the diagonally opposite rear wing and a single door pressing suiting either side of the car until pierced for the handle. The front and rear bumpers were also identical, a grille being added at the front while at the rear the spare wheel slotted through an identical oval. But only the non-handed door panels were carried through to the production car and to improve both looks and luggage space it was decided to mount the spare wheel in Continental fashion. Entry to the 'boot' could only be gained by folding forward the rear seat-back; a far from popular feature that undoubtedly reduced its handiness as a 'shopping' car, but a feature that Nash claimed added strength to the body and avoided ingress of both dust and water.

The skirted wings had been shown to save some 4bhp at 60mph on the larger Nashes but they increased the car's turning circle and, in the case of

When asked, the American public said they would prefer a car with something like a 100in wheelbase. Unknown to them, Nash was about to launch exactly that – the 'compact' Nash Rambler of 1950 – seen here. After the launch of the Metropolitan, the 'compact' Rambler undoubtedly hindered sales of the 'sub-compact' and the not-all-that-much-cheaper Metropolitan.

the Metropolitan, seemed an unnecessary hindrance to a car that was so-named because of its supposed suitability in congested areas. Nash, for example, had calculated that the five boroughs of New York would be able to park 1¼ million more cars if they were all the size of the Metropolitan.

William Flajole claimed to have designed the car specially for women. Indeed, the sales literature offered it as a car for career girls: airline stewardesses, nurses, schoolteachers and secretaries. "Drive your husband crazy," they suggested, "and he'll buy you a Met. Fun to own, fun to drive and fun to live with."

George Romney, Mason's second in command, recalled the 'showings' of the NXI prototype. "Yeah, we used that to test the water to see if there was a volume market for such a car. We had meetings clear across the country, from New York to Los Angeles. Sure there was interest but not enough to warrant tooling up for it when we were trying to concentrate our own efforts on the Rambler."

So to develop the Metropolitan without breaking the bank Mason came to England and negotiated a contract with Leonard Lord, whereby Austin and body-builders Fisher & Ludlow (then about to be taken over by Austin) would produce the car using largely A40 and A30 mechanical parts. Nash held the exclusive marketing rights. The only UK sales permitted initially were to American servicemen stationed in Britain.

"Nash didn't seem to have the finance or facilities to produce the car themselves. Some of their plants seemed to be very much on a shoe-string with body panels and so on hooked up on old nails," recalled Ted Price, managing director of Fisher & Ludlow, who flew over to Kenosha to negotiate the original contract of 1952.

John Conde, assistant director of public relations for Nash, spoke of the Metropolitan as a 'no-risk venture' for them. "We didn't have to fork out a fortune for tooling and the labour rates were far cheaper in England. Not only that, Austin had the know-how for the smaller car. It had a very peppy engine, always started easily in winter and could certainly keep up with other cars on the freeway. Being so small it was easy to wash and clean. I thought the ride was good for its size, not exceptional but certainly acceptable, and I thought the colours were rather attractive."

Austin ex-apprentice Dick Perry did not quite agree on either of the last two points. Speaking from behind his desk as managing director of Rolls-Royce in the 1980s he exclaimed, "Oh the wretched Metropolitan – the handling and the colours!"

Yes, those colours certainly caused a stir in the

The second Longbridge-built pre-production Nash Metropolitan – a hard top version – photographed at Austin's Longbridge works on 29 December 1952.

UK. In 1953, about 50 per cent of the cars in Britain were black and most of the others were not all that much brighter. Ted Price remembered that Austin nearly had kittens when they came back from the States with the colour samples for the Nash, "but Austin distributors in the US had already impressed on us how discontented they were with the drab colours they had been receiving. They definitely wanted brighter stuff."

Arthur West of Austin's experimental department was certainly not impressed with the handling. "The narrow track and large overhang of the body made it like riding on a water bed. But that was the type of suspension they wanted. Presumably it suited the Americans."

Although the Metropolitan used Austin mechanical parts it was otherwise designed by Americans for Americans. Ben Benbow, the senior Austin draughtsman on the Metropolitan, recalled, "We simply worked to Nash specifications. Wallace Berry, their development engineer, came over from the States and we adapted their drawings to suit the Longbridge facilities. We engineered the car for mass-production."

The surface development of the body was done in the USA on aluminium plates. Eric Bailey, Benbow's right-hand man on the Metropolitan, remembered those layouts. "The sheets of coloured aluminium had been scribed with a silver pen. Ben and I then

spent a great deal of time determining all the body jig and fixture points for the Austin factory."

The first British-built Metropolitan was put together in Austin's experimental department. George Coates described the operation. "We were waiting for the body from Fisher & Ludlow on Christmas Eve 1952. A little Yank from Nash kept on asking when the 'carcass' was going to arrive. He wanted to take the car to London for Christmas Day. The body or 'carcass' as he called it, arrived at lunch time. It was already trimmed and painted and our job was to motorise it. It meant working all night so the folks at home were none-too-pleased. A bloomin' night and a half that was. It was snowing quite heavily. We had tarpaulins around the car so that people couldn't see it and that did keep out some of the draught. Barry Wood and Maxi Oliver had been to the Hare and Hounds for a drink and I can still remember the bloomin' sparks Barry was producing with the welding torch. Well, it was Christmas Eve. When the Yank returned the same night to take the car to London there was about four inches of snow. We'd only had time to take it up Rose Hill to test it so we tried to persuade him not to take it, but off he went."

That first Metropolitan was soon in the States

Assembling early Metropolitan body shells at Fisher & Ludlow in 1953.

undergoing testing and development in American conditions.

Production cars came off the lines from the autumn of 1953 and 3,000 were shipped to the USA and Canada in preparation for the Spring 1954 unveiling of the car by Miss America. Austin billed the launch as, "The momentous arrival of America's newest and most exciting automobile." They were proud, they said, to have been entrusted with "the task of engraving the hallmark 'Made in Britain' on the first truly light car ever built to American design for American motorists."

When Nash merged with Hudson in 1954, to form the American Motor Corporation, the Metropolitan became available under both Nash and Hudson badges. When the Nash and Hudson names were eventually phased out the Metropolitan became a marque name in its own right.

During its seven years of production, the Metropolitan was continually improved, the 1,489cc B-Series engine of 1956 being a particularly welcome change. Surprisingly, the almost universal agreement that the car required an opening boot was not attended to until 1959. Although there were large numbers of complaints about the early cars, water leaks in particular being a very sore point, the Metropolitan proved a fairly successful venture, a total of 104,377 being produced.

The amount of effort expended by American

Motors in 'selling' the Metropolitan was a strange mixture of innovative endeavour and almost total indifference. James Watson, Nash's sales manager for the Metropolitan, certainly did his best, even running a club with its own newsletter. All those who bought 'Mets' were entitled to free membership. The club motto, *Motores Prudentiores*, (more responsible motorists) was said to express the Metropolitan owners' desire to conserve vital natural resources such as iron, oil and rubber, a 'green' idea way ahead of its time, particularly in America, the land of plenty.

A club badge fixed to the licence plate of each car depicted not only these scarce resources but also a bank book to stress the car's low capital and operating costs. A British lion and American eagle at the top of the badge acknowledged the car's transatlantic parentage. Views expressed in the club's newsletters showed that many owners had taken to the little car in a big way. But those letters also show there were reasons other than the increasing popularity of the Volkswagen for the relative mediocrity of Metropolitan sales. Several years after the Metropolitan's launch, owners were expressing their amazement at the number of people who took a considerable interest in their car but who said they had been totally unaware of the model's existence.

That was hardly surprising. Apart from the

The 1,500cc Metropolitan convertible and hard-top for 1961. The following year, American Motors announced their contract with BMC had come to an end, the growth segment of the market having centred on the Rambler concept.

publicity at the car's launch in 1954, the first nation-wide advertising campaign for the Metropolitan did not take place until February 1960. James Watson reckoned this was because of the uncertainty of supplies due to strikes in the UK. No doubt this was partially true but all the same, it is not entirely convincing.

You see, George Mason had only lived for some seven months after the Metropolitan's launch. His place at the head of American Motors was taken by George Romney. Romney's description (to the author in 1993) of his own efforts to champion 'compact' cars lets us see that he viewed the 'sub-compact' Metropolitan as something of an irrelevance. "There was a difference between my view of the future for the Rambler and Mason's view. Mason thought of it in terms of supplementing the Nash/Hudson line but I viewed it as the car of the future in this country. At the first dealer meeting after I took over I quoted from Ibsen that, 'He is in the right who is clearly most in league with the future.' I said, 'The Rambler is in league with the future.' The cars built by the big three had been getting bigger and bigger and using more and more gas. I caught the attention of the car-buying public by, number one, calling their cars gas-guzzling dinosaurs, and number two, by pointing out that the Rambler had the room of the bigger cars but was economical.

We increased our penetration of the market by almost 400 per cent in an eight-year period, largely with the Rambler. The Metropolitan helped a little but that was a minor factor. It may have drawn

customers into the showrooms. They came in to eye-ball the thing. Yeah, floor traffic we called it. It played its part in that respect but it didn't play a major role. Certainly it was Mason and I who kind of pioneered the shift away from the gas-guzzling dinosaurs but it was Mason who thought there might be a market not only for a Rambler type car but also for a genuinely small car. That's why the Metropolitan was developed but I didn't quite share his enthusiasm for the Metropolitan"

It also seems that American dealers were not particularly keen on pushing an imported car against the home-grown product. Jack Miller, of Miller Motor Sales in Ypsilanti, recalled his allocation of Metropolitans. "If you bought lots of big cars you also got Metropolitans and six-cylinder Ramblers. If you didn't you got lots of V8 Ramblers which you had a heck of a time giving away. The 'Met' was a pretty good little car. We had a preacher here in town, a big heavy-set guy, and he bought a little coupé and drove it to Detroit every day on the expressway and just beat the bejeebers out of it but it lasted real good. But see if you had somebody shopping for price you could put him into the base Rambler two-door with a proper back seat for actually less money if you took a short deal."

Considering what it was up against, the Metropolitan was surprisingly successful.

Images of that other car for the Metropolis, Austin's FX4 taxi cab have been beamed round the world in television news bulletins for the last 40 years, making it as symbolic of Britain as 10 Downing Street, 'Big Ben', Buckingham Palace or the Routemaster bus.

Andrew Overton, business development director for the retail side of LTI (London Taxis International) explained in 1995 how Austin became involved in the cab trade. "My great uncle Will Overton, of Mann & Overton, sold cabs in London from 1906 onwards, but in 1928 he did the deal of a life-time. He persuaded Herbert Austin to modify his Heavy 12/4 chassis so that it would comply with the London 'Conditions of Fitness' by turning in a 25ft circle and then selected a number of coach-builders to produce bodies for that chassis."

This agreement led to Austin and Mann & Overton dominating the London taxi scene with LTI Mann & Overton still being the main suppliers of the London cab today.

After the Second World War, Mann & Overton wanted a cab with an up-to-date all-steel body. Austin could provide the chassis but not the body so an agreement was made whereby Carbodies of Coventry would build a body for the Austin chassis.

This Metropolitan Club badge was first issued to 'Met' purchasers in 1957 but is still used today by the Metropolitan Owners' Club of North America.

Half the tooling costs were paid by Mann & Overton, 25 per cent by Carbodies and 25 per cent by Austin. Later, both Carbodies and Mann & Overton came under the LTI umbrella.

The resultant Austin FX3 taxi was launched in June 1948 and remained in production for ten years but in 1956, Eric Bailey, who had just finished his work on the Nash Metropolitan, got the surprise of his life. Jim Stanfield, Austin's chief body designer, asked him to style and design an FX3 replacement. It was most unusual for the body designs depart-ment at Longbridge to be entrusted with styling a vehicle. Exterior shapes were usually conceived in Dick Burzi's department. Clay models would then be presented to management for approval and only then would body designs be asked to 'engineer' the body for production.

In this case, however, it seems that Dick Burzi's lack of interest in styling anything as mundane as a taxi saw Eric Bailey being handed what he regarded as a wonderful opportunity to do his own thing.

Of his work on the new taxi, Eric recalled, "Jim

One of the first Austin Taxis built on an adapted 12/4 chassis. The chassis was modified at the request of Will Overton in 1928 to comply with the London Metropolitan Carriage Office's 'Conditions of Fitness'.

A typical London cab of the 1930s – a 1936 Austin 'Low Loader'.

An early Austin FX3 cab (built 1947/59) passes Buckingham Palace.

Stanfield asked me to produce a full-sized wooden model to meet all the requirements of the London Metropolitan Carriage Office. I was lucky to be working with Phil Baker, a senior chassis man, who had already 'fathered' the FX3 and was able to give me guidance. The full-sized model was identical in every way to an actual cab and the doors opened to give access to a fully trimmed interior."

When it came to devising the exterior style, Eric had a free hand. "I didn't envisage anything too radical, just a pleasant shape that would cause no offence to anyone. The interior space requirements called for vertical glass planes so the scope for styling was very limited."

The headlamp arrangement and the upright grille on Eric's original sketch owed something to the days when he worked for Vanden Plas on the early Princess. Although this sketch set the basic style of the cab, it was felt that the large flat areas of the bodywork would look rather featureless. "To give it more character," said Eric, "we moved the headlamps to the centre line of the wings and introduced the feature line along the side of the body. This produced a more distinctive appearance and also introduced the possibility of using two-tone paintwork, which was then all the rage."

Eric produced a two-tone sketch in red and white crayon (see colour section) and a full-sized model painted to match it. So, could his choice of colours have been influenced by the schemes for the Nash Metropolitan on which he had just finished work? "I just wanted it to show up really well," said Eric. "I also produced a sketch with a one-piece wraparound backlight. That backlight may not have been applicable to a taxi where people might want privacy but in any case, Mann & Overton seemed so pleased when they viewed the red and white model that my alternative suggestions were never shown to them. The taxi was produced almost as I had drawn it although the Austin 'wavy bars' I had used on the grille were changed for a chicken-wire affair that I never did like."

With the model approved the project was handed over to Jake Donaldson, then chief designer at Carbodies. Visiting Carbodies with Eric Bailey in the 1990s was like entering something of a time warp. Charlie Law, one of the modellers who, in 1957, made wooden models of all the body panels for the FX4 taxi, was still there. It was from Charlie's models that the dies were made for the press tools and he was able to show us the same presses and press tools still churning out almost the same panels as they had done 35 years earlier.

To give the impression that the FX4 had barely

Eric Bailey's initial 1956 sketch for the FX4 – the front-end treatment owed much to his Vanden Plas days.

changed since its 1959 introduction would be wrong. Under that familiar skin the cab was regularly modified to suit prevailing needs. Even the apparently unchanged body panels had all been altered to allow, for example, for new and safer door handles or easier access to the interior.

In 1982, British Leyland decided they did not want responsibility for the Austin FX4 any longer so from then on Carbodies became the manufacturer. Up to that time the cab had been powered by BMC engines but Carbodies then had to resort to the Land Rover's 2.2-litre diesel engine. It was not a great success, as Peter James, who succeeeded Jake Donaldson as chief designer at Carbodies, recalled,

Eric Bailey's FX4 cab became as much a symbol of London as the Routemaster bus.

Austin of England

Eric Bailey (left) and Andrew Overton discussing LTI's Nissan-engined but FX4-derived Fairway Driver Plus in 1994.

"As an engine there was nothing fundamentally wrong with it but driving in London is a punishing business and Land Rover engines rarely get to the mileages clocked up by London cabs. A cabbie might do 35,000 miles every three months. Wear in the fuel pump drives was forcing the Carriage Office to fail cabs because of smoking engines."

Andrew Overton spoke of the ensuing search for a suitable engine. "In 1984 we approached Ricardo, the consultant engineers, and asked them to decide which would be the best engine in the world for the London taxi. They plumped for a Nissan engine but at that time Nissan couldn't provide an automatic transmission to go with it so Carbodies were forced to adopt the Land Rover 2.5-litre engine. This was significantly better but required a lot of maintenance. Nissan later came back to us and offered their 2.7-litre diesel engine with a matched automatic transmission. It turned out to be a superb engine. Cabs have done 4–500,000 miles on the same engine. Injector servicing has gone out of the window. That engine doesn't require it. In 1989, with the introduction of both the Nissan engine and wheelchair accessibility we redesignated the FX4 as the Carbodies Fairway."

Carbodies had previously made several abortive attempts to replace the FX4 with a completely new design. In one of these, Jake Donaldson hatched a scheme that put two extra doors into a Range Rover body. The project, known as CR6 (City Rover 6) for which several prototypes were produced, was abandoned in 1985 but the board of Land Rover thought enough of the idea to ask Carbodies to 'engineer' for them what eventually became the four-door Range Rover.

It was only in October 1997, 39 years after the cab styled by Eric Bailey took to the road, that LTI launched their new TXI cab. The cab's running gear is similar to that of the later Fairway and although many new safety features are incorporated, and there is much-improved wheelchair access, the overall style shows an obvious attempt to try to retain something of the somewhat idiosyncratic charm of Eric Bailey's 1956 offering

According to Andrew Overton, "The shape of the old FX4 had become something of a cult and a major asset. There isn't another country in the world which has a licensing regime that results in a purpose-built taxi. It is clearly something the world enjoys when it comes to visit Britain and should be maintained at all reasonable costs."

Tony Aksentowicz, Carbodies' senior body engineer agreed. "If we had changed the shape too much we could have had a problem. The first thing people do when they come from abroad is get into a London cab. From the tourists' point of view the cab is a hell of an attraction."

Eric Bailey can be excused the odd chuckle. A cab has an expected life of some ten years and perhaps a million miles, so even with the TXI now on the market, he can be sure that his 1956-styled cab will still be plying its trade in London and elsewhere well into the new millennium.

12

Going chassisless – the A30, A35 and Austin-Healey Sprite

"We would sometimes find ourselves talking a totally different language from that of our superiors."

KEN GARRETT

Immediately post-war, any plans to replace the pre-war Seven were put on hold. If dollars were required, then offering the Americans a car that emulated the Austin Seven or American 'Bantam' was hardly the way to obtain them. America had given those cars the thumbs down in the 1930s.

It was the collapse of plans for a merger with Morris which eventually got the A30 on to the mainstream Longbridge drawing boards in 1949. Figuring that if he could not join them then at least he could try to beat them, Lord gave the go-ahead for the A30 as a competitor to the Minor.

Ken Garrett, who devised the A30's structure, stressed that this design was not only Austin's first chassisless car but also, "the first truly chassisless car to go into quantity production anywhere in the world." Ken felt that such a claim was worth putting forward, "since it will place the car on the list of those marking historic technical milestones."

In 1951, the A30's lively and economical over-head-valve engine, its independent front suspension and 12-volt electrics, undoubtedly placed it up with or ahead of most of the competition. But was Ken Garrett seriously nominating this charming but dumpy little black-pudding of a car as a world leader? Had he gone off his trolley?

Certainly not the latter and as editor of *Automobile Engineer* for 21 years and co-author of *The Motor Vehicle* (Butterworths), Ken obviously knows his automotive onions.

He divides cars into three categories. Those with a separate body and chassis; those of integral or unitary construction where some sort of chassis frame is integrated into the structure; and those, like the A30 and many modern cars, which are of truly chassisless construction, having no semblance of a chassis whatsoever. "To the best of my knowledge", said Ken, "all the so-called chassisless cars earlier than the A30 had what amounted to a chassis frame of some description welded to the underside of the body. Even cars that have a sub-frame to take the engine and suspension loads do have a frame and therefore are not truly chassisless."

Austin certainly blew their own trumpets loudly enough in October 1951 when they boldly proclaimed the A30's launch as the 'Greatest Event in Post-War Motoring', but this was more of an attempt to tell the world that, "once more we have an Austin Seven", and thus bathe in reflected glory, than to announce the car in its own right as a world leader in body-engineering. It made sense to slant their advertising thus because the pre-war Seven had a wonderful reputation. In any case, would the public of 1951 really want to know that this new Austin was devoid of any chassis whatsoever, with no lovely heavy girders to stop the thing falling apart? In those days it was a debatable point.

It was certainly a much-disputed matter during the A30's development. By 1948, although Len Lord was convinced of the merits of chassisless construction, some of his more conservative senior engineers viewed such a prospect with trepidation. Their concern was understandable. Lord had proved time and again that if anything went wrong he did not sack the tea boy.

Not a man to be side-tracked by the faint-hearted, Lord secured the services of Ken Garrett and Ian Duncan. Both men had been in the aircraft industry and so stressed-skin construction was right up their street. Ian found his way to Longbridge by interesting Len Lord in a miniature car of his own design, the Duncan Dragonfly. That car was not only of unitary construction, but employed front-wheel drive to mini-sized wheels. It also had independent rubber suspension that had been designed in conjunction with Alex Moulton. Bear in mind that we are talking of 1948, not 1959, and you will see that Ian Duncan was a man of futuristic ideas.

Seen as interlopers by some of the senior engineers at Longbridge, Ian and Ken found it an uphill battle. It was not long before Ian's radical proposals for front-wheel drive and rubber suspension went out of the window but, as he pointed out, "the basic work was still relevant to the car whether in its original front-wheel-drive form or for the rear drive derivative."

Ian was responsible for producing the general layout of the car and Ken Garrett was charged with devising the actual structure.

Said Ken, "We would sometimes find ourselves talking a totally different language from that of our superiors, some of whom were still hankering after a separate chassis. Our talk of shear flows, Wagner beams and tension fields must have been a little disconcerting to men who had spent their lives building traditional motor cars. I failed to realise

that they weren't understanding me. Ian was a more mature bloke than I and was able to put over the arguments so much better. He was a clear-thinking, logical engineer, who could work out various ways of doing things, analyse them all and then decide which was best. He wasn't just good, he was outstandingly good."

Being the first to tackle a truly chassisless car, and with his immediate superiors frightened of his proposals, didn't Ken ever think he had bitten off more than he could chew?

"No. I knew I could do the job but it was a question of persuading other people to believe that I could. We had done the same sort of thing on aircraft, using sheet metal to take the same sort of loads. Nobody believed our ideas would work, until Les Hughes, the assistant chief body designer, suggested making a quarter scale model of the structure in cartridge paper. Much to their surprise it was stiff even in paper, but if they could have fitted a chassis underneath they would still have done so."

The paper model demonstrated how the whole structure would be of sheet steel, suitably shaped and supported, to take all the loads. Each side of the vehicle was formed by the front wheelarch, dash side, sill and rear wheelarch. The four sheet steel crossmembers, were not just structural. Each had been cleverly designed to perform an extra function such as supporting the rear springhangers, transferring the vertical loads from the front suspension

The Duncan Dragonfly in Austin's Experimental Department in 1949. After finding that the Dragonfly could outpace an A40 over the Lickey Hills, Lord paid Ian Duncan £10,000 for it and sent him off home in the A40. Part of the deal was that Duncan would work a three-year contract at Longbridge on the design of Lord's proposed Austin Seven replacement.

A hand-built A30 prototype being assembled in 1950. This first chassisless Austin was "one of the world's first truly chassisless cars", claimed Ken Garrett, the entire structure being of sheet steel that had been suitably shaped and supported to take all the loads.

into the sills or supporting ancillaries such as the radiator. No piece of metal was to have a free ride and there would be no semblance of any chassis frame.

With integral or unitary construction, the stiffness is mainly derived from a frame welded in or on the body. As this frame will only be some 100mm or so deep, it is still relatively flexible. In a truly chassiless car the body panels themselves are the structural members and may be half a metre or more in depth and thus impart great strength and torsional stiffness to the whole structure.

After the launch of the A30, the experimental department at Cowley could not resist the temptation of testing one for torsional stiffness. The test results are particularly interesting because we can

use them to compare the Morris Minor, a car with a chassis frame welded into the floor, and therefore of unitary or integral construction, with the truly chassisless A30.

As Cowley chassis engineer Jack Daniels put it, "We had built up a full history of the torsional stiffness of all sorts of cars. It was a fairly simple and crude test for twisting and bending, but we were staggered to find that the A30 body had a torsional stiffness of about 13,000lb/ft per degree of deflection. The Morris Minor gave a figure of only 4,500lb/ft per degree, and we considered that more than adequate."

As for Ken's claim of the A30 being the first truly chassisless car, it does seem to have been the first in the UK but Lancia enthusiasts might claim the Lambda of 1921, with its ultra-simple straight-sided monocoque construction, to have been the world's first.

Since making that claim, Ken also discovered that as he worked away on the structure of the A30, a design team at Saab was busy with a 'small car

Austin's famous over-head valve A-Series engine first saw the light of day in 803cc form in the A30 in 1951. This is the much-improved 948cc engine and transmission that was introduced with the launch of the A35 in 1956. Inset: Eric Bareham, in the author's garage, inspecting the innards of a 948cc A-Series engine.

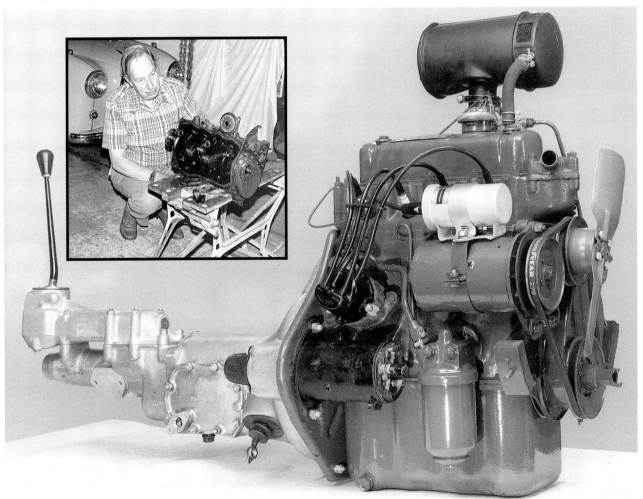

Leonard Lord commissioned industrial design consultant, Raymond Loewy, to produce the initial styling models for the A30. Holden 'Bob' Koto, one of Loewy's stylists, first produced this quarter scale clay model, seen here with a scale model of the Austin Atlantic in the background.

project' that became the Saab 92 of 1950. According to Ken, "Saab's design team included some of its aircraft engineers, which would account for the similarity of their approach to structural design to that of mine. It would appear from illustrations that the Saab 92 was indeed chassisless and was therefore the first truly chassisless car in the world, beating the A30 by a few months."

The A30's engine was certainly ahead of the game. Most small cars of the day, including the Morris Minor, were still being turned out with relatively primitive side-valve engines (which the small Fords would use for a further decade) so the A30's new and efficient overhead-valve unit was a considerable factor in the car's favour.

As late as May 1949, engine designer Eric Bareham was still considering the possibilities of using a side-valve engine but the Austin A40's 1,200cc overhead-valve engine was proving so reliable and efficient that it was decided to produce a scaled down version of that engine for the A30. As Eric Bareham generously pointed out, much of the credit for the engine's efficiency must go to the combustion chamber and valve port shapes that were devised by Harry Weslake.

Eric was remembered by Ken Garrett, and indeed is known to the author, as "a very modest and most likeable character". He is certainly self-effacing. Speaking (in the 1990s) of his remarkable engine he only recalled its faults. "Yes, the crank was under-

Bob Koto in the 'Woodshop' at Longbridge, with his full-size clay model for the A30, including an alternative frontal treatment. Prior to the work by Loewy's men on clay models for the A30 and A40 Somerset, all full-scale models produced had been in wood.

sized on the A30. It wasn't overstressed on the figures, but the 948cc version transformed that engine. I didn't like the back end of the A-Series block. In fact I didn't like the front end either! The back end was a solid mass of metal, full of oilways for the relief valve and so on – pretty horrid – and there's a great mass of metal at the front end too. The water pump is set in at the front and below that the corner is just solid metal. It had to be so but I didn't like solid lumps of metal all over the place. It was throwing metal away for no return really and anyway, I thought it should be more elegant than that. The sump was a bit messy too but then sumps generally are. It is not easy to design an elegant sump. It was our first venture into a split line on the crankshaft centre and gave a very deep drawn sump. It is a difficult thing to put together with those semi circular-corks. They have got to be just right for length and specification. The separate side joints aren't easy either. I wasn't very happy with the oil pump where it was but it seemed to work OK."

Good grief, could Eric be talking about the A-Series engine, one of the greatest small engines of all

The A30 as launched. A car with pleasing lines and attractive detail – not an easy thing to achieve in so small a car. Dick Burzi deserves the credit. Although Koto's designs were well-received it seems that Lord preferred a more traditional 'English look'.

time? Produced in both in-line and transverse configurations, it has provided the motive power for vehicles as diverse as the A30 and Montego. With almost half a century of sterling service behind it, the engine soldiered on towards and into the new millennium in A-Plus form, but will be superseded by a completely new unit in BMW's new Mini. Figures kindly provided by Anders Clausager show that by the end of 1999, almost 14 million A-Series engines had been produced.

To style the A30, Leonard Lord turned once again to Raymond Loewy. Bob Koto, one of Loewy's stylists, produced the first clay models. Speaking of Koto's offering, Ian Duncan remarked that "it was very attractive indeed and would have sold like wildfire, as it would have had very exceptional style for so small a car." Austin management, however, decided they could reduce costs by shortening Koto's proposal by 4½in. Co-incidentally with that operation, they asked Dick Burzi to restyle the car with more resemblance to other Austins.

Ian Duncan observed that shortening the car required the rear seat to be placed above the rear axle and he felt that the resultant increase in height not only spoilt the original design but also meant that some of the metal saved by reducing the length was simply put back in adding to the height.

Despite these constraints, Dick Burzi produced a

car of quite pleasing lines and many attractive details – not an easy thing to do in so short a car. Even he suggested, "Bob Koto's design was probably of better styling proportions but management decisions to chop off the tail of a car were just a fact of life that we stylists had to put up with. Even my version was altered several times before Len Lord was happy with it."

From the motoring press of late 1952 and early 1953 we can see that those who road tested the A30 were more than prepared to give it a good write-up. Even Bill Boddy of *Motor Sport* wrote favourably about many aspects of the car, although when it came to the handling he had reservations. "In a car which goes along so very willingly, handling qualities are of considerable importance. It must be said at once that the Austin Seven [or A30] does not possess such good controllability as its near-relation, the Morris Minor. It has a narrower track and is higher, so that steering it on a wet road and in a strong cross wind, or at its terminal velocity downhill, is rather like what we imagine tightrope walk-

The A35 was launched in 1956. Minor styling changes included a new front grille and larger rear window but mechanically the car was transformed. The 948cc engine, with its lead-indium bearings and higher compression ratio, gave the car a then enviable power-to-weight ratio of 40bhp/laden ton.

ing to be – all right if you keep going straight. The suspension is soft, giving a comfortable, pitch-free if somewhat lively ride, but this induces considerable roll-oversteer which spoils the cornering properties … Very pleasant high-geared steering largely offsets this, and perhaps the fairest way to express the matter is to say that the A30 is controllable but not enjoyably so."

With that *Motor Sport* report we see the first comparisons being made with the legendary road-holding of the Minor. Perhaps Austin management's preoccupation with the idea that the new 'Seven' must emulate the old had led to excessive constraints being placed on its designers. The width of the A30 had been arrived at as the minimum required to seat two abreast without undue discomfort and with the tenor of the pre-war Seven very much in mind.

For the Minor, Issigonis chose torsion-bar front suspension and rack-and-pinion steering, and placed the engine well forward to ensure a very stable car. His late decision to widen the Minor by 4in was for aesthetic reasons but must also have imparted a considerable extra measure of stability. The A30's designers were not allowed such freedom and the A30, being some 6in narrower, was going to be hard pressed to compete in this respect.

Ironically, at the same time as Len Lord's Morris

Minor competitor came on stream at Longbridge in the spring of 1952, a merger was finally concluded between Austin and Morris. One of the first results of this meant the A30 would have to share its lively and economical engine with its arch rival.

In 1956, with the launch of the A35, the engine capacity was increased from 803 to 948cc. Even more importantly, the specification included full-flow oil filtration and lead-indium bearings. The new engine could not only cope with the higher compression ratios that were being demanded by the introduction of higher octane fuels but could also stand up to the hammering that even small cars were being subjected to on the developing autoroutes and autobahns of the Continent. Austin's post-war baby was now no slouch. Indeed, comparing the power-to-weight ratio of all British and Continental cars of under one litre in 1956 we find the A35 tops the lot with 40bhp/laden ton.

The uprated engine and transmission was also used in the Morris Minor. Indeed it was the Minor that benefited the most. Although heavier and therefore not quite so nippy, its wider track and superior suspension meant it could handle the extra power and speed with ease. Not so the lighter and narrower A35, the handling characteristics of which could certainly catch out the unwary. Although the A35 is a car that loves to be powered hard all the way through a corner, chickening out halfway is not to be recommended.

Funnily enough, the A35 was raced very successfully with many of the most famous names in motor racing cutting their teeth on one. Frank Williams, Jackie Stewart and John Barnard are just three who had an A30 or A35 as their first car. From the stories they tell, we can see that they all had great affection for the car and whether on or off the track, their right foot was usually flat to the floor.

Formula 1 World Champion Graham Hill once described how, instead of braking, he would throw the car into the corners and keep his foot hard down. "I found that I was going into Stowe Corner [at Silverstone] flat out at 6,300rpm – 90mph – and coming out at 4,800rpm – 70mph; all the momentum was lost in negotiating the corner. The best technique for cornering the A35 was to put on a full half turn of the wheel going into a bend, to set up the car in a drift, and then come back to a quarter turn, after which there was generally no further need to move the wheel until the corner had been negotiated." Perhaps not a technique to advocate for mum going shopping or the district nurse on her rounds but Graham did not just use his car for racing, it was also his personal transport. He drove it

to all the European circuits including Spa, Le Mans, Rheims and Monza as well as to Monaco for his first Grand Prix in 1958.

Graham was part owner and founder of Speedwell Conversions who marketed tuning kits for a number of family saloons. Naturally his A35 had the full Speedwell treatment: lightened flywheel, balanced crankshaft, gas-flowed head with bigger valves and heavier springs, twin SU carbs, high-compression pistons and a special camshaft. It also had competition dampers, a front anti roll bar and Ferodo VG 95 brake linings. In this trim the car would sing along all day at 6,000rpm with complete reliability, never once letting Graham down. For the trip to Monaco, he fitted a 3.7:1 differential which allowed 85mph cruising at under 5,000rpm. It was the ability of his modified A35 to perform this dual role of racing saloon and long-distance hack that endeared it to him.

Including the commercial variants, over 223,000 A30s and 354,000 A35s were produced between 1951 and 1968. A35 saloon production ceased in 1959.

The A30-A35 era was one in which all manner of experiments were undertaken at Longbridge. An all-aluminium A30, powered by an all-aluminium A-Series engine, was produced in a joint project with the Aluminium Development Association. Although nothing came of it it was, by all accounts, a remarkably good car.

A project that got much nearer to production was an infinitely variable hydrostatic transmission that was developed in A35s. Before it was perfected it fell out of favour when the coming of the Mini presented the difficulties of adapting the transmission to a transverse engine. The transmission was developed in the East Works research and development department. Jim Stanley and Dave Wild were two of those who road-tested the transmission in an A35. On one run they unwittingly found themselves in a rather compromising situation.

According to Jim Stanley, "I could have ended up in gaol with that thing. Dave Wild was a fantastic guy but the sort who always had somewhere he wanted to go. This particular day he reckoned he'd got to get some 'regs' as he called them from the motorbike scramble people. So off we set for this little village in Buckinghamshire and had to ask all over the place to find the particular farm where the guy lived. When we eventually got there, Leatherslade Farm, there was a 'For Sale' notice up but our old boy lived down the bumpy farm track. When David saw all his old motor bikes he was about stoned out of his mind. We spent well over an

In 1951, Austin produced this prototype A30 convertible but decided not to put it into production. The car suffered quite a serious accident in 1956, being hit amidships by an A90 Atlantic while being rallied by Joe Edward's son, Michael. Fully restored, it is now on loan to the Heritage Motor Centre at Gaydon.

hour there before beginning to negotiate the rough track again when all of a sudden we lost the drive. A pipe under the car had caught on something and all the transmission oil was pouring out from underneath the car. It was specially imported oil so we emptied the tools out of the tool box and bunged that underneath to save what we could. We repaired the pipe using a hose clip and had to put the old oil back in. Of course, it's supposed to be perfectly clean and you know what the bottom of a tool box is like, but we bunged it all in and got the car back to the works. All well and good except that we had only chosen to visit Leatherslade Farm on the same day as the Great Train Robbers.

Dave arrived at work next morning with a newspaper in his hand, saying 'Read it, read it, read it! Look where the bloody robbers were, Leatherslade Farm.' Not a stone would be unturned, they said, to track them down. We'd even been to the local post office to ask where the farm was and we must have left our tyre marks and oil all over the place. We thought we'd had it. Dave was really worried. I mean, how could we tell Roger Lewis, our gaffer.

He didn't really mind where we went as long as we were putting miles on to the car but we were supposed to be in the Cotswolds. I only told Roger about it the day I retired from the department."

Arthur Whitaker recalled that episode too. "It was only ages afterwards that they dared to tell us about it. Roger Lewis was the senior foreman in the East Works experimental department and was well respected by everybody. We'd work all night for him. If the work was there we used to pull our fingers out and get it done. He was as good a gaffer as you could possibly get. If you told him you wanted to do something he would always say it was all right but if you did something without asking him he had a knack of finding you out. He'd got a hell of a temper if anybody let him down so Jim and Dave were sweating on the top line for months and months."

Neither the A30 or A35 was ever produced in drophead form, other than a lone A30 prototype convertible, but Len Lord did toy with the idea of using the A30's mechanical parts for a small sports car. After Dick Burzi had produced several clay models, a running prototype was built in 1953. This car was quite a departure from Austin practice in that it had a glassfibre body mounted on a tubular space frame.

Ray Tustin recalled helping Eric Bailey to produce the drawings for the A30 Sports. "Johnnie

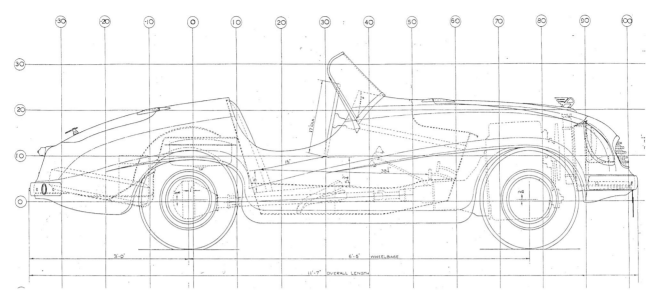

This drawing and rare photograph show Austin's attempt to use a spaceframe, glassfibre body and the A30's mechanical parts to produce an A30 Sports in 1953.

Rix ran round in it for quite a time. He used to take it home nearly every evening in the summer so we barely got a chance to drive it ourselves. He seemed to like it more than any other prototype we made. He was dead keen to develop it and although Len Lord seemed keen on it too, it was decided that glassfibre just wasn't on for volume production."

Before Austin had got too far down the road with their A30 Sports project, Donald and Geoffrey Healey came up with their proposal for the 948cc-engined Sprite. This is the Gerry Coker-styled prototype known as Q1 that Healey brought to Longbridge for approval.

Len Lord solved the problem by suggesting to Donald Healey that because sports cars were forever getting larger and more expensive, there ought to be scope for a much smaller one. Healey had been thinking along the same lines but it was only after this prod from Lord in 1956 that he did something about it, the end result being the Austin-Healey Sprite.

By that time, the project could benefit from the 948cc engine and transmission, a much more suitable unit than the 803cc version for sports car use.

Healey's stylist, Gerry Coker, came up with the shape. "DMH [Donald Healey] wanted a small simple sports car that a chap could store in his bike shed … the original design had retractable headlights, but these were scrapped due to their cost."

Having the run of BMC's parts bins, Geoffrey Healey plumped for the Minor's fully hydraulic rear brakes rather than the A35's hydro mechanical setup. The Minor's more positive rack-and-pinion steering was also chosen in preference to the A35's

Healey's car went into production in 1958 with very few modifications as the Austin Healey Sprite. Replacing the flip-up headlamps of the prototype with the fixed 'frog-eyes' not only saved money but gave the car an appealing personality all of its own.

much woollier steering-box and idler arrangement.

Bernard Johnson described two problems with the Sprite prototypes. "Developing the Frogeyc with its quarter elliptic rear springs was a little tricky. There was no structure aft of the heel board and when the thing crashed through on to the bump stops it crippled itself. You could see the marks on the wheel arch. To get the Sprite into production we had to strengthen it up. I did a lot of the pavé testing on it. It was only a twin carb version of the standard 948cc A-Series engine but we had quite a bit of trouble with the cooling system. Healey had mounted the radiator up front and the fan was miles away from it. On our own prototype the fan stirred the fug up a bit but couldn't cool it. At MIRA it was hopeless. It would boil round the banking but when we took Healey's original prototype round it was a treat – never boiled at all. They looked the same but our buying office had used a different radiator supplier and the gills weren't so well soldered to the tubes. They weren't conducting the heat away. We took the rad out of Healey's and put it into ours and it was fine. Problem solved."

In all, some 300,000 Austin-Healey Sprites and MG Midget derivatives were produced, cars that offered the joys of sports car motoring to many who would otherwise have been unable to afford it.

13

A mixed marriage – the British Motor Corporation

"You know what BMC stands for, don't yer? Bugger my competitors!"

LEONARD LORD

"We knew nothing," said Joe Edwards of the 1952 merger which produced the British Motor Corporation, "until we read the statements in the papers. I don't disagree with mergers, but Len Lord brought Austin and Morris together as enemies, putting one against the other by talking of those at Cowley as, 'Those people in the country. They all live on a bloody farm down there.'"

Lord was undoubtedly responsible for intensifying Austin/Morris rivalry but can hardly be blamed for its existence. Since William Morris began producing motor cars in 1913, Austin and Morris had always competed head on for their share of the market, Morris usually managing to out-sell Austin comfortably from the early 1920s to the early '30s. But the rivalry went deeper than that. In 1927 William Morris had succeeded in buying Wolseley from under the nose of Austin. Being the man responsible for shepherding Wolseley into car manufacture in the first place, Austin was far from pleased.

It was only after Morris's purchase of Wolseley that Len Lord entered into the equation, initially as the saviour of Morris. As Cyril Hodgkins, in the Cowley experimental department recalled, "There was a bloke at Wolseley called Len Lord; well, that's all he was to me in 1933, a bloke from Wolseley. You see, Morris Motors had become rather fragmented. There was the body department, trimming department, sub-assembly department, erecting department and so on, people with their own spheres of influence, little cliques everywhere and sales had plummeted to a level where Austin was selling more cars than we were. During this crisis, Lord came from Wolseley to Morris as managing director and kicked out all the people running those little

Lord Nuffield (William Morris) in his office at Cowley in 1950.

empires. He sorted the blighters out all right. In the three years to 1936 he bought the latest gear-cutting equipment from America for Wolseley to begin producing all the parts for Nuffield's cars: rear axles, brakes and steering gear.

Eventually they decided that Wolseley might as well assemble the units as well and send them to us ready to go on the cars. It was all very logical and very sensible. Lord also decided that Morris cars were over-engineered. They were too. Designs introduced by Landstad in 1920 were still extant in the 1930s. All the bearings were enormous, so Lord reduced them by about 60 per cent. He went through everything like that; did an excellent job; gave us the Morris Eight in 1935 too – and probably saved the company with that. Lord was a person who made instant decisions. He would come along and bust the impasse – do something whether it was right or wrong. I disagreed with that. Second thoughts are always best, but his saving grace was that if he turned out to be wrong he was big enough to admit his mistakes. You see some of the things he had to decide were hellishly difficult, not really capable of being resolved."

Of course, Herbert Austin and William Morris (later Lord Nuffield) had spawned two very different companies. Austin had always perceived his factory as that 'single machine that could produce a car from start to finish' but Morris had a completely different approach. As Geoffrey Iley, production manager of Morris Motors in the late 1950s, explained, "Bill

Len Lord's Morris Eight of 1935 owed a great deal to Ford's Y-Type but it did a great deal for Morris Motors. "He probably saved the company with that" said Cyril Hodgkins.

Morris had the nous to expand his business using other people's cash. He procured everything on 30 days' credit. By careful stock control and swiftly converting the bits into a motor car which he then sold for cash, he always had ample working capital. Financial engineering if you like. Simple but brilliant. This led to an essential difference in ethos between Cowley and Longbridge. At Cowley it was accepted that if you didn't work according to a plan, if you didn't have the paperwork right, then sooner or later you would fall over; so for God's sake get everything written down. Longbridge was the antithesis of that.

The Longbridge philosophy was, 'we'll do it now and we'll sort out the paper work later – if we bother.' Longbridge was run on the phone or by dashing round and kicking people: do this and do that and don't argue; and somehow it got done. They worked miracles. They could get on the phone to this shop and that shop and knock up a prototype body in 48 hours. Cowley couldn't have thought of doing that. They would have required all the drawings first."

When Lord fell out with Morris and left Cowley in 1936 he told Cyril Neale in the experimental department that he "would see to it that grass would grow once again on the streets of Cowley." Other declarations by Lord, such as his oft-quoted threat to "take Cowley apart brick by bloody brick" and the fact that he subsequently joined the opposition at Longbridge, offended not only Lord Nuffield but Cowley men in general. Such enmity meant that the on-off on-off negotiations prior to the 1952 merger were seriously hampered by an animosity that had gradually ingrained itself into all levels in both

companies. The fact that Leonard Lord and Lord Nuffield had barely been on speaking terms since the parting of their ways in 1936 cannot have helped things either.

In the end, however, it was the Nuffield board who maintained their opposition to the 1952 merger long after Nuffield himself had agreed to go ahead. Indeed, Lord's daughter, Pauline, felt that the differences between her father and Nuffield have been much over-stated. "When we were in Australia I wanted to swim on Bondi Beach so dad and Lord Nuffield came down to the beach to keep an eye on me. They sat on a concrete step, eating ice cream cones and happily discussing all sorts of things to do with the merger."

Although other meetings between Lord and Nuffield may have been far less harmonious, an ageing Nuffield does seem to have realised that he was no longer a match for the dynamic Lord. Very soon after the merger, although accepting the presidency of BMC, he quietly backed out of the lime-light.

With Leonard Lord assuming the roles of both chairman and managing director of BMC, Morris men were justifiably concerned that he was about to have his way with them. But in truth, many Cowley men were to do quite well out of the merger and found Lord's direct and forthright approach more predictable than that of the increasingly inconsistent and cantankerous Lord Nuffield.

What they saw as Lord's uncouth nature did rankle, however. "I and many people at Cowley only knew of Len Lord by reputation," said Eric Lord, then works superintendent at Cowley. "In the early days of BMC, the only time that I saw him in action was at a Nuffield function at Grosvenor House where he stood up and said, 'You know what BMC stands for don't yer? Bugger my competitors.' Well, there was dead silence. Believe me, that had not been the way in the old Nuffield Organisation. To my mind that typified the man and of course what the boss man says determines the attitude of others."

At the time of the merger, Nuffield's vice-chairman and managing director was Reginald Hanks. According to Cyril Hodgkins, "Reggie was a rather pedestrian sort of chap, very reliable, but didn't have any vision and when Lord took over in 1952 he just seemed to sink without trace. Lord and he just did not get on, probably because Hanks was known to have been dead against the merger. Vic Oak, a very good man, was still chief designer. It was he who had constantly sheltered and fostered Issigonis since his arrival in 1936 but even Vic did not become part of the merger, really. He left in 1953. Issigonis was then

Probably the earliest Morris still in existence, a 1913 Morris Oxford. Whereas Austin took great pride in producing cars from start to finish, William Morris "had the nous to expand his business using other people's cash. Financial engineering if you like" – Geoffrey Iley.

made chief engineer at Cowley for a while but was not thrilled about the post-merger prospects and took himself off to Alvis."

As deputy chief engineer of the Nuffield Organisation, Charles Griffin saw something of these happenings. "I attended monthly engineering meetings at Longbridge with my director of the day, Vic Oak. Johnnie Rix was the boss engineer at Longbridge and these two great men had got too old to be sensible, too set in their ways. To bring the two companies together demanded that even as engineers we should practice the art of compromise; but neither was capable of compromising. They even started arguing about whose part numbering system we were going to adopt. Longbridge had already planned for the introduction of computers, not just for part numbers but for the payroll and everything else, so it was obvious that the Austin numbers, which were already fed into the system, ought to be adopted. These two ancients simply couldn't agree on this so it had to be referred to Len Lord. The rest of us knew that they were virtually sacking themselves."

Bob Grice, then Austin's chief experimental engineer, spoke of how several post-merger arguments centred on the testing of cars. "After the merger Lord put me over Morris Motors experimental as well, so I had the whole of BMC. That gave me something to sleep on. Lord and Harriman used to call me Myski because there was a Russian tough guy called that. One day Lord said, 'Myski, the best thing we can do is find you an office at Cowley.' We went down there and when Lord asked for the keys to Nuffield's old office he was told that no-one was allowed in there. That did it. Lord said, 'Don't tell me what I can or can't do. I want the keys.' We walked in to find Nuffield's old buttoned couch and an ancient telephone. Lord said, 'Right Myski, from now on this is your office.' It turned out that S. V. Smith (a Cowley man who eventually became technical co-ordinator of BMC) had always fancied it, so you can imagine what it was like being set up in there over that bunch. I had a rough time. Cowley was in trouble with the Riley Pathfinder. I had to reject a lot of things for redesign and I put one of my 'stop notes' on it to halt production. I had three cars brought to Longbridge and had only been working on it three days when Lord phoned to ask when I could release it back into production. I wasn't very popular with Lord or Cowley but the car had awful brake judder, terrible steering wheel shake, very heavy steering and dreadful roadholding."

The Pathfinder had been designed at Cowley by Gerald Palmer when chief engineer of MG, Riley and Wolseley cars. Soon after the merger, Palmer was moved to Longbridge as group body and chassis designer for BMC. The problems encountered on the introduction of the Pathfinder meant that his

An early split-screened mock-up of the Riley Pathfinder. Problems with the Pathfinder and its Wolseley 6/90 stablemate saw designer Gerald Palmer getting his marching orders from Leonard Lord.

good fortune did not last long. According to Charlie Griffin, "Palmer was a good designer. He had been responsible for the Jowett Javelin and the MG Magnette but he certainly came unstuck with the Riley Pathfinder. It was essentially a bad motor car and was the reason why Gerry had his comeuppance really. He had to move on over that."

Palmer himself explained how Leonard Lord had actually confronted him over a report on the Wolseley 6/90 saloon, the C-Series-engined derivative of the Pathfinder. The report was published in *The Autocar* of 16 September 1955. Many years later, Palmer still had the report as handed to him by Lord; all the passages Lord was unhappy with were clearly marked in red crayon. Said Palmer, "Not long after that I was given the push. I got my marching orders at just about the same time as Lord brought back Issigonis in 1955."

Even after Palmer's dismissal things were far from harmonious between the Longbridge and Cowley road-proving departments. "When Cowley brought out the little Wolseley 1500," said Bob Grice, "I had four brought up to Longbridge and produced a list of things that were wrong with them and sent it up to Harriman with another 'stop note'. S. V. Smith at Oxford wasn't going to wear that stop note at any cost so I took Harriman and Joe Edwards out in one and frightened the life out of them coming down Rose Hill. I warned them to brace themselves for a crash stop – Harriman was sitting by the side of me – but, as I expected, I got a repeat performance of the pedal coming away from the bulkhead and we lost all braking. They believed me after that. Even on

The Wolseley 1500 was another car which produced aggravation between the Longbridge and Cowley road test departments. Lord had instigated this project as his replacement for the Morris Minor. Drawings exist showing the boot of one version badged as an Austin A40 replacement too. The success of the Minor 1000 saw the project move up-market to produce Wolseley and Riley versions but in Australia they produced it as a Morris Major and Austin Lancer, the latter version being shown here.

normal braking the car hopped about because the position of the damper mountings was wrong. They had to re-do the fascia too because when big Jim Stanfield got into the car he knocked off several switches with his knees."

After the formation of BMC one might have expected Lord to hatch radical plans for the restructuring of the whole corporation: rationalising the model range, simplifying the supply lines, concentrating production in fewer and more efficient plants and marketing the products through a unified franchise. That such a master plan was never devised meant that many of the possible benefits from the merger simply never materialised.

Immediately after the merger Lord did bring together a group of planning engineers to see what suggestions they might make. Eric Holbeche was one of them. "About eight of us were quietly closeted in the 'Kremlin' so that no-one saw what we were doing, myself and two or three others from Longbridge, technical and planning people, and someone from each of the Nuffield factories, considering ways in which we could rationalise."

Joe Edwards recalled one of the first results of that exercise. "That's when we put the A-Series engine in the Minor. It took me ages to persuade George Harriman. I remember leaning out of the window of the Kremlin and saying, 'We've bloody well got to do it George.' He had been buggering about but eventually, after about three weeks, he said, 'Do it then. Get on with it.' The Minor never looked back after that."

That decision, although eminently sensible, suited neither Austin nor Morris die-hards. Cowley tester Joe Gomm held a fiercely partisan Cowley view. "That 803cc engine was the biggest load of rubbish we ever had. Let me tell you here and now, our testers could wear out those Austin engines in no time at all. At under 3,000 miles they would bring them in with clapped-out bearings, whereas you could flog our 918cc side-valve engine flat out for 20,000 miles without trouble. We also had a good gearbox on the side-valve Minor but the Austin gearbox would jump out of gear as fast as you could put it in. What really upset us was that we had the Wolseley Eight overhead-valve engine scheduled for the Minor and weren't far off putting that into

Putting the A30's engine into the Morris Minor did not please Cowley tester, Joe Gomm. "That 803cc engine was the biggest load of rubbish we ever had." Here we see Joe in his nineties with the Minor he bought from the Cowley experimental department – the first Minor to be fitted with the 1,098cc A-Series engine.

production. That was a beautiful engine."

Blindly supportive of Cowley or not, Joe was a good sport, so it was well worth an attempt to really wind him up. What had he to say about the irrefutable fact that, in the first full year of Austin-engined Morris Minor production, the sales increased by nearly 50 per cent? With a big smile he retorted, "Pull the other one," and then carried on to try to score more points for Morris by claiming, "You know it was my boss, Walter Balding, who instigated the development of the 948cc engine." When asked how highly he rated the 948cc version of the A-Series engine he rather grudgingly conceded its virtues, albeit with a broad smile. "Well I suppose it was better than the 803 and I suppose it wasn't a bad engine," but after a pause for reflection he made another little dig in the Longbridge direction by harking back to the 803cc unit, saying, "I'm afraid we Morris people expected cars to do 100,000 miles, not 3,000."

Although Cyril Hodgkins was an ardent enough Cowley supporter he held very different views from Joe's. "The 918cc Morris engine was good in its day but it was a bad policy decision to fit it to the Minor. The Austin engine was a big improvement. With the side-valve unit the timing was critical. A degree either way and you'd either lose all the power or get outrageous pinking. Whoever decided on using that engine buggered the first Minor up for four or five years. Issigonis had a hell of a run-in with Tom Brown at Engines Branch who managed to persuade the directors to adopt the side-valve engine instead of the flat-four that Issigonis originally wanted to develop. The secret of the A30 engine was the gas-flow of the Weslake head and ports. It revved effortlessly to 5,000 or 6,000rpm, but the 918 peaked at

about 4,000. Even as a Morris man I give unqualified praise to the Austin engine. Not many Morris men would say that, but I learnt to be very objective. As an engineer, one has to be. It's no good being biased because it comes home to roost eventually."

Eric Lord took a fairly balanced view too. "I was disappointed that we weren't going to use our Wolseley engine but we could see that there was a greater demand for the Minor than we could have possibly met with the Wolseley engine. As a production man I was very happy to have the 803cc Austin unit, very happy."

Over at Longbridge, George Coates saw things quite differently. Almost 40 years after the event, it still upset him that the Minor had benefited so much from the Austin engine. "Don't forget, the bloomin' thing had an Austin main spring, the A-Series engine. That was the biggest mistake ever, letting Morris get their hands on that."

BMC's medium car range undoubtedly benefited from the post-merger decision to standardise on Austin's new B-Series engine. However, the larger cars (apart from the Vanden Plas Princess limousines, which used the D-Series engine) would all rely on the six-cylinder C-Series engine developed in 1954 by Morris Engines of Coventry.

Having decided not to disturb the dealerships, partly to avoid the wrath of the more powerful distributors and dealers and partly because of the risk of losing sales to competitors, BMC continued to produce the full range of Austin, Morris, MG, Riley and Wolseley motor cars. Such diversity was only made feasible, as we shall see in later chapters, by rationalising on body shells, in particular by 'badge engineering' the Farina range of both family and executive saloons of 1958 onwards.

A consequence of the merger was that all BMC design was centred on the Austin drawing office at Longbridge, hence the ADO project numbers that were issued from the mid-1950s onwards. Some Cowley men were adamant that those letters stood for amalgamated drawing office but their protestations did not alter the fact that it was the Austin drawing office that took over the driving seat.

It was hoped that the adoption of a new logo would help signify the unity of BMC. "Do you know where the BMC rosette came from?" asked John Cleaver with a chuckle. "From Sir Leonard's cattle. We were trying to devise a logo and had done all sorts of schemes but no-one could decide which was best. Lord, was pretty impatient. He always called a spade a spade but in very decorative language. He said, 'Look, I've got another appointment and as you can't make your bloody minds up we'll use this.' He threw a rosette across the table that he'd been awarded for his Hereford cattle and said, 'that's what we'll use, in red, white and blue.'"

New logo or not, there was not always unity on the shop floor. Mike Sheehan, who had just finished his Austin apprenticeship about the time of the merger, but who later became director and general manager of Longbridge Operations, clearly remembers Austin folk talking of Morris men as though they were bitter enemies. "Although only a young lad, I remember thinking it was all a bit silly. When people went down to Cowley they talked as though they were going out to war."

Geoffrey Rose, an ex-Wolseley man, spoke of being moved to Longbridge in 1953. "After the merger there had been a lot of, I don't want to say clashes of personality, but perhaps I should. Harriman was anxious to have somebody with a tinge of Morris about them so I went to Longbridge as works manager of the car division. Talk about Daniel in the lions' den. But Joe Edwards, who was

Cyril Hodgkins thought quite differently to Joe Gomm. Seen here working on a Plasticine model for the proposed post-war Morris range in the Cowley development department, Cyril admitted that, "even as a Morris man I give unqualified praise to the Austin engine."

then works director, was my immediate boss and made it clear to all the Austin people that Geoffrey Rose wasn't one of those terrible people from the Nuffield Organisation who just had to be endured. He got them to give me their full support. What Joe said was law at Longbridge. He was well respected and very well liked."

Cowley men were understandably annoyed to see the Longbridge plant being given preferential treatment at the expense of Cowley, as Eric Lord remembers. "Our production lines became very outdated because the money we were making at Morris Motors was being spent on modernising Longbridge."

Longbridge man Paddy O'Reilly pointed out a further adverse consequence of centring things on Longbridge. "It meant that in the heavy press shop we eventually made something for every model that was made at Longbridge or Cowley. As the trade unions gradually became all powerful, the blokes in the press shop soon came to realise that they could bring the whole company to a halt at the drop of a hat."

Geoffrey Iley's main disappointment was that, even by the early 1960s, neither Lord nor his successor George Harriman, had managed to cash in on the possibilities offered by the Austin-Morris merger. "If a car had a Nuffield badge on, it still had

November 1956. The new exhibition centre at Longbridge was able to house BMC's whole range of cars. By that time, BMC had standardised on engines while common body designs would follow later. The Minor and A35 used the A-Series engine; the Austin Cambridge, Nash Metropolitan, Morris Oxford/Cowley, MGA/Magnette/Wolseley 15/50 all used the B-Series. The Austin Westminster, Healey 100-Six, Morris Isis, and Wolseley 6/90 used the C-Series. The Austin Princess limousine used the D-Series. The odd car out in the photograph is the Riley Pathfinder which used a Riley 2.4-litre four-cylinder engine until the Pathfinder was replaced by the C-Series-engined Riley Two-point-Six in 1957.

to be made at Cowley or Abingdon. Those with an Austin badge had to be built at Longbridge. There had been minuscule alterations to that rule for the Wolseley 1500/Riley 1.5, the Austin-Healey 3000 and the Sprite but those were very much the exceptions. The Mini, 1100 and 1800 were built in two places. So were the Austin Westminster and Wolseley 6/110. It was just the way things had always been. It was never questioned until I did so. I was too late to stop the first Morris 1800s being built at Cowley but I damned soon put a stop to that and we got all the 1800s built at Longbridge. I stopped Mini production at Cowley; that all went to Longbridge. I brought all the mid-range Farina saloons to Cowley, all the Austin Westminsters and Wolseley 6/110s to Cowley and we used the 1100, as the model in most demand, to act as the balancer. If there was a significant alteration in demand for one or other vehicle we

would try and spread the agony around the group – keep as many in work as possible – by using the quantity of 1100s built at Longbridge and Cowley as the final balancing act in the equation."

Whether Lord fully cashed in on the merger or not he certainly could not be accused of lacking commitment to the success of both Austin and BMC. In the mid-1950s, when credit squeezes left new cars stockpiled everywhere, he spoke with ebullience of his plans for further expansion. "Wearisome tales are going the rounds of the imminent decline of the British motor industry … These plans speak for themselves: we do not share this fashionable defeatism. They show – we want them to show forcefully – that we look forward to the future with every confidence." This was not just talk. When Austin and Morris had merged in 1952, their combined annual output stood at some 275,000 vehicles. Under Lord's guidance, and before his retirement from the chairmanship in 1961, BMC had reached an annual output of over 700,000 vehicles and were planning to produce 1,000,000. Lord's efforts were rewarded with a knighthood in 1954, and a peerage in 1962, when he became Lord Lambury.

But perhaps even his lordship would have appreciated the even-handed view of Dan Warren of BMC Service. Discussing the behaviour of BMC personnel in the post-merger days, he leant forward, and with a knowing smile, quietly confided, "Believe me, there were Austin bastards and Morris bastards!"

14

A car is born – from GS5 to Cambridge

"By the time the engineers and management had finished with my designs, there was only that much of me in any car."

DICK BURZI

By 1954, the rather bulbous Somerset and Hereford were beginning to look a little overweight. Fuller figures were beginning to go out of fashion in cars as well as girls, so the Somerset and Hereford were replaced by Burzi's Cambridge and Westminster, cars that brought a lower, leaner look. This was derived, in part at least, from Bob Koto's initial proposals for the A30.

At the launch of the Cambridge in 1954, Austin produced a publicity booklet entitled 'GS5 into Cambridge', describing how the Cambridge, initially known by its type number of GS5, was gradually transformed from a handful of sketches into the fully fledged car.

The styling took place in Burzi's new studio which was tucked away behind the 'Kremlin'. An ideal location as far as Len Lord was concerned. Every morning and evening, and sometimes in between, he would pop in to see how the clay modelling was progressing. From a balcony he could survey the scene from above and almost invariably would suggest an alteration or two.

Burzi obtained this studio in somewhat bizarre fashion. A keen photographer himself, Lord had quietly planned it as a new photographic studio for the works photographer, Ron Beach. With the building complete Lord said to Ron, "Come with me." Entering the new building, Lord said brusquely, "There you are. What do you think of that?" Not knowing what the building was meant to be, Ron simply said, "Fine." "I expected more reaction than that," said Lord, "it's your new studio." Taken aback, Ron found himself saying, "Mm, well, I don't know about all those roof lights." "What's

the matter with them?" asked Lord. "I don't want windows in a studio," said Ron. "I create my own light." "You are never bloody satisfied," said Lord and stalked off shouting, "All right then, I'll give it to Burzi. He'll appreciate it." Lord was right. Burzi was in like a shot.

"Naturally Ron Beach was kicking himself," said Aubrey Edwards of Austin's publicity department, the recounter of the above tale. "Ron came to me saying, 'I've just lost a studio to Dick Burzi.' When he told me what had happened I said, 'You twit. You could have got a bloody spray gun and sprayed the glass black.' He said, 'I just didn't think.' He did eventually get a studio in the Kremlin but about a quarter of the size; you could only just get the larger cars in with the bumpers almost touching the wall. He had to make do with that for the rest of his working life."

Hardly able to believe his good fortune, Dick Burzi quickly got the studio underway with the original 'renderings' for the Cambridge: quick colour impressions in both coloured chalks and paint. In earlier days Burzi would have then produced a quarter scale model in Plasticine entirely on his own which would have been followed by a full-sized model painstakingly crafted in pine by the woodshop.

For the Cambridge it was to be different. The experience gained working on models for the Somerset and A30 with Loewy stylists Tucker Madawick and Bob Koto, saw Longbridge importing their own modelling clay from America and Dick Burzi overseeing a team of clay modellers who produced a whole series of alternative quarter scale

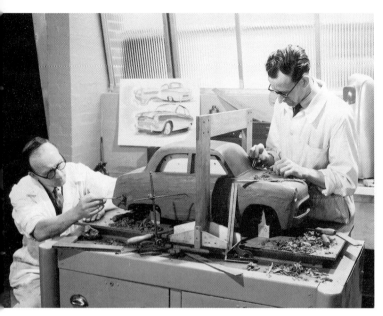

Albert Nokes (left) and Jack Clare at work in Dick Burzi's new styling studio on a quarter scale proposal for the GS5 Cambridge. Jack spent 50 years at 'The Austin' from 1932 until 1982.

modeller to vary the light and so pick up any blemishes or faults of line. A modeller or 'clay scraper' would pare away at the clay with a variety of tools, most of them home-made from hacksaw blades and other bits and pieces. Management would view a selection of quarter scale models and the preferred style would then be produced in full size. A full-scale model would require up to two tons of the reddish brown clay to be gradually added to the armature. To avoid any cracks in the clay the studio had to be kept at a constant temperature.

"We didn't paint many of the clay models," said Ron Griffiths, "because it made it much harder to reclaim the clay when the model was finished with. Clay modelling was a messy business. You tried to keep your feet out of the clay scrapings otherwise they piled up on the bottom of your shoes. That parquet floor in the studio might have looked nice but it was a devil to keep clean. It was more of a show floor than a practical floor."

Jack Clare was working on a model of the Cambridge when in came Lord. "He just said, 'I want that higher,' pointing to the bumper. When Lord left Burzi said, 'Leave it where it is, he won't know any different.' Next day Lord walked in and eyed up the model and then with a doubting voice

clay models. That same clay was then used to produce the initial full scale model. Using clay throughout meant that even a full-size model could be rapidly changed at the whim of management. Reworking a wooden model took a great deal longer.

The men in the woodshop (or 'wood-butchers', as the modellers irreverently called them) still provided a wooden armature as a base for the clay. The models were built on turntables to allow the

The wooden 'armature' for the full-scale model was mounted on a turntable and gradually covered in clay. The '10-inch lines' on the base, in conjunction with an overhead bridge, allowed any point on a model, and therefore the drawings that were produced from it, to be accurately determined.

asked me, 'Have you raised that bumper?' I think he noticed my hesitation because without waiting for an answer he handed me half-a-crown, saying, 'Hold that, I'll bet you haven't.' He proceeded to prove his point with the use of a ruler. He'd obviously measured it the day before. Then Burzi got out his rule and instead of putting it correctly he sort of bent it on the floor to give the reading he wanted. But Lord wasn't a mug; he just took back his half-a-crown and walked away."

In his retirement in Italy, Dick Burzi placed a thumb and forefinger about half an inch apart as he confided, "By the time the engineers and management had finished with my designs, there was only that much of me in any car." Of course it was much the same for designers and stylists everywhere, but Dick's frustration was often increased by the way Len Lord might approve of a design after George Harriman, Lord's deputy, had shown his dislike for it or vice versa. Between the pair of them they managed to take out their differences on poor Dick. On more than one occasion Lord, who fancied himself as a stylist, intimated to Dick that he could have managed perfectly well without him, insinuating that he was an inheritance from Herbert Austin that he could have done without. As Jack Daniels put it, "Burzi was between the devil and the deep blue sea. It was an extraordinary situation because he never really had any official position." Fortunately, Dick was such a genial and easy-going character that not even Lord, who would sometimes refer to Dick as the ice cream vendor, could help but enjoy having him around.

In the 'GS5 into Cambridge' brochure, much was made of the fact that Kay Petre (ex-racing motorist, motoring correspondent and lady extraordinaire) had been employed as a colour consultant. She got the job after persuading Lord that Austin cars were extremely dull compared with other cars of the day. As Sam Haynes put it, "The next thing we knew she was our consultant colour stylist." According to Joe Edwards, "Kay's ideas were too advanced for the day; she wanted pinks and blues as opposed to our blacks and browns. As a lady she got a rough ride. The blokes were simply not used to having someone powdering her nose in the corner of the studio."

"She certainly brightened up the cars," said Dan Warren, "and did some excellent work on trim co-ordination. But she came unstuck when she followed the fashion of the time that had gone barmy on rust colours. Her proposed rust-coloured A30 didn't go down well at all. She didn't last long after that."

After the full-size clay model of the Cambridge was 'approved' by management it was up to Jim Stanfield, the chief body designer, to transfer the design to the drawing boards.

Peter Nokes took the templates required from the clay models. "I would make a rough cardboard template at each 10in line along the car. You made the cardboard virtually fit the contours of the model and then laid it on a piece of plywood, drew round it, cut out the plywood template on the bandsaw and then spoke-shaved it to a perfect fit, a template for each 10in line. We only took templates off one side of the model to ensure that both sides were exactly the same on the drawing."

As usual, the bodies for the first six GS5 prototypes were produced by hand in South body experimental under Dick Gallimore. Phil Stanworth recalled, "Gallimore was a working boss. He was as bald as a badger so he wore his trilby all the time. He was a brilliant chap but he could be an awkward sod. If he was busy when you wanted to speak to him you would have to wait and wait. You'd often get so cheesed off that you'd give up. As you walked away he'd say, 'What do you want?' As you bloody walked away."

Awkward or not, the ability of Dick Gallimore's men to knock up a prototype in almost no time at all was meat and drink to Len Lord who would often ask them to alter things here or there and thus by-pass the designers and stylists to get his own way.

Barry Brecknell spoke of producing the wooden patterns from which the press tools for the production bodies were made. "The most frustrating part of working in the pattern shop was that you couldn't visualise what any new car was going to look like. I was only given the drawing of a panel in orthographic projection. They had a commissionaire on the door of the experimental department so you couldn't get in to see any of the models that might be taking shape. I managed to get in occasionally by writing out a requisition such as, 'Required, one piece of mahogany, 3ft long by whatever.' If you added a fictitious signature the bloke on the door wouldn't know that the requisition was a duffer, so you could walk slowly through the shop taking in what you could from the corners of your eyes.

"Our pattern shop was one of the biggest in the country with about 120 pattern makers on the day shift and 40 or 50 on nights. The wooden patterns had to be accurate to within two to three thousandths of an inch. If anyone made a mistake or misread a drawing they were put through quite an ordeal. They might have spent months on a pattern but if it was returned by the checker it was known as

The new GS5/HS5 Cambridge photographed at Longbridge in 1954. The ground behind the car slopes down from what had been Austin's Flying Ground on the top of Cofton Hill. Soon after this, Austin photographer, Ron Beach, was furious to find iron railings being erected immediately behind where the car stands. His efforts to persuade management to make a section of the fence removable so that his photos could be free from background distractions were to no avail. Later in the book you will see further photographs, all with the offending railings spoiling the picture.

a 'shitter'. If it wasn't up to standard the checker would ceremoniously carry it back to the culprit's bench with every eye in the shop following him all the way. Everyone would grab something suitably resonant, a bit of tin or something, and as the checker put the pattern on the poor bloke's bench they would all hammer the benches and rattle tin cans. It was pandemonium.

"From our slightly over-sized wooden patterns they would make rough metal casts of the press tools. Howard Clare's woodshop would produce models in Honduras mahogany for each body panel too and these would be bolted to the faceplate of a Keller Copy Miller. As a stylus traversed the mahogany model a cutter took the same path over the rough casting of the punch or die and milled it to the exact size. The punch would then require a great deal of hand finishing but would eventually be used to press out panels by the thousand."

The A40 and A50 Cambridge both utilised BMC's new B-Series engine, the type symbol GS5

applying to the 1,200cc A40 Cambridge, and HS5 to the 1,500cc A50 version.

Although the totally new body for the A40/50 Cambridge was of unitary construction it was not quite as chassisless as that of the A30, at least not in its final form. Both Ken Garrett and Ian Duncan had left Longbridge before the body design took place and their skills in chassisless construction seem to have been sorely missed.

According to Bernard Johnson, "We had a lot of trouble with the Cambridge. The first ones had no chassis under them at all and they cracked up – fell apart in a big way in Spain. Most of the tools for the panels had already been produced so they just had to strengthen it by what was virtually a chassis welded on underneath. Johnnie Rix was in charge of the thing."

Chief tester Bob Grice was most unhappy about the problems with the original prototypes. "I had a hell of a row with Rix over the failure of the GS5. In fact I put Rix on a plane home from Spain and rang Harriman and told him why. When I got back a week later we had a meeting with Lord and I said, 'As far as

Top: Austin's first use of colour in their sales brochures was in 1919 when they suggested that one of the, 'Pleasures of Peace' could be "Seeing the world in an Austin Twenty Touring Car."

Bottom: This painting by Robert Johnston depicting Herbert Austin's 'Motor for the Millions' was used in Austin's Golden Jubilee booklet produced in 1955.

Sir Herbert Austin's first scheme for the Seven

By 1932/33 the Seven (opposite), Ten-Four (above) and Light Twelve-Four (below) accounted for 80 per cent of Austin's output.

The AUSTIN SEVEN

THE LITTLE FRIEND OF ALL THE WORLD

The Austin range for 1937.

SEVEN · TEN · TWELVE
FOURTEEN · EIGHTEEN · TWENTY

You buy a Car...but You Invest in an Austin

The New AUSTIN TEN

Leonard Lord introduced his new 8, 10 and 12hp cars in 1939.

The 16hp was not introduced until 1945. Here we see Leonard Lord signing a 16hp saloon which represented Austin's 1,000,000th car, in 1946.

By 1947, Austin's all-new post-war cars ranged from the A135 Princess to the A40 Devon and Dorset. The original artwork for the Princess, shown above, was found in a skip at Longbridge. Hence the part missing from the front wheel!

The painting below by Robert Johnston, nicely captures the spirit of the ships that were supposedly 'waiting' for Austin's exports.

Above: This A90 Atlantic prototype – with one-piece Perspex screen – covered 5,000 miles in France, Belgium, Holland, Germany, Denmark and Sweden, in July 1948.

Below: Carbodies of Coventry produced over 7,000 A40 Somerset drophead coupés between 1952 and 1954. They also produced 266 A70 Hereford coupés, 1951–53.

Above: This example of Austin's A40 Sports was prepared for the 1951 Earl's Court Motor Show. The car owed its styling to Eric Neale of Jensen.

Below: An A40 pick-up sporting Austin's post-war livery of claret and blue on a stone-coloured background – the colour used for the jacket of this book.

Above: According to Nash, the Nash Metropolitan 1500, seen above, offered, "American standards of comfort and performance" with "European craftsmanship and economy."

Below: Eric Bailey had just finished work on the Nash Metropolitan when he was asked to style the FX4 taxi. This is his first colour sketch from which a full-size model was constructed.

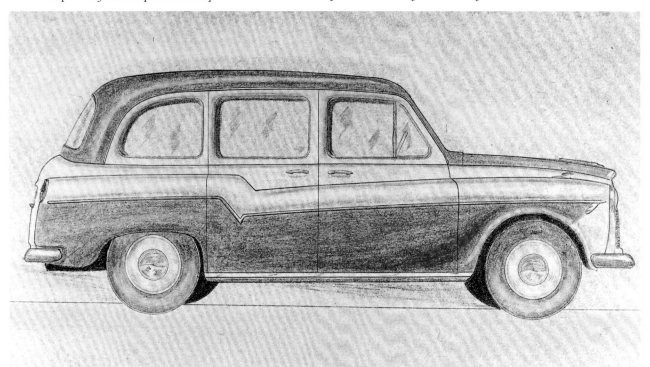

Above: The A30 of 1951 was not only Austin's first chassisless car but one of the first truly chassisless cars in the world.

Below: A cut-away drawing illustrating the car's chassisless construction and mechanical layout.

Above: Stylist Dick Burzi (standing) discusses the initial renderings for the GS5 Cambridge with Mark Young. Artist Robert Johnston is nearest the camera.

Below: A selection of quarter scale clay models from which the final style was chosen. Opposite: Nissan sales brochures for their Yokohama-built Somerset and Cambridge.

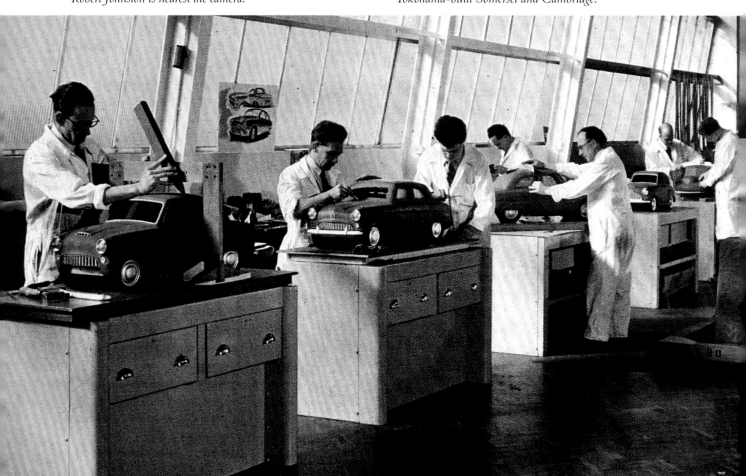

オースチン'A40'サマーセット 仕様書
サルーン

AUSTIN A50 CAMBRIDGE SALOON

NISSAN MOTOR CO., LTD.

Farina's A40, the Countryman version of which is seen above and the A55 MK II below, provided quite a departure from previous Austin styling.

Opposite page, top: The Farina Aerodynamica of 1967 could have turned the technically advanced 1800 of Issigonis into a very stylish car. Middle: Michelotti proposed this face-lift of the 1800 in 1969, seemingly to cater for much earlier thoughts of 'Roverisation'. Bottom: In 1973, Andy Duthie sketched this proposal for an Austin Princess Countryman.

The new AUSTIN SE7EN

DER NEUE BMW-KLEINWAGEN

Top right: In 1929, BMW announced "Der Neue BMW – Kleinwagon" – "The New BMW – small car", their version of the Austin Seven-based Dixi. Top left: The Issigonis-designed Mini of 1959. Below: So near yet so far. In 1999, BMW were preparing to launch another "Neue BMW – Kleinwagon" – a new Mini to replace the Issigonis car – and to build it at Longbridge. Unfortunately that is no longer the case. (See Chapter 27.)

I'm concerned I'm not going to pass designs I consider unsatisfactory. You can make your own choice, Sir Leonard. It is either Mr Rix or me.' All he said was, 'Oh!' Then he and Harriman went out and discussed it. Anyway they pensioned Rix off and that was when Lord brought Palmer up from Cowley."

That test of the 1,200cc GS5 in Spain in December 1953 had not only shown up serious flaws in the body, there was also much bottoming of the suspension. The steering and handling were considered to be very poor too, particularly when fully laden on twisty mountain roads. The 1,200cc engine was also found to be somewhat inadequate for the size of the car. Petrol fumes were also a problem, entering the body compartment from the boot. Whoever designed the fuel filler seems to have done it on an off-day. Placing it inside the boot was not a good idea, particularly as the filler pipe could not always cope with the flow from certain pumps and simply overflowed into the boot.

Twelve months later, when a pair of HS5 Cambridges with much reinforced underpinnings returned to France and Spain for further testing, they were deemed to be a considerable improvement on the earlier prototypes.

Some of the early production cars still gave problems, however. Joe Gomm of the Cowley road test department took great delight in claiming, "Longbridge used to send us what they couldn't do themselves. In 1954, Leonard Lord sent us an Austin Cambridge that the police were refusing to accept because of terrible body boom. At Longbridge they had been trying to get rid of the boom but eventually told Lord it was inherent in the design and couldn't be cured. 'Send the bloody thing to Cowley,' he said, 'and see what they can do with it.' It even boomed with the car stationary so we put it over the pit and my son, Leslie, ran the engine. When he got the boom going I prised a bar against the rear cross member that held the engine and gearbox. The noise stopped immediately. The cross member was so thin you could see it vibrating. I took it off and spot welded two pieces of 16-gauge metal either side of it. We had the car back at Longbridge in no time at all, completely cured. Lord

was delighted. He sent the car back to the police in Hull and they said, 'Get them all like that and we'll accept them'."

Accompanying the A50s on the second trip to Spain were two A90 Westminster prototypes. The A90 Westminster used an enlarged version of the Cambridge body and the new 2.6-litre C-Series engine. On the earlier trip one GS5 had been fitted with an A70 engine but the steering and handling proved to be very poor and there was excessive boom and body vibration. Austin had already received many complaints of boom in the A70 so decided that to put an A70 engine in the GS5 would only result in further serious criticism. On the second test, however, the strengthened bodies coped quite well with the smoother six-cylinder C-Series engine.

The Westminster was 8in longer and 2½in wider than the Cambridge but the doors were common to both cars. Although the A90 was almost 6in narrower than the A70 it replaced, its rear seat was 4in wider. The extra width of the seat was largely due to the longer wheelbase of the A90 which allowed the seat to be placed forward of the rear wheel arches.

Bill Hooper, who was in charge of Austin's West Country sales, was not happy with a couple of Cambridge features. "Those pull down windows broke your finger nails and that petrol filler cap in the boot was ludicrous. Before the launch I put those points to George Harriman but he said, 'I'm afraid we've got all the panels struck for it.' He said,

The A90 Westminster used the same doors as the Cambridge and a similarly styled but enlarged body. The new six-cylinder C-Series engine offered a smooth performance. The two-tone arrangement on this prototype was not used on the production cars.

In early 1956, Austin introduced the A105 with twin SU carburettors and high compression engine as a faster, more luxuriously equipped version of the A90 Westminster.

'The window goes down easily enough.' I said, 'Well it might be all right when it's new and it might be all right for clumsy guys like you and me but ladies are not going to like having their finger nails broken.' In early 1955 they had to bring in wind-up windows and they solved the problem of the petrol fumes at about the same time by clipping off the front corner of the boot and turning it into a separate lockable petrol filler door. Later in the year they also replaced the semaphore trafficators with flashing indicators."

The relatively poor sales of the 1,200cc version of the Cambridge meant that when the A55 (HS6) Cambridge was introduced in January 1957 the smaller-engined version was dropped. An exception to that, according to Anders Clausager, was a

1,200cc CKD version that was built in Ireland and sold as an A45.

What had been a simple and effective line on the A40/A50 bodyside was picked out and extended rearwards on the A55 with a somewhat fussy chrome strip to facilitate the application of the optional two-tone paintwork. The boot was larger and had a lower loading height. The rear wings lost their infamous 'cow-hip' styling and perhaps lost a little bit of character in the process. The wrap-around rear window certainly allowed a better view of the road behind and the dished steering wheel showed the beginnings of concern for the safety of the car's occupants.

A similar restyling job which produced the A95 and

The Cambridge evolved into the A55 in 1957 with its re-worked rear end and larger, more easily loaded boot. The chrome side-strip allowed for the increasingly popular two-tone colour schemes.

A re-worked tail also appeared on the A95 and A105 Westminsters of late 1956, which also sported a rather neat side flash in a contrasting colour that was matched to the roof. The A105 (seen here) featured fog lights and fancier, all-enveloping wheel trims. From 1958/59 there was also a Vanden Plas version with walnut fascia panel and window frames, leather seats and luxurious carpeting. Although this series of cars was arguably the most stylish of any of Dick Burzi's designs, Austin would soon be looking for further outside help with the styling of their cars.

A105 of late 1956, seemed to suit the larger cars well. Chrome strips to demark each edge of the coloured side flash on duotone models produced twice the number of potential rust-welcoming rivet holes, but the coloured flash certainly looked well, as did the new grille. The twin carb A105 was given virtually the same body treatment as the A95 but sported fog-lamps, whitewall tyres and fancy wheel discs.

The A105 had virtually the same power unit as that of the Healey 100-Six. A 1,200-mile *Motor Sport* road test of the A105 in February 1958 described it as a handsome, spacious and comfortable high-performance family saloon at a competitive price. They felt it carried on the tradition of the 1919 Austin Twenty, describing the 2.6-litre, six-cylinder engine as very smooth and willing. "So silently does the 102bhp engine idle that only the absence of the ignition warning light indicates that it is running. This commendable silence of running is a feature of the A105 and when motoring in top gear at moderate speeds the ticking of the clock can be heard clearly … when the accelerator is depressed a splendid surge of smooth power wafts this spacious saloon forward."

They found the column gearchange the weakest feature of the car and stated rather brusquely that "Whoever designed the Austin gearbox, together with its gear linkage, should be quickly found other employment." No doubt Harry Gardner would have cringed a little at that and must surely have been hoping that Len Lord wouldn't read that edition of *Motor Sport* and underline the complaints in red crayon before summoning him to his office as he had done with Gerald Palmer. On the A105 the overdrive changed the 4.1:1 top gear ratio to 2.87:1 and allowed it to cruise at 80mph at under 3,000rpm.

From 1958/59 there was also an A105 Vanden Plas – the start of otherwise standard Austins being turned into luxury cars by the careful addition of much veneer, leather and shag-pile carpeting at the Kingsbury Works. "It all started," said Roland Fox, "when Lord rang us up and asked if we'd make him an interior for his A105 Westminster as his personal car. He gave us a car and we sent it back within a fortnight with our own woodwork, paintwork and leather upholstery. We made a decent job of it and he was so pleased that he said, 'You want to make some of these.' So we did, and sold quite a few, not big numbers of course, about 500 I think, but it went down very well indeed."

The restyle and longer wheelbase of the A95 and A105 of late 1956 undoubtedly produced a sleeker looking car. But beauty, of course, is in the eye of the beholder and, as we shall see later, doubts expressed by one royal personage eventually led to Austin and BMC seeking further outside help in the styling of their cars.

15

Letter from Tokyo

"I have already started work in our body drawing office in the Nissan Motor Company, and I am endeavouring to make cars and trucks as well as you, applying invaluable knowledge and experience which I have been given in your factory."

KAORU SANEYOSHI

Humble words but of historic importance. They were contained in a letter sent from Japan in 1954 by Kaoru Saneyoshi to Les Farmer, the chief rate-fixer for many years in Austin's Longbridge press shop.

Saneyoshi was one of those sent by Nissan to Longbridge in the 1950s, when Nissan were planning to build Austins in Japan. So soon after the war, not everyone at Longbridge took kindly to seeing Japanese about the place but Les Farmer did his best to befriend them. In his letter, Kaoru Saneyoshi thanked Les for the kindness he had shown to both him and his colleague, Takuro Endo.

Les Farmer recalled, "Saneyoshi and Endo were particularly interested in how we got such output from the press shop. They couldn't understand why the men worked so hard. They used to stand there open-mouthed watching the men feeding blank after blank into the presses that churned out panel after panel. In trying to explain the piece-work system I eventually drew a donkey and a carrot. They understood that. At night they just sat in their lodgings so I invited them round to our place. They brought some Japanese green tea and insisted that we drank it with them. They were obviously very grateful and wrote to me for quite a considerable time afterwards."

In 1993, when Nissan Headquarters in Tokyo was sent a copy of Saneyoshi's letter, they kindly advised that Messrs Saneyoshi and Endo were still hale and

Part of the letter sent by Kaoru Saneyoshi from Japan in 1954 to Les Farmer.

and I am endeavouring to make cars and trucks as well as you, applying invaluable knowlege and experience which I have been given in your factory.
I shall stop for today, but I wish to write you again, when I shall have interesting news.
Hoping to hear from you.
Please remember me to your wife. I hope you and all your family are very well.
I remember
Yours Sincerely
K Saneyoshi

Kaoru Saneyoshi (left) and Takuro Endo (right), being entertained in 1954 at the home of Les Farmer, centre, chief rate-fixer in the Longbridge press shop.

hearty and would be happy to be interviewed. Several others from Nissan's Austin Department of the 1950s also offered to help piece together the story of those times. A trip to Tokyo made it abundantly clear that many of Nissan's post-war whiz-kids had cut their teeth in the Austin Department that was set up in their Yokohama plant in February 1953. The man responsible for the localisation plans to build Austins from 100 per cent Japanese parts was none other than the 1993 chairman of Nissan, Yutaka Kume. Takuro Endo had not done too badly either. Beginning as a young engineer at the Yokohama plant, he had risen by 1993 to the presidency of Nissan Diesel. Another of those involved, Teiichi Hara, eventually became Nissan's executive managing director in charge of exports.

Nissan chairman, Yutaka Kume, explained, "Just after World War Two we were not permitted [by the occupying forces] to turn out passenger cars and this produced a technical void in Japan. American and European countries were making great strides so eventually there became an urgent need to bridge this gap or disparity vis-à-vis Western countries. We yearned for the technology that was available, especially in the UK, and that we Japanese lacked."

By the time Nissan was given the go-ahead to produce cars in 1948 it had become obvious that co-operation with another motor manufacturer was essential. A tie-up with Volkswagen was considered but in those days a new German-Japanese alliance of any sort was a non-starter politically.

In early 1953, Nissan president, Genshichi Asahara, proudly announced to his employees that he had signed an agreement with Longbridge to build Austins in Japan. He had a good right to be proud. The Austin Motor Company was then one of the largest exporters of cars in the world and news of Longbridge's state-of-the-art assembly facilities had spread far and wide. Austin engines too, were noted worldwide for their efficiency and reliability.

As for the agreement with Austin, Teiichi Hara recalled, "Austin offered us every possible assistance. They also agreed to us using their patented technology and, most importantly, allowed us to use that technology in other Nissan products. That's why we worked so hard. We paid no royalties in the first year, but in the second year it cost us 2 per cent of our retail sales figure and 3 per cent from then on."

Signed at Longbridge in December 1952, the agreement ran for seven years. Initially, Nissan were simply to assemble CKD A40 Somersets, but it was agreed that subsequent to that they would build the A50 Cambridge from a gradually increasing

Nissan's Datsun Thrift (built 1951–54) provides clear evidence of the 'technical void' spoken of by Yutaka Kume. The car relied on an antiquated pre-war chassis and pre-war side-valve engine. The bodies, made by outside suppliers, suffered from structural weaknesses too.

percentage of Nissan-produced parts. An exchange of personnel was also agreed.

Saneyoshi and Endo's visit to Longbridge was part of that exchange. Takuro Endo saw his time at Longbridge as something of a pioneering mission in rebuilding international relations. "Generally speaking it was fun, but there were one or two men on the shop floor with tattoos on their arms who said they had fought the Japanese in Burma. They asked me where I was during the war and I honestly answered that I was a student and did not fight in the war. But I certainly have no bad memories. In fact my memories of the British people still give me great comfort."

Shinkichi Shimada, who became operations manager in Nissan's Austin Department, did have an awkward moment at Longbridge. "I was sitting in the exhibition hall looking at a new car when a chap came along and pushed me off the chair using his hips. I thought I had to bear it because we were defeated in the war. Other than that, I should say they were all good-natured people."

Stan Woodgate, of the Austin Export Corporation, used to lunch with the export sales people and sometimes with the Nissan representatives who were studying Longbridge methods. "George Harriman would be there at times with a management team that in comparison to the Japanese seemed like boisterous, fourth-form school boys. The Japanese were steady, properly educated, clued-up blokes, determined to do it right. Just ordinary men, but each had his own specific job to do."

Takuro Endo's responsibility, as he related to the author in 1993, was to study the Longbridge press

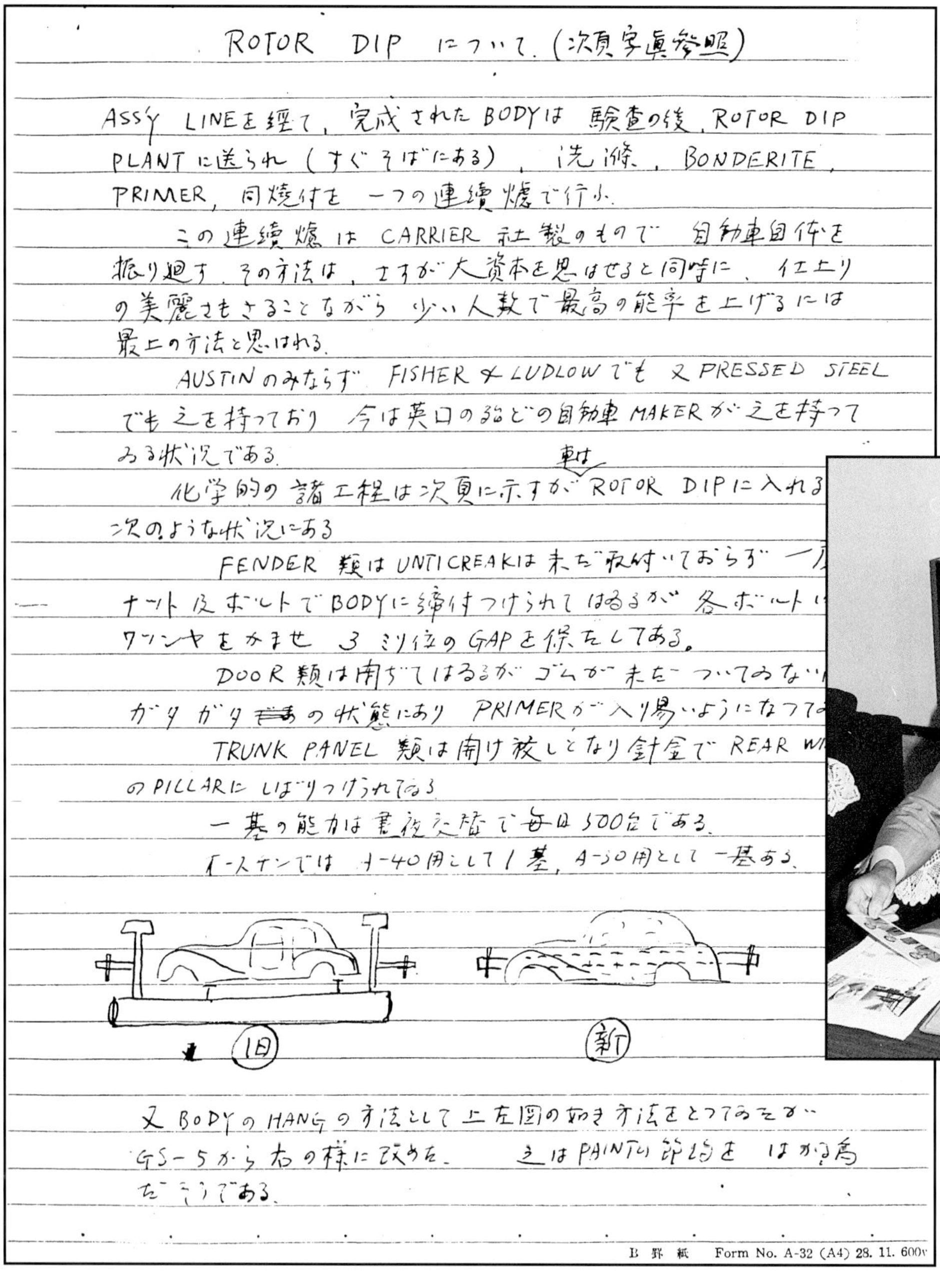

ROTOR DIP について (次頁写真参照)

ASSY LINE を經て、完成された BODY は 検査の後、ROTOR DIP PLANT に送られ（すぐそばにある）、洗滌、BONDERITE PRIMER, 同焼付を 一つの連続炉で行ふ。

この連続炉は CARRIER 社製のもので 自動車自体を振り廻す。その方法は、さすが大資本を思はせると同時に、イエ上りの美麗さもさることながら 少い人数で最高の能率を上げるには最上の方法と思はれる。

AUSTIN のみならず FISHER & LUDLOW でも 又 PRESSED STEEL でも 之を持っており 今は英口の殆どの自動車 MAKER が 之を持っている状況である。

化学的の諸工程は次頁に示すが ROTOR DIP に入れる前 次のような状況にある。

FENDER 類は UNTICREAK は未だ取付いておらず 一方ナット及ボルトで BODY に締付けられてはるが 各ボルトにワンヤをかませ 3ミリ位の GAP を保たしてある。

DOOR 類は閉ぢてはるが ゴムが未だついてない ガタガタの状態にあり PRIMER が入場いようになって

TRUNK PANEL 類は開け放しとなり針金で REAR W... の PILLAR に しばりつけられてる。

一基の能力は書後交替で毎日 500台である。

イーストンでは A-40用として 1基、A-50用として 一基ある。

(旧)   (新)

又 BODY の HANG の方法として上左図の如き方法をとってあるが GS-5から右の様に改めた。 之は PAINT の節約を はかる為 だそうである。

B 野帳   Form No. A-32 (A4) 28. 11. 600v

Takuro Endo, president of Nissan Diesel (inset), with mementos of his time at Longbridge. His responsibility was to study the Longbridge press shop and body assembly plant. This is an extract from the many reports he sent back to Tokyo and which he still treasures today.

shop and body assembly plant. "We studied different sections week by week and I wrote a report each week to send back to Tokyo. I still cherish those reports today. They were very informative and not only gave stimulus and interest to those back in Japan but provided the technology for the Nissan Motor Company of the future. The Longbridge plant was brand new and we aimed to build such a plant in Japan. Mass-production was a new experience for me. I joined Nissan in 1948 when they were producing between 200 and 300 units a month. Longbridge were producing 6,000 units a week. I had great admiration for the orderly way which they produced this large volume of vehicles. If we had not learnt such a system from Austin we could not have competed in the period that came after that, the period we call 'Motorisation' in Japan, where the volume of car sales increased dramatically."

The first Nissan-built A40 came off the line on 4 April 1953, the parts having arrived in Yokohama exactly one month prior to that. Only a further 208 cars were completed that year because the early days of the Austin agreement turned out to be the most tumultuous days in the whole of Nissan's history. The American occupying forces had encouraged the development of trade unions as a move towards a more equal and less feudal Japanese society. The

The first truckload of Austin parts arrives in Yokohama in March 1953.

unions spread rapidly and gained a considerable hold.

To mass-produce Austins, Nissan needed to reorganise their factories completely and to introduce simultaneously a whole host of new practices. The unions put many difficulties in the way of such progress and production became either spasmodic or impossible. Tired of incessant bargaining, Nissan management decided to meet the unions head on (something British management would only do 25 years later) and are said to have provoked a final showdown by locking out the workers and encouraging middle-management to form a new union, one that was more sympathetic to company needs. After a 100-day strike in mid-1953 the new union was formed.

Yutaka Kume found himself caught up in that strike. "It is a painful memory to me personally and I remember it very clearly because at the time I was just a new member of the company. I was locked out with the rest and production was halted for a long time. It was a strike of major proportions and taught

Sorting the consignment of parts which initiated Somerset assembly in Japan.

Austin engineer, Herbert Bailey, supervises the mounting of the first Somerset body on to its chassis at Yokohama.

us that neither the company or the union had anything to gain from such strikes. We wanted to prevent this kind of thing happening again. Labour and management came to the recognition that we had to maintain and improve close communications and co-operate wherever possible."

The new union was certainly an important feature in Nissan's subsequent success. With the strikes over, everything went ahead smoothly.

By August 1956, when Nissan's new transfer machines finally began producing cylinder blocks and cylinder heads for the 1,500cc B-Series engine, the localisation of car production was complete, only three years and nine months from the commencement of the agreement. The transfer machines were built by Hitachi Seiko, along the lines of those at Longbridge, and gave a dramatic boost to Nissan's engine-building capabilities.

Yutaka Kume recalled their efforts to establish 100 per cent local production of the Cambridge. "We

Celebrating the completion of the first Yokohama-built Somerset, April 1953.

would produce a sample part and send it to Austin who would subject it to their tests and evaluation. We would then receive approval or rejection. Sometimes we sent things three or four times and still met with a rejection."

Austin's almost excessive strictness in these matters was explained by Eric Holbeche, who was involved in the project at Longbridge. "In those days nobody was very happy about our association with the Japanese. In fact some people were quite upset. Not only that, the Far East had a reputation for shoddy goods, so George Harriman insisted that every part, right down to the last split pin, was sent to England to be tested and approved before we agreed to its deletion from the CKD (completely knocked down) pack."

Norman Horwood, who was responsible for co-ordinating the programme with Nissan, found himself instructed to tell them, for example, that the door rubbers were unacceptable because they had a chalk 'bloom' on them. "I thought it a bit ridiculous because every bit of rubber that went into our cars had a bloom on it. The Japanese didn't complain, they just sent further samples which were far better than those we were using. In effect we were forcing them to work to a higher specification than our own. I've often wondered whether it was we who ensured that the Japanese were going to beat us on quality."

When that suggestion was put to Yutaka Kume a gentle smile spread over his face and his head and shoulders assumed a rhythmic nodding motion, no doubt brought on by rueful thoughts of the difficulties of getting parts accepted by Austin, but his only utterance was a quiet, "Perhaps so". He then continued, "In 1956 we succeeded in completing our schedule for local production of Austin cars. I was manager of that department, so that gave me a lot of pleasure. We learned a great deal from Austin, particularly in the fields of design, engineering, and materials. We speedily learnt not only how to make cars but learnt the technology to produce engines and bodies. That progress was very important to us."

Nissan made very few alterations to the Longbridge-designed A50 but found they had to strengthen the chassis and suspension to combat the

Nissan's first chassisless car was the Yokohama-built Austin Cambridge. The first bodies required a considerable amount of hand finishing.

complaints of Japanese taxi drivers, likened by some to Kamikaze pilots, who found any weaknesses in a very short space of time. Between 1953 and 1960 Nissan built 21,859 A40 and A50 saloons, approximately 2,000 of these being A40 Somersets. They also produced 1,045 Nissan-designed Cambridge estate cars.

The most lasting benefit to Nissan from the Austin tie-up lay in Austin's lively and efficient B-Series engine. Not only did they gain the technology to build it efficiently using Austin-like automatic transfer machines but it was also agreed that they could use derivatives of that engine in the vehicles Nissan designed themselves as successors to the Cambridge. Nissan designers had intended to build their own small engine in the mid-1950s but when they hired Donald Stone, an American consultant, he basically told them they would be barmy not to simply vary the bore and stroke of the Austin engine to provide whatever capacity they

Nissan did not just try to emulate Austin, they tried to go one better. On their de luxe versions of the Cambridge they offered an exterior trim based on that of the Austin A105 ie two-tone paint, fog lamps, white-wall tyres etc. From 1958, their de luxe cars had the side stripes and two-tone colour treatment that Austin used on the A95/A105 from 1957 onwards, and even added the silver-coloured side flash of Austin's Vanden Plas version.

required. This was excellent advice because it meant that all their engines could be produced on the same transfer machines. Between 1955 and 1972 Nissan powered part of their range with almost 2 million B-Series derived engines in four different sizes.

Figures kindly provided by Anders Clausager show that Austin and BMC also produced between 3.7 and 4 million vehicles with B-Series engines. A total production of between 5 and 6 million engines is quite a tribute to Eric Bareham's original B-Series design.

What did Eric, a former chief designer of engines and transmissions for BMC, have to say on being given those facts and figures? Those who know his quiet ways will not be surprised that he simply uttered one word: "Blimey!" In fact he then went on to suggest that most of the credit for Austin A-Series and B-Series engines should be given to Austin's chief designer, Johnnie Rix, and that he, Eric Bareham, "simply did the drawings". While it is true that Johnnie Rix did make many of the major design decisions, Eric's colleagues insist that he was a highly skilled and enthusiastic designer rather than a mere pencil pusher and definitely deserved much of the credit for the design processes by which both the A and B-Series engines evolved.

Wesley Hunt, assistant designer to Eric Bareham, gave an interesting aside to the B-Series story. "Our

chaps in Australia had inspected some of the Yokohama-built Cambridges and told us how clean the engines were. We always had trouble with the front crankshaft seal, but the Jap engines were bone dry. We got hold of a complete set of the gaskets they were using in Japan and I got Coopers, the mechanical joints people, to have a look at them. We copied the Japanese seals wherever we thought they were better, particularly the timing chain cover, and we then had far fewer leaks."

It seems then, that after the Second World War, the old order of things in Japan had been so severely disrupted that a demoralised Japanese nation needed to be shown, step by step, how to rebuild its motor industry. Once shown the way, however, their confidence and expertise blossomed dramatically and they were soon producing innovative designs of their own. Equally important was their preparedness to invest continually in new technology and their deep desire to counteract the Far East's earlier reputation for producing shoddy goods.

Edwards Deming, one of the first to preach the importance of quality in the 1950s, had found his words falling on deaf ears in his native America. The Japanese, and Nissan in particular, welcomed him

with open arms. His exhortations that quality ought to be central to any company's philosophy made good sense to them. It was impossible, he told them, to put a price on the value of a satisfied customer or to calculate the cost of a dissatisfied one. The enthusiasm with which the Japanese responded to his teachings made Deming one of the first Westerners to realise that the Japanese motor industry would soon be a formidable force in world affairs.

As President of Nissan, Yutaka Kume was present at the opening of Nissan's UK plant at Sunderland in September 1986. "We invited the Prime Minister, Mrs Margaret Thatcher, and many others who had supported the project. That day gave me supreme pleasure."

The Sunderland factory soon became the largest exporter of UK-built cars and since 1992 has even been 'carrying coals to Newcastle' by exporting certain UK-built Nissans to Japan. For the last three years of the 20th century it was also hailed as the most efficient car plant in Europe.

Yutaka Kume's proposal to build a UK plant was initially met with derision in Tokyo. Had he not been prepared to stick his neck out, not, it would seem, a common trait in the Japanese executive, the UK plant might never have materialised. At Nissan's Tokyo headquarters, he explained what happened. "There were considerable differences of

A Quality Circle? Not really, just members of the All-Japan Datsun Car Club inspecting a Yokohama-built Somerset in 1993.

In 1993, Yutaka Kume, Nissan Chairman, inspects memorabilia from their Austin Department of the 1950s.

opinion and much vacillation amongst us. Many thought that UK industry was too strike-prone. When I submitted the proposal for the UK project and mentioned the availability of very high quality human resources, the others laughed at me. They actually laughed at me. They said the 'British Disease' was well known. My answer was that the large nationalised companies might be strike-prone but the private companies would have failed long ago if their employees were on strike very often."

But why, in the light of the previously mentioned dissent, should Yutaka Kume have continued to champion the UK for a European assembly plant rather than some other Continental country? Without hesitation he replied, "Firstly the UK Government and UK people extended a hearty welcome. Secondly, your parts manufacturing industry is the most developed of all European countries and your financial institutions are very well developed too. The fact that English is spoken is also important for us Japanese. Your provisions for higher education are good, so there are many people with a high educational level which means that

high-quality labour is available. Finally the UK wage level was reasonable compared to other countries on the Continent. Although those are the reasons, also at the back of our minds was the fact that the UK was the country where Austin was and they had taught us how to make cars in the first place. I know we had that in our hearts."

When Kaoru Saneyoshi, the writer of that "Letter from Tokyo", was asked if he had succeeded in his aim to build cars as good as the British, he replied in a typically polite Japanese manner: "I didn't believe that Japan could ever compete with Britain, but that was our aim, to produce cars as good as the British."

Note that he had not actually answered the question, presumably settling for the fact that the considerable successes of the post-war Japanese motor industry had already done so on his behalf.

Did President Kume ever reflect on how in 1953, Austin was showing Nissan how to build cars and then, 40 years on, they, and other Japanese firms, were showing the world how to go about things? "It especially impressed me that the Austin Motor Company was such a fine company and kind too in teaching us how to build cars at Nissan. All of us at Nissan are very much indebted and I think we must keep that modest feeling even now."

Although, for a short while, in 1932/33, the earliest Datsuns built by Nissan did look remarkably similar to the Austin Seven it should perhaps be mentioned here that the cars were very different mechanically. Even the early Datsun's resemblance to the Austin was very short lived because by 1934, Datsun styling was betraying a strong American influence. Whatever may have been written elsewhere, Nissan have made it very clear that they had no licensing agreement with Austin until after the Second World War, nor did they build their own bodies on imported Austin chassis.

Some of the earlier confusion may have arisen from the fact that Nihon Jidosha, the pre-war Austin agents in Japan, did build and sell vans, saloons and tourers based on the Austin Seven chassis. However, these cars had no links with Nissan other than the fact that Nippon Jidosha built completely different bodies for Nissan during the same period.

So, with Nissan engines now powering our London taxis and thus taking over the one-time domain of Austin, Nissan's erstwhile tutor in engine design, and with much use being made of the slogan 'You can with a Nissan', perhaps it is as well that within this chapter we have at least recorded that once upon a time, 'You could with an Austin'.

16

50 years on – a golden day at 'The Austin'

"Let's roast an ox, Sam. It would be nice to roast an ox and give them all a slice of beef."

LEONARD LORD

Austin's first 50 years had, to all intents and purposes, been under the direction of only two men, first Herbert Austin and then Leonard Lord.

Unlike Herbert Austin, Leonard Lord was more feared than revered, but as an astute production engineer he succeeded in turning Longbridge into one of the most up to date factories in the world. By 1955, 50 years after its foundation, the factory had grown from 2½ to 260 acres and production had increased from some 120 vehicles a year to more than that in every working hour.

In his efforts to ensure that the Golden Jubilee of the Austin Motor Company would be celebrated in style, Lord's largesse knew no bounds. He even chartered planes to fly in dealers and distributors from all over the world on a money-no-object spree.

Clements of Bromsgrove, who for many years built motor show stands for Austin, was asked to transform the Works, especially the gala day area, into a riot of colour.

Sam Haynes was delegated to organise the festivities and his account of the preparations illustrates rather nicely that it was Lord who determined almost everything that happened at post-war Longbridge. "I thought I'd got everything pretty well in hand," said Sam, "but with the Jubilee almost upon us my telephone rang. 'That you Sam?' 'Yes, Sir.' I knew who it was because it was a special phone. 'Come up and see me Sam.' So up I went to Len Lord's office and he said, 'Now then Sam, sit down and give us one of your cigarettes.' He liked a Woodbine for a change. He said, 'About this Jubilee. Let's have a fair Sam.' I said, 'A fair?' He said, 'Yes, you know, roundabouts and things like that.'

Naturally, I said I would do what I could and down I went. A few minutes later the 'phone rang and it was a question of 'Come up and see me again Sam.'

Artist Jean Beddow works on the 25ft diameter likeness of Sir Herbert Austin which formed the centrepiece of the Works' decorations.

Kenneth Horne arrives in the 1908 Austin 100hp Grand Prix car, obviously giving the throttle a bit of 'welly' to amuse the crowd – and frighten, it seems, Leonard Lord.

This time it was, 'Let's roast an ox, Sam. It would be nice to roast an ox and give them all a slice of beef.' I wondered where the hell I was going to get a fair and an ox-roasting from at this stage. Anyway, I made some enquiries, found someone in the know,

Harry Austin (left) and Leonard Lord, prepare to unveil the plaque at the start of the 50th anniversary celebrations.

and we got it all together. We managed to build seating for 16,000 people outside the car assembly building. Our 22,000 employees could each apply for two sets of tickets and on the night before the Jubilee they were selling for about £3–4 apiece in the pubs of Longbridge and Northfield."

The celebrations duly honoured the memory of Herbert Austin. Medals were struck in both pewter and gold, showing Herbert on one side and on the reverse the image of his first car and that of the latest Austin Cambridge. A medal was sent to Clements so that Jean Beddow, their commercial artist, could reproduce it as a 25ft diameter plaque which formed the centrepiece of the Works decorations.

To paint a faithful reproduction of the features of Lord Austin on so large a scale was far from easy. When next to the 'workface' Jean could see little of the effects of her handiwork, but solved the problem of continually running up and down the ladder by a craftily placed mirror in the Bromsgrove workshop where she executed the commission. Turning round to the mirror she could quickly check on how things were looking.

Saturday, 9 July 1955 still holds happy memories for many, but it began a little worryingly for Sam Haynes. "When I looked out first thing it was belting down with rain but fortunately the sun soon came out and people piled in and filled all the seats. Thousands had to stand because something like 35,000 attended altogether."

In his opening address, which included a welcome to the Lord Mayor of Birmingham, Lord played to his audience by telling them, "He hasn't come in an Austin, so we can blow him a raspberry." The ensuing enthusiastic raspberry blowing was only silenced when, with a terrific roar, the 1908 Austin 100hp racer burst upon the scene and was driven enthusiastically through the crowds by the then star of radio, Kenneth Horne, on his way to take over the commentary for the day.

To start the proceedings the large plaque of Herbert Austin was unveiled by Harry Austin, then 79 years old but still a superintendent in South Works. Herbert Austin's daughter, Irene, then presented long service awards to a select band of 15 men who had served Austin for 46 years or longer, those with a half century of service being Harry Austin, Bobby Howitt and Alf Depper.

Ivor Greening, of Austin's publicity department, had organised a cavalcade of cars for a 'drive past' in the afternoon. "I got my list together a week or two before the event. Several old cars had to be tuned up and checked over and I got on to 'Doc' Weaving and asked if we could have a special appearance of the

The post-war 'Flying A' and the Austin 'Winged-wheel', which dates back to 1906, were both used to decorate the viewing platform set up alongside CAB 1. Note the 'Austin of England' script on the car assembly building.

turbine-driven Sheerline. It was all in pieces at the time but he said, 'No problem, we'll put it together for you.' On the Friday afternoon I was summoned to the chairman's office and asked to bring the list of cars for the cavalcade. Len Lord took a look and remarked, 'That's a bloody good show,' but when he got to the bottom and saw the Sheerline he said,

'Out, out with that one.' 'Oh,' I replied, 'I thought that one would make the day.' 'No,' he said, 'We can't have that one, it's too noisy.' Of course you couldn't argue with Len Lord. Even when I explained how 'Doc' Weaving had gone to all the trouble of assembling the thing, it didn't make any difference. On the day itself I was waiting for the

CAB 1 is on the left in this view of the crowds at Jubilee Day as veteran cars are put through their paces in a motoring gymkhana. In the background is the metal framework of the new reception and exhibition building then under construction.

Winner of the J40 race, Alan Swadling, receives his car from Lady Lord as Leonard Lord looks on. Note the tie that Alan remembers flapping in his face all those years ago.

coming up Low Hill Lane and into the Works by way of the car despatch gate. When the signal came I had to move off in an old landaulet and still didn't know whether the Sheerline had tagged on to the end of the parade or not.

"Apparently with the Jubilee going so well Len Lord had looked over to Doc Weaving and said, 'Can you get the turbine in?' This was only about ten minutes before the parade. You can imagine what hit the headlines the next morning. It was a case of, 'Austin show their turbine car.' It was its one and only public appearance but it overshadowed the whole Jubilee." Unabashed, Lord lapped it all up, proclaiming to the press, "We brought the Sheerline out because we wanted to give our guests a glimpse of motoring in the future."

Any noise the Sheerline may have made was undoubtedly surpassed during another event that day, a race in Austin J40 pedal cars for employees' children. The race was accompanied by an ear-splitting soundtrack of racing cars at their limits and a hilarious commentary by Kenneth Horne brought enthusiastic cheering from the crowd. Preliminary heats had eliminated all but the top ten drivers. Alan Swadling, who won the race, remembered it as a serious business because the winner was to receive a J40. "You could choose your own car for the race, so

signal to lead off the parade when I heard the whine of the turbine. It still chokes me today. I couldn't believe it. I couldn't see it but you could hear it

The end of a memorable day. Children play on the export packing cases as the chefs do their best to cope with the steady demand for helpings of roast ox.

my father put several cars on their sides to check if everything ran freely. He chose number 11, a white car. We were given crash helmets that had been made by the experimental department and I still remember the smell of the helmet, a rubbery, fibre-glass type smell. I felt the bees' knees with the helmet on and was getting quite keyed up by that time. We even had to run across the road in a Le Mans-type start. That suited me because I used to run for 'The Austin'. On Sports Day I ran for North Works because my father was a foreman on A-Series engine-build. After I won the J40 race I hardly knew what was happening except that I remember Leonard Lord's tie flapping in my face, when he stooped over the car, and I can remember stopping to talk to one of the policeman on the gate on the way home. Everyone was looking at me. I mean those cars were quite a thing to see then. I pedalled it all the way home, blowing the horn. I couldn't wait until it got dark to go out in it and try the lights."

The story behind those Austin pedal cars, produced at Bargoed by Welsh miners disabled with pneumoconiosis, is delightfully told in David Whyley's book, *Austin Pedal Cars* – see Bibliography.

After the pedal car race and with the main proceedings over, the fun-fair came into operation. As Sam Haynes explained, "We'd managed to get all

Emil Frey and the stained-glass Swiss warrior which is still in the 'Kremlin' keeping an eye on production quality.

sorts of side-shows and rides, including a beautiful steam roundabout with those great big horses that go up and down. A whacking great thing it was, the biggest I'd ever seen. When it was announced over the loud speaker that the fair was opening it produced a sudden rush of hundreds of people all heading to clamber on the big horses. Naturally they were all approaching from the one side and when they jumped on, the whole roundabout collapsed sideways. That was the end of that. It never ran at all, but fortunately nobody was hurt."

The ox-roast was a little more successful. It had been roasting away quietly all day until an announcement that Leonard Lord was about to cut the first slices signalled the final attraction of a memorable day, a day which had seen the biggest party ever thrown in the British motor industry.

Emil Frey of Switzerland was one of the Austin distributors flown in for the celebrations. He brought with him a gift of a stained-glass window panel that was later installed above the main door of the 'Kremlin', immediately opposite the car assembly building. It is there to this day but what few people know is what Emil disclosed in Switzerland when in his nineties. "That piece of stained glass shows a Swiss warrior and when Len Lord told me where he would place it I said, 'Excellent. Our Swiss Warrior will be able to keep an eye on the quality of your cars.'"

Even on this day of great celebration, Lord was being offered food for thought.

17

Putting on the style – the Farina era

"The next one I hear call it a van will get the sack."

___

GEORGE HARRIMAN

Although Dick Burzi's easy-going charm made him a very popular figure at Longbridge, there were those who were not altogether happy with the designs emerging from his studio. Those intimately involved in the design process realised that Burzi's creations were usually compromised to a greater or lesser degree by the heavy hand of Lord. Indeed, a general feeling began to emerge that as long as Lord meddled with the styling they would never be able to develop a top-flight range of cars.

When Joe Bache of the Austin Export Corporation plucked up the courage to suggest to Len Lord in person that their cars would probably be much more popular on the Continent if they

The Duke of Edinburgh chats to the men on the Cambridge assembly lines before putting the cat among the pigeons on his visit to Longbridge in late 1955.

commissioned Pinin Farina to do some styling, Lord brusquely replied, "We don't want any more damn foreigners, we've enough of them already."

Lord's eventual capitulation was seemingly triggered by the Duke of Edinburgh during his visit to Longbridge in December 1955, as Joe Edwards recalls. "The Duke was very friendly and chatty but Lord had an enormous inferiority complex, so we hadn't gone very far on our tour of the Works when Lord said, 'You will have to excuse me your Highness, but I've got some other business to attend to.' He'd got bugger all to do but he left Edinburgh with George Harriman and me. That suited us down to the ground. We spent the rest of the morning showing him the assembly lines and he met all the chaps. He was very good at that sort of thing. Eventually we got back to the cocktail room in the Kremlin and in came Len not knowing quite what to say. By that time we had built up quite a relationship and Edinburgh was laughing and talking to us and Lord was being ignored. You could see his agitation building up. 'Should we go and eat?' he asked. We had a very nice dining room in the Kremlin. So we sat down, Lord, Edinburgh and his PR man, George and I – nobody else.

"Edinburgh was going on about how impressed he was with the assembly lines and the automation and Len suddenly asked him, 'What do you think about this Champ we are making?' 'Oh,' said the Duke, 'I think it's very good.' Len said, 'Well, I've seen you and the Queen going round in Land Rovers waving to everybody. You ought to be in an Austin Champ.' Well! Edinburgh has very long fingers you know, and he pointed at Lord and said, 'Be careful what you say.' He was obviously very

Farina's first task was to bring his creative flair to the re-packaging of the A35's running gear in an all-new body style to produce the A40 Farina.

The result. Austin styling took a quantum leap forward. Although this initial mock-up was deemed to have far too little strength above the waistline, the basic style, including the possibility of a contrasting roof colour, went into production largely unchanged.

Still known under its code name ADO 8, this pre-production prototype was photographed at Longbridge on 17 October 1957. It stands exactly where Ron Beach photographed the A40/50 Cambridge in 1954. No wonder those railings nearly drove him to despair.

annoyed. It was like a bombshell. Of course George and I were killing ourselves with inner laughter but we got our heads down and although Len apologised the lunch went very quietly after that. It was simply Lord's inferiority complex. He was nervous and just wanted to get in on the action but didn't know how. Eventually Len said, 'Let's go and have a look at the models down below in Burzi's studio.' So we all trooped downstairs and after Len had shown him the models the Duke said, 'Sir Leonard, I think you ought to have another look at things because I'm not sure these are up to the foreign competition.' Old Len just didn't know where he was. Eventually Edinburgh went and the next day Len sent for Farina. That's why Farina was brought in. He flew in one morning and went away that night with an £84,000 contract for designing our first Farina cars. Not many people know that but I assure you that it was the Duke of Edinburgh's comments which brought it all about."

Those who had been pressing for Farina to be consulted were certainly proven right. His repackag-

ing of the A35's running gear showed considerable flair. The crisp clean lines of the resultant A40 Farina saw Austin styling take a quantum leap forward. Farina had managed to combine style with practicality by daringly venturing into a new, 'two-box' format that anticipated later hatchbacks. His rearward extension of the roof line meant that, even in this small package, it was possible to provide adequate headroom for the rear-seat passengers and increase luggage-carrying capacity at the same time.

Having achieved such progress, it is understandable that George Harriman was greatly annoyed to hear people referring to the new car as a van, but when Austin men first saw it they were quite shocked. Barry Brecknell was doing his National Service at the time and when he called in to see his pals in the pattern shop they asked him, "Have you seen the bloody matchbox we are producing?"

"When I saw it myself," said Barry, "I couldn't believe it was an Austin. Previously we'd had rounded bodies but this was square at the front, square at the back and square at the bloody sides – amazing."

The retention of the A35's tried and tested mechanical components meant that the A40 Farina sailed into production with very few problems. Its public debut was at the Grand Palais, Paris, in October 1958.

Announcement day, 18 September 1958. It was quite a tribute to Farina that his efforts should be acknowledged in the very name of the car. With the new Austin A40 Farina outside the Longbridge exhibition hall are Leonard Lord, Battista Pininfarina, George Harriman and the stylist's son, Sergio Pininfarina.

Here we see white and black-roofed Mk II A40s being assembled at Longbridge. The A35 van beyond shared many mechanical components with the A40. Innocenti of Milan assembled the Mk I A40 Farina from 1960 onwards. It was their criticism of the car's ride which led to most of the improvements on the Mk II cars introduced in September 1961.

Funnily enough, the main complaints came from Italy. When Innocenti of Milan assembled the Mk I A40 from 1960 onwards they immediately began receiving criticisms of the harshness of the front suspension on rough roads. Innocenti, in turn, demanded that Longbridge should improve both the ride and handling.

According to Bernard Johnson, "I think they placed the car in a slightly higher slot in the market than us. We drove a car down to Italy and worked with them to sort things out. The telescopic rear shock absorbers and a front anti-roll bar that we developed were introduced on the Mk II version."

Farina was also entrusted to restyle Burzi's A55 Cambridge to produce what became the A55 Mk II Cambridge of 1959, the mechanical components of which had already been well proven on the Mk I. The Farina-styled car, complete with its fashionable rear fins, was developed under the code name ADO 9. Being twelve inches longer and two inches wider than its predecessor, the Austin A55 Mk II was a much roomier vehicle.

Variants of Farina's mock-up were soon devised

too. Indeed, it was with their Farina-inspired mid-range cars, all using the B-Series engine, that BMC's rationalisation plans made their greatest strides. With the majority of Austin and Nuffield distributors so determined to keep their pre-merger identity we can

Innocenti went one further, however, providing their A40S Combinata with a full lift-up tailgate. Austin's own Countryman version of the A40 Farina was initially proposed for Australia. The split tailgate might have been ideal for carrying surfboards but it did make the loading of heavy cases rather difficult.

Farina's first offering for BMC's mid-range of cars had this ugly, over-ornate front end which seemed completely out of step with what was otherwise a car of very clean lines.

A combination of proposals from Farina and Dick Burzi produced a front end that was more acceptable from Austin's point of view. Other than moving the Austin badge to the grille and adding a bonnet motif, this is basically how the Austin A55 Mk II went into production in 1959, using the 1,489cc B-Series engine and other mechanical parts of the Burzi-styled A55.

Sid Goble of Cowley was responsible for the styling of BMC's other variants of the mid-range Farina styled cars. Here is his proposal for the Riley 4/68. Other than the shape of the overriders and the two-tone arrangement on the rear wing, this is basically how the Riley went into production.

hardly blame Lord for deciding to simplify the situation by supplying them with 'badge-engineered' cars. It was Sid Goble who was given the brief of producing the Nuffield versions at Cowley. "There weren't really any stylists at Cowley," said Sid, "but because of my pre-war work with H. J. Mulliner, anything that required styling was given to me. Eventually S. V. Smith gave me the title of chief stylist at Cowley, presumably so that he could talk to Burzi about his chief stylist, Sid Goble. From Farina's design for the Cambridge I had to develop designs in ascending order of price for the Morris Oxford, Wolseley 15/60, MG Magnette, and Riley 4/68. I was only allowed to alter the bonnets and grilles of each car and had to produce any further differentiation by playing about with the trim, fascias and paintwork. Although there were different sidelights I got away with the same pressings for the front wings. One draw die could produce all the rear wings because we simply used a different clipping tool to produce the variations for each model. Farina wasn't involved with these variants at all."

Although this rationalisation of the mid-range BMC cars made excellent economic sense it did not please everyone. Derogatory headlines such as, 'BMC's five-car trick', began appearing in the motoring press. One correspondent to *Motor Sport* in March 1959 declared himself "horrified by BMC's Farinacious Magnette." Another felt that "whatever styling is adopted, Farina's or Joe

The Austin A60 Cambridge, as launched in 1961, with its toned-down fins and generally softer lines, was a much-improved car mechanically too. The wider track and 1,622cc engine produced a more stable and satisfying car to drive.

Snook's, BMC cars would feel and behave similarly due to uniformity of engines, transmissions and suspensions." He therefore hoped that they would "transfer all the staff who are occupied in dreaming up new distortions of the old radiator shells to the testing department. Then perhaps their new models would not show quite so many maddening and stupid faults."

However, as Bernard Johnson of the experimental department pointed out, "the mid-range Farinas were well-received and didn't give much trouble because we pinched the engine and transmission out of the long-tailed A55. When we'd put 13in wheels on that, it had given problems with ground clearance, so on the export models we had to revert to the larger wheels. With the Farina models we took such pains to see that the ground clearance was adequate that it ended up rather too high. Before the launch, George Harriman decided the space above the tyre in the wheel arch had to be reduced, so we put an aluminium block between the axle and the spring. The spring went under the axle, so adding the block lowered the car. We decided that if anybody ran into ground clearance difficulties then their local agent could take the blocks out and throw them away. Harriman was right to be concerned about the showroom look of the unloaded car. It did look too high. I mean, even a tank of petrol weighs some 70 or 80lb. Of course, the first mid-range Farinas were basically built on the previous A55 chassis and were a bit narrow-gutted. The A60, with its wider track and the B-Series engine enlarged to 1,622cc, was eventually a far better car."

Although rather harshly described over the years as 'grey-porridge' motor cars, the mid-range Farina-

In 1959, Farina's styling was extended to BMC's ADO 10 project which produced a new range of executive saloons, The Austin A99 Westminster (subsequently the A110), the Wolseley 6/99 (later the 6/110) and Vanden Plas 3-litre were all powered by a 3-litre version of the C-Series engine.

styled cars performed well for both BMC and its customers, some 900,000 being produced. Indeed, one could argue that the Farina-styled Cambridge and its Nuffield derivatives, with their well-proven mechanical parts, were at least as "dependable" as any car the company had ever produced.

Geoffrey Iley, production manager at Morris Motors, added a little spice to the story of getting the range into production. "We couldn't get certain parts for love nor money. Sam Smith virtually lived at Lucas to ensure we got the bits for our cars in case Longbridge got them first. They had their chaps doing exactly the same thing so it was a case of buying the foreman a drink or whatever because Cowley and Longbridge were fighting for identical components. Design parentage for that model [ADO 9] had been given to Longbridge so they chose the suppliers of any components common to all versions. In the pre-launch months I had desperate trouble getting the common bits. Many were from Austin suppliers that we had not dealt with before. The stainless steel finisher for the windscreen had been given to Pianoforte Supplies. We hadn't dealt with them at Cowley and we phoned, wrote, sent guys down, but could we get samples? Could we hell. I simply couldn't build a car. You can't put a new car outside without a windscreen. It was driving me mad so I jumped in the car and drove over to their office. They virtually set the dogs

on me. Eventually a chap came out and said, 'You just don't know, do you?' I said, 'Don't know what?' He said, 'About Morris.' He took me into his office and produced a book of press cuttings from just before the war.

"Apparently at that time, Morris decided to produce their own bright metal trim and cancelled their orders with Pianoforte Supplies overnight. No consultation, no compensation, nothing. To add insult to injury they placed adverts in papers local to Pianoforte trying to persuade tool setters and so on to move to Oxford. So they said, 'None of those bastards are ever crossing our threshold again.' Eventually they grudgingly produced me one or two bits and we began to build the cars."

Further progress with BMC's rationalisation plans was seen in 1959 when Farina's styling was extended to the ADO 10 project at Cowley. The resulting Austin A99 Westminster, Wolseley 6/99 and Princess 3-litre, were to form BMC's new line-up of executive saloons and were all powered by a 3-litre version of the C-Series engine.

Roland Fox described how, in the design period, Lord had suggested that Vanden Plas should make a higher quality version of both the Westminster and the Wolseley 6/99. "We had actually started assembly of both cars when we had a phone call from Lord to say that he wanted us to cancel the Austin and Wolseley versions and make a Princess instead. The motor show was only three months away so I wasn't very pleased. In fact I very nearly exploded at the thought of the disruption it was going to cause but I asked for time to think about it. After I had cooled down I thought, 'He's right you know.' It was actually a brilliant idea of Lord's to associate a prestige name with a quality car that could be produced at an attractive price. So I said, 'OK we'll do what we can.' It meant we needed a new radiator grille. I suggested to John Bradley that we made it a cross between a Bentley and an Alvis and we took one up to show Leonard Lord – just held the grille in front of a Westminster and he told us to go ahead. It eventually became the Vanden Plas Princess 3-litre and it turned us into quite a big producer. It took us several months to get it into production because we had to have new bonnets and grilles and so on but we eventually got production up to a hundred a week."

Production levels were to be a serious bone of contention when the successor to the Princess 3 Litre was announced in 1964. The idea was not only to combine the vast engineering resources of BMC with Vanden Plas craftsmanship, as in the Princess 3-litre, but to add one further enticing ingredient, a

Rolls-Royce engine, thereby offering a unique blend of quality, comfort and performance at a competitive price.

Roland Fox described how things did not quite go according to plan. "By 1963 Leonard Lord had retired and Harriman wanted us to do the 4-litre R. He wanted us to go hell for leather with the thing. Lord had suggested using the Rolls engine once before but I told him the Austin engine was perfectly adequate and advised against it. Later on Harriman resurrected the idea and he seemed to want to do it so much that I gave in and we agreed to plan to produce 100 a week.

"At the Longbridge press preview in the summer of 1964, Lewellyn Smith of Rolls-Royce and I were sitting with George Harriman on the top table in the exhibition hall. Someone asked how many we were going to make and Harriman said, 'Two hundred a week.' Just like that. The press hand-out said we would produce 100 a week so they naturally wanted to know which was the correct figure. 'Two hundred a week,' re-affirmed Harriman. When he sat down I said to him quietly, 'I can only do 100 a week.' He said, 'BMC can do anything old boy.' We

The Vanden Plas Princess 4-litre R of 1964–68 was powered by a Rolls-Royce engine that was a light alloy, six-cylinder version of their military 'B' range of engines. With its slightly more sophisticated styling, luxurious interior and the added cache of the RR engine, the car was expected to be a considerable success.

The Princess 3-litre of 1959/60 became known as the Vanden Plas Princess 3-litre from May 1960. The cars were built at Cowley but sent to Kingsbury for luxurious trimming and finishing, and had a radiator grille which, according to Roland Fox, was a cross between [that of] a Bentley and an Alvis.

were then building the little Princess 1100 as well so we were absolutely flooded out.

"The 3-litre had been almost trouble-free but from the very beginning the Princess R engine caused considerable anxiety. That particular Rolls engine was horrible. When we started them up they made a dreadful noise. I called Lewellyn Smith to say that there was something seriously wrong with the carburation. Tuning the engine was almost

impossible. On tick over it sounded more like a diesel tractor and it was quite a while before it was sorted out. What with water leaks, cylinder liners which worked loose and cylinder head studs which pulled out of the block during normal tightening, the thing was a disaster. At the same time, Harriman was sending poor old Geoffrey Rose down to Rolls-Royce to chivvy them to increase the production of the darned thing so they were having to employ new and inexperienced labour.

"When we were building as many as we possibly could at Kingsbury, about 120 a week, Harriman said, 'All right, we'll make some down at Morris.' As a result an awful lot of cars got stuck in showrooms and those that were sold required a great deal of rectification work. The thing was a flop. They were storing finished cars at Oakley Aerodrome not far from Aylesbury. It was a dreadful sight to see hundreds of cars that we had so lovingly produced just stood out in the open. Even with about 1,400 of them stood outside, George Harriman was still demanding more and more to be produced.

"During a celebration after Harriman got his knighthood, Lord asked me, 'Have you taken over Duples yet?' They were the coach people at Hendon. I said, 'Good heavens no, we don't need to do that. What we need to do is to take over another airfield.' He said, 'What do you mean?' I said, 'Well

A success it was not to be. After being constantly badgered by dissatisfied owners, Leonard Lord decided to remove the BMC 1 numberplate from his own 4-litre R. Here we see Dennis Bush, waiting to pick up Lord in BMC 1 outside the Longbridge reception building in May 1964.

most of our cars are simply going into storage on an airfield.' It had obviously been kept from him because he had a go at Harriman and everything came to a halt. Bang. We cut production right down until the faults were sorted out and the cars already produced had been absorbed. But the damage done to sales was incalculable. Eventually it was a very nice car, but because of all the troubles it made an enormous loss."

With the chaotic situation of so many unsold cars in storage for so long it seems that more than one repeat purchaser was incensed to find that their new car bore an earlier chassis number than the one they had just traded in.

Leonard Lord's attempts to "fly the flag" by using a 4-litre R as his own chauffeur-driven transport came to grief after adopting the appropriate registration number of BMC 1. "Father had the number changed," said his daughter Pauline, "because wherever he took the car he was harassed all the time by people wanting to complain about their own car."

Although the introduction of the Farina-styled cars in 1959 meant that BMC had at last considerably simplified and rationalised its range of vehicles, any benefits from doing so did not last long. At about the same time as Lord had bowed to the pressure to bring in Farina in 1955 he had also given in to those who were suggesting that BMC cars had fallen behind technically. The result, as we shall see in the following chapters, was a completely new range of front-wheel-drive cars that would be introduced from 1959 onwards and marketed alongside and in competition with their rear-wheel-drive stablemates. So much for the benefits of rationalisation.

18

The Mini –
wizardry on wheels

"Leave it. It is unique."

SERGIO PININFARINA

In the early 1950s, during the aftermath of war, the British motoring press was loath to criticise British cars. Patriotism, understandably, was the order of the day. Bill Boddy of *Motor Sport* was probably the first to break ranks. His championing of the

The project known as Maximin was developed at ERA between 1956 and 1959. Do not be fooled by the rather fussy Burzi-styled body, the basic rear-engined, rear-wheel drive platform offered some very advanced engineering, giving unrivalled room and ride comfort for the car's overall size. Although 1ft shorter and about 5in lower than an Austin A55, it had 1½in more ground clearance and would seat six people. By the time the car ended up at Longbridge the Issigonis Mini had already shown that the future lay in front-wheel-drive cars.

VW Beetle seemed an almost treasonable offence in those days but we can hardly fault his perception. Others eventually joined him in complaining bitterly about the lack of inventiveness in British car design.

According to Geoff Cooper, then liaison officer at Longbridge, "Most of the Press were soon blowing off about 'another load of boxes on wheels' and how it was about time we came up with something different."

In 1955, Leonard Lord found himself driven into a corner at Earl's Court by Laurence Pomeroy, technical editor of *The Motor*. When Pomeroy suggested to Lord that it was high time he progressed from cart springs and built something a little more inter-

esting, Lord replied, "You bloody well tell us what to build and we'll build it."

'Pom' took Lord at his word and was soon enunciating his ideas for a relatively compact and light-weight rear-engined car in which a cunningly designed and located engine and transmission would allow seating and luggage accommodation for six people. Hence the name 'Maximin' for a project that Lord and Harriman delegated to David Hodkin and his team at ERA of Dunstable in 1956.

The criticism of BMC cars had obviously bitten deep. At the same time as sanctioning Pomeroy's project Lord also introduced another adventurous dimension to Longbridge design by persuading Alec Issigonis to return to the BMC fold.

"Len Lord was determined to get hold of Issigonis," said Alex Moulton, "but Issigonis only agreed provided he could have a free rein to develop new ideas and could also have access to the work we had already been doing on rubber suspensions. So in 1956 we formed Moulton Developments which provided Austin-sponsored research for the development of rubber suspensions for the exclusive use of BMC."

John Sheppard had worked with Issigonis at Alvis since the spring of 1952. "Alvis told us they hadn't the money to produce the car we had been working on so Issi asked me to join him at Longbridge. The two of us shared a little drawing office in the Kremlin and we began concocting XC 9001 which would have been a mid-range car and thus somewhat in competition with the Maximin project."

Chris Kingham was another who followed Issigonis from Alvis to Longbridge. "When I got to Longbridge XC 9001 was already a runner. Its 1,500cc aluminium engine was really one bank of my Alvis V8 engine. I didn't know that Issigonis had taken the drawings and reproduced it at Longbridge, albeit as a straight-four single-overhead-cam engine, but using the same cylinder head and valve gear."

Although Issigonis was about to turn the motoring world upside down with his front-wheel-drive Mini, Gil Jones recalled, "XC 9001 was front-engined and rear-wheel-drive but it had a wheel at each corner which gave it excellent handling. At that stage Issigonis was still considering whether front-wheel drive was the right approach. Anyway, when the Suez crisis blew up Lord decided he ought to build something to beat the German bubble cars that were springing up everywhere. Both XC 9001 and the thing Hodkin was working on at ERA were put on the back burner."

"The petrol shortage brought on by Suez produced a hell of a scare," said Sid Goble. "At the next motor show, Sidney Smith, who was then technical director of BMC, tapped me on the shoulder and said, 'Go and have a look at the Goggomobil, that's the car of the future.' We soon had all sorts of weird and wonderful ideas floating around and Charles Griffin and Reg Korner were asked by Lord to set up a small car project at Cowley."

Charles Griffin, who was then chief experimental engineer at Cowley, explained that Sidney Smith had briefed him to produce a motor car that could be marketed for £300 or less. "We produced a little car down at Cowley very quickly. A transverse rear-engined thing with the engine ahead of the axle so

When Issigonis returned to BMC from Alvis, "the two of us began concocting XC 9001," said John Sheppard. "Issi always thought it was very elegant – very Citroenish."

the weight distribution wasn't too bad. It was made of bent pieces of rod and all sorts of simple things and we got it to a price of about £295. We showed it to Lord when he made one of his visits to Cowley and it was then that he told Issi, 'You'd better drop that bloody thing you are doing (XC9001) and see what you can do to stop this thing they are building at Cowley.' Issi then built his Mini and they had a showing of the two cars and very sensibly the Mini was chosen."

During most of the Mini's design period, Austin's chief designer was officially Jim Stanfield, who had held the post since the departure of Johnnie Rix. Stanfield had been Austin's chief body engineer on the chassisless A30, as Eric Bailey explained. "Until then the body didn't affect car design too much so it had become traditional at Longbridge that the chief designer of cars was a chassis man. Jim Stanfield was the first body man to become chief designer but we hardly had time to congratulate him when Issigonis arrived with a bang. Although Sidney Smith was nominally in overall charge of BMC engineering and even Stanfield was theoretically above Issigonis in the pecking order, after the arrival of Issigonis, Stanfield was never allowed to exercise his authority. A little later on he was conveniently moved out as a director of Fisher & Ludlow."

Charles Griffin, who had become the chief engineer at Cowley, explained what happened. "Issigonis then became chief engineer at Longbridge with both of us supposedly under S. V. Smith. Sidney was not an engineer so Issigonis was really running the show. Eventually Issigonis was given the title of technical director of BMC with Sidney Smith looking after the administrative side as director of engineering."

Alf Dolphin recalled the first tentative ideas for the Mini being discussed in Burzi's studio. "Vic Everton came in with this guy who had a rather large nose. They placed a sheet of plywood on the floor with a set of Morris Minor seats bolted to it. They were sticking bits of wood over the seats and making sure they could get in and out. I asked John Sheppard who the other chap was and he told me it was Issigonis. Issi kept saying, 'Don't take any notice of us. We are not interested in taking your job. We are only interested in this project.' That Heath Robinson affair was the beginning of ADO 15, the Mini."

Although both Bill Boddy and Pomeroy were still championing rear-engined, rear-wheel-drive cars, Issigonis preferred to think everything out from first principles and was soon, as Geoff Cooper put it, "throwing out ideas like a dog throws off fleas."

Gil Jones recalled a discussion he had with

Engine designer Wesley Hunt recalled this twin-cylinder version of the A-Series engine being tried in a Mini prototype. "Ben Benbow did the layout at Longbridge but it was made at Engines Branch, Coventry by Bill Andrews. Standard A-Series parts were used wherever possible. It ran quite well but, to be honest, I suppose it was a little rough for a production vehicle."

Issigonis on the merits of front-wheel drive. "He had certainly decided that the rear-engined car with its oversteering tendencies was basically unsound. He argued that an engine placed well forward provided good dynamic stability and promoted understeer which gave safety in cornering. As for aerodynamic stability, we knew that a front-engined, front-wheel-drive car was intrinsically far more stable in cross winds than a rear-engined car."

Although brilliant, Issigonis was undoubtedly fortunate. In Jack Daniels, Chris Kingham and John Sheppard, he had co-workers on the Mini project with the ability to translate his ideas into reality. As Jack Daniels modestly put it, "Issi's was the inspiration and mine was the perspiration."

According to John Sheppard, "Issigonis knew what he wanted and made sure he got it. He'd come round holding an ounce weight and say, 'Have you saved that for me today?' Weight was very critical. The Mini had to be ten feet long – no more, no less. He was very pedantic like that and very domineering. 'This is how I want it. Go away and do it.' When it went into production it was a quarter of an inch over ten feet long. That really annoyed him."

"When building the doors for the first Mini," said Doug Adams, who had taken over from Dick Gallimore in body experimental, "I asked Issi how he was going to get the water away. He hadn't really thought about it but said, 'Ah! We'll have a piece of tube there and there and a rubber tube to come out of the bottom.' That was how it was designed. Then you had to send for the draughtsman to draw it. Issi sent for me one day and said, 'I want that much taking off the grille.' He was holding his thumb and finger a little apart. I said, 'About three eighths?' He said, 'I said that much.' I couldn't get a figure out of him. He wouldn't commit himself. We thought he was crazy many times but it was quite exciting. In any case, you couldn't go any higher. He was the boss."

Early in 1956, Alf Depper said to Ian Smith, "All right our kid, follow me." They jumped in Alf's A35 and drove up to 'A-cell' where the Mini project was

This XC 9003/ADO 15 Mini prototype with an A35 grille had its engine with the carburettor facing forwards. Terrible icing-up problems meant the engine had to be turned through 180 degrees and an idler gear introduced to maintain the correct direction of rotation.

underway. "I got up there and saw these strange looking cars," remembers Ian. "They'd made two by then with A35 grilles and transverse engines but with the manifolds at the front and distributor at the back. They had no boot lid at all. Everything was stowed behind the back seat. Issi was the gaffer and had his office in the Kremlin but he used to come down each day like God walking in. In the workshop were Ron Hale, John Wagstaff, and Alan Garrard, just the four of us. In those days Issi never spoke to the workforce, only to those he really had to. All the rest of us were just numbers, minions. He would be right next to me and say to Jack Daniels, 'Mmm Jack, tell him I want this done Mmm,' and Jack would turn round and say, 'Ron, we want this done.' Ron would then turn round and say, 'Ian …' It had to go through a bloody chain."

Chris Kingham recalled his own work on the Mini. "My task was the transmission. Having been told from the word go that we had to use the A-Series engine, everything was wedded to that. We started off with the engine the other way round but had terrible problems with carburettor icing-up in particular because we had no radiator between the

engine and the fresh air. It meant we had to turn the engine through 180 degrees fairly early on.

"The big unknown factor was running a gearbox on engine oil. Prior to that transmissions were still using thick gooey stuff. We didn't know if the tooth pressures would destroy the oil film and lead to excessive rates of wear. It came as a very pleasant surprise when the results showed a positive gain from using light oil.

"At first we used a two-gear primary drive but on turning the engine round we had to introduce an idler gear to retain the correct direction of rotation. Incidentally, that was one of the reasons why the car became a practical proposition. With the original two-gear train the gears were twice the diameter of those in the three-gear train and on the early proto-types we never cured the problem of gear whine. I'm pretty sure that even if we hadn't had the trouble with icing-up we would have turned the engine round to introduce the idler gear. Using those smaller gears was a critical factor in reducing the noise to reasonable levels.

"A great deal of work was done in relation to the small wheels and the durability of the tyres. All this was utterly new. There were problems accommodating adequate brakes within such a small wheel. How to exclude water from a tiny drum in a tiny wheel so close to the ground wasn't easy either. The 10in diameter wheels were necessary to be in proportion to the rest of the car but also minimised the unsprung weight and the amount of intrusion into the car of the front wheel arches. They also improved the steering lock.

"Issigonis had little faith in professional road testers. He thought they drove too well so he had a pool of drivers that he allowed to sample the proto-type vehicles. They had been chosen specifically because Issi considered them bad drivers. Bill Appleby (in charge of engine design) and Harry Gardner (in charge of transmissions) were two of these and were allowed to drive the Mini as early as anybody. They didn't, of course, know why. Issigonis was proved dead right because the first time Appleby and Gardner went on the road in a Mini they turned it over on the far side of Lickey Hills. We never knew how they managed it."

Wesley Hunt took up the story. "Harry Gardner was actually driving. It had the 948cc engine and was a bare car so it easily flipped. Gardner cut his head and I think Issigonis panicked because they decided to use a short-throw crankshaft to reduce the capacity to 850cc. He thought it was going to kill people but when you think of the later 1,275cc Cooper it makes that look a bit silly."

Quite a contrast in wheel sizes. A prototype Mini, with its 10in wheels, and devoid of any telltale badges, on test in Spain in 1959.

Dennis Harold saw some of the problems of engineering the car for production. "For the floor-mounted starter switch Issigonis tried to insist that I had a bare aluminium rod along the bottom of the car from the battery to the switch. I said, 'But it is live from the battery. If a mechanic gets a spanner across it there will be a firework display.' We had one or two little upsets with him like that. For right and left hand steering we always drilled alternative holes in each body for the wiper motor and so on to be mounted as required. Issigonis had to approve every hole in the body so I went down and showed him where we were going to put the wiper, the steering and so on. He said, 'OK, fine.' The next morning he poked me in the chest with his bony finger and said, 'You have been drilling holes in my motor car. What's this?' It was where the wiper motor would go for left hand steering. 'You didn't mention that.' Oh dear, he wasn't happy about those extra holes.

"With any new design we always consulted the assembly superintendents so that they could give it the once over. They often made useful suggestions but when Issi found them looking at the Mini he told them to clear off. He said he didn't want production people looking at it because they would try to convince him to change the design and he wasn't going to change it. Of course that annoyed the production men and as soon as any of his designs reached the track the balloon went up."

The balloon certainly went up over the water leaks recalls Barry Kelkin. "The first three Minis that came off the tracks were letting in water. When we drove Issi round through the puddles where they were preparing the site to build CAB 2 the

XC 9003 or ADO 15, as shown to George Harriman. "Spend another few quid on it and jazz it up a bit," he said. After the addition of wheel discs and a chrome strip along the wheel arches and sills he accepted it was ready for production.

water was actually seeping up his tweed trousers. He got very irate and shouted, 'Stop. Stop. There isn't a problem.' Even though the water was actually wicking up his trousers he just didn't want to believe it. We had to liaise with Jim Percival from Fisher & Ludlow to alter the tooling almost overnight."

After declaring that no-one had yet told the

Wizardry on wheels. The Mini was launched upon the world from Tony Ball's top hat. Said Tony, "The Austin version was launched as the incredible Austin Seven with the V of the Seven put on its side as a figure 7. The Morris version was more of a problem. We already had the Minor – so we had to devise a name smaller than a Minor. The alliteration made Morris Mini Minor an obvious choice. We thought that the Austin Seven would catch on but people abbreviated everything to the 'Mini' and it was so successful that we dropped the Austin Seven bit and referred to them both as Minis."

proper story about the water leaks, John Sheppard demonstrated to the author, the building of a Mini floor-pan. "Issi wanted to make the car so simple that anyone could build it. The idea was that if we sold it as bits, you took a floor, then you put a heel-board up, then you put a toe-board up. Notice what I've done. I've put that on top of that. But as you go along the front flange catches the water. Between each spot weld you have an ingress. Every prototype had been subjected to quite extensive water tests without shipping water because Ron Dovey's shop were so good that they had welded and sealed them properly. But when they went into production, it would be, 'How did Villa get on yesterday?' Some of the spot welds would be six inches apart."

The reaction of Longbridge men to their first sight of the Mini varied considerably. According to Ron Hale, "When Harriman saw the first pre-production Mini stood in our shop, all polished and ready to go, he said, 'What a bloody mess. We'll never sell that. Spend another few quid on it Alec, and jazz it up a bit. Put some chrome plate on it or something.' That's when they put the wheel discs on and the chrome strip around the wings."

Later, when Lord, Harriman and Issigonis showed Farina the finished product he was asked if he could suggest ways in which it could be improved. "Leave it," he said. "It is unique."

Issigonis had no time for stylists, claiming that they were employed to build in obsolescence, but after that diplomatic reply by Farina the pair of them became firm friends.

Tony Ball was only a 23-year-old personal assistant to the sales director, Jim Penrose, when Leonard Lord and George Harriman called him into Dick Burzi's studio. "Just to be in their presence was a bit nerve-wracking. Alec Issigonis was there too so, believe me, it was like being with the Father, Son and Holy Ghost. Lord said, 'Come here young man, we want to show you something.' They pulled back a curtain and there was the Mini. They asked what I thought of it. I was staggered. I said, 'It's magic.' This was about six months before the car was launched and they wanted to know how I would go about it if they gave me the job of launching it. I said, 'Well, I'd love to develop a 'magical' concept, perhaps build a huge top hat and launch the car from that, and perhaps use a 'wizardry on wheels' theme to emphasise the car's ingenuity.' It all clicked immediately. One of those flashes of inspiration that you sometimes get. Of course, when you are in the presence of the mighty you can't suck your thumb and say I'll come back to you in three weeks time. You have to be positive.

Fortunately they decided to run with my idea. At the actual launch in the Longbridge showroom we played the tune, 'That Old Black Magic.' I was stood in front of the closed top hat in magician's garb and after a few wisecracks on the theme of 'wizardry on wheels' I waved my wand and the hat was pulled open by two pretty young ladies from the Aston Hippodrome.

"From the Mini emerged my wife Ruth and a friend, and three of the biggest men I could find. My son Kevin, was also in there as a babe in arms. We had a couple of dogs and great stacks of luggage, including two sets of golf clubs and the baby's potty. They got out one at a time from this tiny car. All the luggage had been packed around them and inside the door pockets and under the seats and it was all taken out progressively to show that the car, tiny as it was, could contain all this stuff. It was very effective."

Certainly, the Mini's 1959 launch did manage to silence most of the critics, even Bill Boddy congratulating BMC for 'pulling their finger out.' But much of the Mini's magic was initially dispelled by post-launch troubles, some of which could have undoubtedly been avoided had Issigonis been prepared to listen to those testing the cars.

Ben Benbow recalled the handbrake of an early Mini seizing in snowy conditions when Issi was driving it. "When we stopped him to tell him that

his back wheels weren't turning he said, 'Oh we don't worry about little things like that,' and carried on sledging."

Bernard Johnson recalled a trip with a pre-launch Mini which showed up serious water leaks that went uncorrected before production began. "We flew several cars, including a Mini, to Calais and went down through France to Biarritz, then on through Spain to Gibraltar. It was raining cats and dogs. In Reims we kept the A40 Farina and Mini back and Georgie Coates and I took the Mini brakes to bits. The front brakes were full of mud so we cleaned them out as well as we could."

Barry Wood travelled in that Mini with Alan Moore. "The water was four inches deep by Reims and every time we braked it sloshed backwards and forwards. I had my feet up on the dash and Alan had his trousers rolled up and his feet on bricks."

According to George Coates, "Bernard Johnson punched a nail through the Mini's floor in Lyon and the water flooded the garage and the French garage owner cussed us something awful. After returning home Jim Stanfield asked our shop to try and find the leaks so I put a Mini up on a ramp and put a hose in it. When I went to get Charlie Griffin I

Ben James brings an early Mini through the dust tunnel at the MIRA test track but it was water problems that would trouble early Mini owners the most.

suggested he bring his umbrella. He wasn't very pleased but filling the car up with water seemed the best way of finding the leaks to me. It wasn't just the floor that was leaking. Barry Wood and I went out one night to try and find the source of other leaks. We'd got to find them because people were getting annoyed. Apparently someone wrote in complaining and said they were glad we didn't build boats. We went up the motorway to find out why the rear seat cushion was getting soaked. I was in the back with a torch. All of a sudden I tumbled to it. I said to Barry, 'Have you got your window open? Then shut it. Now open it.' When he opened it the bloomin' spray was coming past the door seal with the suction. It was such a fine spray that it needed darkness and the light shining on it to make it stand out. The spray was actually hitting the rear cushion. We weighed a dry cushion and a wet cushion. It was as much as you could do to drag the wet cushion out of the car. There was about 40lb of water in the cushion; that's four gallons."

Eric Bailey told of how the inability of Issigonis to listen to criticism led not only to customer dissatisfaction but also to tragedy. "Issigonis would only take orders from Harriman so Jim Stanfield never had proper control when trying to 'engineer' the Mini for production. One body-experimental chap had a very rough time over the leaks. They had to find a scapegoat and seemed to pick on him. He had made a full report of the water leaks and sent it to Issigonis but he'd put it in the waste bin. When the production cars were having all the water leaks the chap said to Issigonis, 'Well there is the report that I gave you.' He was told, 'Well, you

didn't emphasise it enough.' That really hurt him."

Sid Bowden agreed. "Yes, that poor guy got the rap for most of it. As a matter of fact it finished him off. He had a stroke. I can vouch for the fact that a report went in every week on the failures of sealing and they were ignored. 'Just get on with it', was Issi's attitude. If only he had listened to other people. There is no question that he was a very brilliant man but in the early years of the Mini I don't think there was a penny profit out of it because there were so many modifications and rectifications to be done."

Arthur West had nothing to do with the design of the Mini but was landed with its water problems. "I spent six months in 1959/60 at Safenwil in Switzerland, sealing 700 Minis at Emil Frey's place. It broke your heart to see a body with all those faults get into the public's hands. People were driving about in Switzerland in gum boots. One man had drilled holes in the floor but of course as soon as he opened his windows the low pressure inside pulled the water in. You see the Mini was low and about as fast as anything on the road. They wouldn't stop production to get it right. Once the tracks started it was always, 'Out, out, out! We don't stop the tracks for anything.' They would turn the cars out at any cost and the cost in this case was that they made a large loss."

"It was a great shame," said Doctor Duncan Stuart of East Works research department, "that Sidney Smith left. In the short period when S. V. Smith was there Issi was kept under control but he had gone by that critical period in which the Mini was being readied for production. I think Smith would have insisted on other views being heard. He would have listened to the production engineers and testers and said to himself, 'Here's an intelligent bloke saying something which isn't the same as Alec is saying so perhaps we had better look into this.' When Smith left, and Issigonis got his job, it was a disaster because although he was a wonderful egg-head he was not an administrator. After that there were very few people who would speak out of turn because they knew that if they had done so they would have been down the road."

There was a funny side to the water leaks. John Cleaver spoke of going round the Middle East with sealing kits. "Imagine telling the Arabs that we'd come to stop water getting into their Minis. 'What water?' they would ask. 'It hasn't rained here for 15 years.' But we had to do them all. I think it amounted to about 8,000 cars throughout the world."

The Mini, of course, was years ahead of its time. Ron Nicholls, then a development engineer at Longbridge, saw it as, "a whole order different from

George Harriman and Alec Issigonis with the new Mini at Longbridge in 1959. With the kudos attached to his new creation and the imminent retirement of Leonard Lord, Issigonis was about to rule the roost.

That the Mini was indeed 'Wizardry on wheels' was clearly shown when Mini Coopers took the Monte Carlo Rally by storm from 1964 until 1967. This cartoon, drawn in 1966 by an unknown Longbridge wag, shows just what depths he thought the French would stoop to when, after the 1966 Monte, the three winning Minis were disqualified by the French officials and a Citroën was declared the winner.

other cars. Its handling dumbfounded people."

"The Mini's integrated engine and gearbox was a bold step", remarked Alex Moulton, "the innovative engineering it pioneered was by and large very sound. You might say that the intermediate bearing of the idler gear was too small and you might say it should have been caught earlier on etc, but basically the concept of the whole vehicle was sound. It couldn't have come from the existing team at Longbridge. Not in a hundred years. I think you can say that. Lord was conscious of that and knew that Issigonis was the only man capable of doing such things."

On announcing the Mini, BMC claimed that, "posterity will regard August 26th 1959 as a landmark in the development of the popular motor car." For once they had not over-stated their case. Virtually every manufacturer would eventually follow the lead given by Issigonis. In late 1999, 40 years after its introduction, the Mini, still in production at Longbridge, was declared the 'European Car of the Century'. After a production run of some 5.5 million, it was expected that its successor would start to roll off the Longbridge production lines at just about the same time as this book is published in Summer 2000. The sale of Rover by BMW has now altered all that. (See Chapter 27.)

As for Issigonis; once he had weathered the storm created by the Mini's early problems, the kudos attached to his revolutionary new creation gave him a stranglehold at Longbridge. With the imminent retirement of Leonard Lord he was, in effect, about to rule the roost.

19

Further innovations – the Issigonis 1100

"I suppose the 1100 was quite something, particularly the performance and reliability of the innovative Hydrolastic suspension."

ALEX MOULTON

Before starting work on the Mini, John Sheppard had worked for a while with Issigonis on project XC 9002. "We started by scaling down XC 9001. I drew out the under-structure, which they built in Dick Gallimore's shop, and it went down to Cowley with all my drawings where it developed into the ADO 16 or 1100 project under Charlie Griffin."

Cyril Hodgkins, who had worked with Alec Issigonis on suspension design at Cowley, both pre-war and right through the Minor project, was the development engineer for the 1100's suspension. "Charles Griffin was a very practical man with enor-

XC 9002 alongside XC 9001. "We started by scaling down XC 9001," said John Sheppard. "I was asked to bring my Morris Minor up and put it alongside because he (Issigonis) wanted five seats in a car no longer than the Minor."

mous energy. He would come directly from Issi's office and get me to develop the things that Moulton and Issi had dreamed up between them. We used a Morris Minor as a test bed for the early ideas on the Hydrolastic suspension. Issigonis and Moulton took it down to Turin and Joe Green and I then took it on a three-week trip to the toe of Italy and back home. We had a heavy rubber tube, or 'python' as we called it, running down the centre of the car which acted as a spring unit and contained the Hydrolastic fluid which consisted of a mixture of alcohol, anti-freeze and inhibitors."

During the trip the 'python' punctured several times before finally bursting open in southern Italy leaving the car running on its bump stops. "We sent an SOS to Cowley," said Cyril, "but had to wait a week before they got a spare to us. In the meantime

Down on the bump stops. Cyril Hodgkins near Lagonegro in Southern Italy where his Minor, fitted with an early version of the 1100's Hydrolastic suspension, burst its rubber python.

we repaired it with a steel tube and hose clips. Having lost the fluid we had to fill it with water. Water does the job fine in summer but would freeze in winter. The 'python' idea was scrapped soon after that and we then had separate units for each wheel. We worked on that suspension for three or four years from 1958 onwards."

In the course of the development of the 1100 it was found that when the front wheels hit anything hard this produced a very disconcerting knock. As the front suspension went up it was creating enormous pressure in the Hydrolastic fluid which was instantly transferred to the rear wheels to keep the car level. This was, of course, the whole idea of interconnected Hydrolastic suspension, but the early configurations needed considerable refinement. As Cyril graphically put it, "In effect you were trying to jack the car up bodily in one bloody fell swoop. We were never quite able to solve the harshness of it although I know we were on the verge of doing so when I retired in 1966. Nevertheless, the Dunlop-made Hydrolastic units were very reliable."

Cyril considered himself very fortunate to have worked under Issigonis but recalled that it was not all plain sailing. "Issigonis had tremendous enthusiasm and was a marvellous man for conceiving ideas. What caused me problems was that he never laid on the means of translating his ideas into reality. He'd found me such a willing workhorse that he seemed

to assume I could do anything. Well I couldn't. I was very versatile I know, but that inspired him to expect me to do more and more with less and less. He was very reluctant to spend any money on tools so we were making things by knife and fork methods. I wasn't the only example of that. Jack Daniels was another who was ever so good at translating Issi's ideas into practical propositions. Issi had the ideas but it was others who did a lot of the donkey work."

Alan Webb began work on ADO 16 in the combined Morris and Wolseley drawing office in 1958. "We had just completed work on ADO 10 (the Austin Westminster) when Bob Shirley and myself started work on the ADO 16 chassis and Reg Job and Alan Parker made a start on the body. Although Bert Raynor, our chief draughtsman, was in charge of the office we were working directly for Griffin and Issigonis. Issigonis used to come down from Longbridge most Wednesday nights, stay with his mother in Oxford and come into the design office on Thursday mornings. Issi would always arrive at nine so Bert Raynor would come round about half an hour before Issigonis to get genned up on what we had been doing. 'Hello boys,' he'd say, 'What are you going to show us this week?' When Issigonis arrived Bert would trot round after him, repeating word for word what we had just told him.

"I would have been working on the layout very accurately for a week, perhaps doing overtime to have everything ready, but many a time Issi would get out a big fat pencil and scribble all over my layout ruining everything I'd done. He'd obviously been in discussion with Alex Moulton. After he had changed everything he would look me in the eyes and say, 'I'll be down next Thursday and it'll all be ready. Won't it?' Of course it meant starting all over again. He was after the maximum interior space so one of the things he altered was the wheelbase. There was too much wheel arch intrusion to the rear seat so he moved the rear wheel back about 2½in. This meant the whole back end of the car had to be redrawn."

Charles Griffin remembered that occasion. "Yes, it was certainly an Issigonis decision to lengthen the wheelbase but he was absolutely right, bless him. The nearer we could get to 60 per cent of the gross weight on the front wheels of a front wheel drive car the more we liked it because they negotiated snow and hills better. The lengthening of the wheelbase also improved the looks of the 1100. Front wheel drive cars with too much motor car behind the rear wheels just don't look right."

Alan Webb was impressed by the work Jack Daniels did on the 1100's suspension. "From what I saw, Jack was the first bloke to fully understand the theoretical working of the Hydrolastic system. He was the first to put it all down on paper. There was a great deal of maths involved. If you changed an arm length or changed the hardness of the rubber in the Hydrolastic unit he could calculate the effects on the vehicle. Issigonis certainly didn't go to those depths. He simply hadn't that sort of ability.

"I don't think Issigonis was very interested in body detail either. He was more of a chassis than a body man. A box on wheels would have done him. Originally, the dash panel, from floor to screen, was going to be in two pieces with a horizontal flange

This mock-up by Morris Motors, seen here being compared with a Minor, "was very plain and uninteresting," said Reg Job, "so they asked Farina to style it."

running all the way round. Because of the fiasco over the Mini's water leaks it was decided to make the panel in one piece.

"The prototype 1100 bodies from Pressed Steel were painted, trimmed and motorised at Cowley in Charlie Griffin's experimental shop. No matter who sat in the prototypes, they usually wanted the steering wheel moved or the pedals altered. It became quite a joke. We almost ran a book for the next position of the steering wheel. Getting the right size of pedal pad to make sure you only hit one pedal was a problem too because it was a fairly confined space. Issigonis had quite big feet so we decided that if Issigonis could use the pedals then anybody could."

Reg Job was project engineer for the 1100's body design. "A prototype two-door saloon was built by Morris Motors' experimental department," said Reg, "but it was very plain and uninteresting so they asked Farina to style it. Farina sent us a full-size mock-up in steel. Even the tyres were made in steel because they couldn't get wheels or tyres of the correct size. It was very badly styled for a production car. It had undercuts on the roof at both front and back – very difficult and expensive to make. Tooling wasn't as sophisticated in those days so, with an undercut at each end of a one-piece panel, it just wouldn't have come off the press. The wind resistance at the front would have been terrific too because it had a very flat grille area with a peak over the headlamps and bonnet. Neither Issigonis nor I liked it very much so we altered Farina's styling quite a bit.

"Some of the body detailing I did for the Morris Minor body was unsatisfactory. Water came in all round the roof and screen. The sills were not too clever either. When I started on the 1100 I was determined that I would make it watertight. Charlie Thompson from Nuffield Metal Products rang me up to say he'd noticed my drawings were nothing

Farina's first mock-up in steel was even shod with steel tyres. Note the peak over the headlamps and grille and the roof protrusion over the windscreen which needed considerable modification before being deemed ready to be engineered for production.

like the Minor. I said, 'I know, and they are not going to be either.' He wanted to make them like the Minor but I refused to allow him to alter them. Three weeks later Issigonis summoned a meeting. There was Charlie Griffin, who knew nothing about body work, Issigonis who knew even less, Leslie Hall, my boss and Ramsey his assistant, Westby the chief of the chassis department and his assistant – about six or seven of them. Their salaries added up to about £80,000 a year when I was on a thousand. Issigonis called me in and I showed him how I wanted to do it to avoid the leaks we had on the Minor. There was a long argument but they wouldn't have it at all. Issigonis looked at me and said, 'All right Reg, make it like the Minor.' I was bitterly disappointed but I had to go back and get my chaps to redraw all the panels. I couldn't believe it. When Pressed Steel took the job over Ken Osbourne, their chief designer, phoned and said, 'What the hell have you been doing with the bloody sections on this 1100 Reg? The water will pee in all over the place.' I told him the story and he said, 'Don't worry, we will do our own sections.' So they turned them out just like I had proposed in the first place."

"I remember Issigonis asking me if we had hinged the boot lid so that it dropped down like the Mini. Well of course we had because he had asked us to do it, but he then asked us to make it open upwards. That might sound a simple request, but for it to open high enough to clear your head it had to be raised and go through 140 degrees. Ordinary hinges would have been useless, so I had to devise a swan-neck hinge out of $\frac{7}{8}$in diameter tubing that I flattened at each end. When Leslie Hall saw it he thought Len Lord would do his nut, but apparently Lord thought it was perfectly all right and so that's how it went into production."

Farina's second offering was still a bit slab-sided but much nearer to the production car.

Reg Job, seen here with his own Morris Minor, was the project engineer for the body of both the Minor and 1100. His own sketches show how he tried to eliminate water ingress into the 1100 body by avoiding the 'mistakes' he had made on the Minor.

ROOF SIDE SECTION

MORRIS MINOR

NOTE - WATER CAN ENTER AT

ARROW A

ROOF SIDE SECTION

1100 - 1300

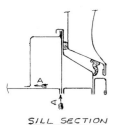

SILL SECTION

MORRIS MINOR

NOTE - UNDER-CAR SPRAY CAN

ENTER AT ARROWS A

SILL SECTION

1100 - 1300

NOTE - INSIDE SILLS AND FLOOR

IS A ONE-PIECE PANEL

Ron Nicholls first saw the 1100 when Charles Griffin brought it up from Cowley to be engineered for production. "It came up to Longbridge as a car supposedly ready for production and then suddenly all hell was let loose. Getting the production processes right was quite a headache. The Hydrolastic suspension was a major problem in the early days. It was very sensitive to very small weight changes and only when the cars were actually coming off production tools did we have a reasonable indication of the true weight. It was quite a job to get the Hydrolastic units sized properly."

Alan Webb and several others who had worked on the 1100 at Cowley were moved up to Longbridge in May 1962. They continued working on the 1100 project in what became known as C-Cell. "There were four of us with a small design office and a little workshop run by Bob Lambert. We never had a head of cell, such as Chris Kingham in B-Cell on the 1800, or Jack Daniels in A-Cell on the Mini, but worked directly for Charlie Griffin who by then was a sort of assistant chief engineer to Issigonis."

It was when the project moved to Longbridge that Barry Kelkin became involved. "The first 1100 was the Morris version with the black crackle finish to the fascia but when we started to produce the Austin version Issi said he wanted a much simpler fascia. He said, 'I don't want it styled. Just imagine you are putting a plank across the car. I want it silver and very narrow. You can put a bit of crash padding on it and a ribbon speedometer.' We made the prototype fascia in 'experimental' and after adding the knobs and switches I put a chrome beading round it. When Issi and Burzi came to have a look at it Issi said, 'It's not narrow enough. What's that bit of bright stuff doing round it?' I explained that apart from embellishing the fascia it hid the joins. After a lot of moaning and groaning he accepted that we really couldn't make it much narrower but he wasn't very pleased with it. It was only when Dick Burzi offered to restyle it that Issigonis decided that my suggestions weren't too bad after all. He obviously didn't want Burzi to run riot with it."

The design work on the engine and transmission, basically an 1,100cc version of that in the Mini, took place at Longbridge under Bill Appleby and Eric Bareham. Charlie Griffin spoke of how ADO 16 had originally been scheduled to go into production with the 948cc A-Series engine. "I dug my heels in on that. Some of the first testing was done with a 950 but it was useless so I had a go at Harriman about it. It was also supposed to go into production with a big cone spring instead of Hydrolastic suspension, the same suspension as the Mini but an

This rear view of a Morris 1100 shows the novel way in which Reg Job produced the swan-necked hinges that allowed the boot to be hinged at the top.

inch bigger in diameter, but that was very harsh. I had a go at Harriman on that too. I was also concerned that projected production levels were unrealistically low. I said to Harriman, 'Look, I need your support, we've got a success on our hands if we handle it properly.' In those days it was going to be tooled for 4,000 a week but once we had the go-ahead for Hydrolastic and had got the engine upped to 1,100cc, I said, 'look, the numbers you've quoted only just replace the Morris Minor at its peak. If this

Barry Kelkin designed this fascia for the Austin 1100. Issigonis did not think it was narrow enough but allowed it to go into production rather than let Dick Burzi "run riot with it".

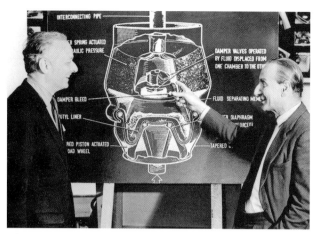

Alex Moulton and Alec Issigonis, with a diagram of the 1100's displacer unit. Moulton considered the 1100's suspension to be one of his greatest achievements.

is going to replace the A40 and Wolseley/Riley 1500s as well, then we need more like 10,000.' We finished up by getting agreement to squeeze it to 6,800 with some scope for more and that's how we went into production. I went down to Pressed Steel to lobby Joe Edwards for the lowest possible body cost so that we could price it right for high volume production."

The 1100's transverse, front-wheel-drive power pack, drive shafts and Hydrolastic units. A new V4 engine had been under development at Longbridge but tooling costs ruled it out.

Eric Bareham spoke of how the 1100 might have been the recipient of a completely new power unit. "A lot of work was done with a Lancia-inspired 1,100cc V4 engine. In fact, that was the reason for so generous a space in front of the eventual engine. The V4 engine and transmission would have provided front-wheel-drive from an in-line arrangement but the idea was abandoned when it was found to be perfectly feasible and much cheaper to enlarge the A-Series engine to 1,098cc."

Charlie Lane, a Longbridge fitter, recalled the driveshaft problems with the early Minis and 1100s. "After several people were killed in Minis and 1100s, attempts were made to sue BMC over the design of the constant velocity joints. It was Charles Griffin who saved the company's bacon on that one. It was he who managed to show that there were always other factors involved; the joints themselves weren't causing the problems. We ran them with balls missing and with broken cages but we found they were fail-safe."

Doreen Schrier, who was the first ever female apprentice at Cowley, was by this time PA to Charles Griffin at Longbridge. She remembered that difficult period. "Everybody was in a state of turmoil. It really could have brought the company down. Sir Alec just wiped his hands of it, but fortunately Charles Griffin had the courage and conviction to treat it logically. It all started when some professor at Cambridge decided the problem was

The Austin version of the 1100 was launched in September 1963, the Morris having been on the market since August 1962. The 1100 offered an amazing package of style, stance, comfort, handling and performance for so small a car.

metallurgical. After that each Mini and 1100 that had an accident hit the headlines as a possible CV joint problem. Charles studied each case and found that they often boiled down to things like deflated tyres or wrong pressures – all sorts of things that were causing people to have accidents. The joints were being broken in the smashes but weren't the cause of them."

Alex Moulton considered the 1100's suspension to be one of his greatest achievements. "I suppose the 1100 was quite something, particularly the performance and reliability of the innovative Hydrolastic suspension. There was a unit that did 200,000 miles on several bodies and engines and all the damping levels were still within the required tolerances, so there was a professional satisfaction in that. Compacting the Hydrolastic down to Mini size wasn't possible in the Mini's development period so the cone spring which I had developed earlier on was really used as an interim measure. We put Hydrolastic on the Mini in 1964/65 but it was taken off again when Stokes

came in and wanted to make economies."

In the case of the 1100, the combined genius of Issigonis, Moulton and Farina had gelled to perfection. Along with those who devised the means of turning their ideas into reality, they had produced a most efficacious blend of style, stance, comfort, handling and performance along with an interior roominess found only in much larger cars. ADO 16 had undoubtedly emerged as a world-beating small family saloon.

Over 2 million 1100/1300 models were produced at a rate which made even Mini sales look sluggish. But after several years at the top of the British sales charts the 1100 was eventually knocked off its perch by Ford's Cortina which not only offered a lot of car for the money but the advantages of a much simpler mechanical layout, a family-sized boot, and the option of a 1.6-litre engine.

The Cortina, of course, was regularly updated. The 1100 was not. Dealers and distributors had been clamouring for a larger-engined version of ADO 16 ever since the car's launch but their wish was only granted with the launch of the 1300 versions in 1967. Before that, those wanting more power in front-wheel-drive form had to make the jump to the much larger and expensive 1800, the subject of the next chapter.

20

Pioneering for posterity – the 1800 and 3-litre

"Perhaps if we had pandered more to accepted taste rather than pioneer for posterity we might have sold a few more."

CHRIS KINGHAM

Chris Kingham was put in charge of the ADO 17 or 1800 project in B-Cell in early 1960. "It was great to be given responsibility for the whole car, not just a component. I will always be profoundly grateful to Sir Alec for that. If you wanted someone stimulating to work with, Alec was the man. I was

Chris Kingham spoke of developing Hydrolastic suspension with Alex Moulton at Alvis. Moulton is seen in his own museum at Bradford-on-Avon Hall with a displacer and python from the Alvis project.

fortunate in having worked with him when it was just the two of us in one small office at Alvis: a drawing board each, a plan chest – oh, and two ashtrays. One gets to know a person fairly intimately when you are thrown that close. So throughout my association with Issigonis I was in the happy position of not having to automatically agree with everything he suggested. I think that was fairly important.

"I spent a lot of time with Alex Moulton on the 1800's Hydrolastic suspension. Alex was another visionary. We did the initial Hydrolastic work at Alvis. After we had devised the dry-cone rubber suspension Issigonis and Moulton went into a huddle and decided they could get some hydraulic damping by taking two of the cones and turning one upside down underneath the other. A big rubber band and a specially made Jubilee clip were used to join the two together. Then we engineered a bleed so that with suspension movement you got a transference of fluid from front to rear. A Jubilee clip was a pretty ridiculous way of joining two main suspension components but it worked perfectly well because all the forces were compressing it."

During the development of the 1800, Sergio Pininfarina came to Longbridge for sessions in the Kremlin styling studio. "Dick Burzi's contribution was to provide the coffee," joked Chris Kingham. "Dick was a nice guy but he embarrassed me at one of these sessions by saying, 'You know everybody says yes to Mr Issigonis except Chris and he always says no.' He said it to Farina and Issigonis when they were styling the cow's hip on the back of the 1800. Fortunately, Issigonis had more sense than to respond."

These slats added to the body of XC 9001, prior to adding modelling clay, show a stage in the process of developing a capacious enough boot for XC 9005/ADO 17, the Issigonis 1800.

Standing next to the car it was meant to replace, this offering from Farina has begun to develop the character of the 1800 although the frontal aspect and door tops have still some way to go. When Sergio Pininfarina came to Longbridge for sessions in the 'Kremlin' styling studio, "Dick Burzi's contribution was to provide the coffee," joked Chris Kingham.

Those railings again. Farina's final version of XC 9005 only required very minor changes.

Ron Unsworth from Cowley joined Chris Kingham as his chassis man on the 1800. "I couldn't have asked for a better person," said Chris, "he was a first-rate engineer with a superbly resilient personality. The Mini and the 1100 both had subframes but I disagreed with subframes. Why beef up the body structure to take the loads transmitted to and from the subframes and then beef up the subframe to take all the suspension loads in its own right. If you throw away the subframe and beef up the body structure you don't have to do the job twice. You also end up with a more rigid structure and far fewer rust traps. In my office in B-Cell I had a sketch Alec had done for 1800 subframes and in fact the first vehicle was built with subframes. But with the heavy 1800 engine the top of the front wheels slowly came inwards and the bottom went out, so we reconceived the whole thing using that massive tube across the bulkhead. It worked very well and was relatively cheap to produce.

"We dabbled for a time with a narrow-angled 2-litre V4 engine produced by Duncan Stuart in the research and development department. It went into a prototype but it was never too seriously considered. The more's the pity because it was a very flexible unit. I'm afraid that at BMC it was a case of, 'how much can we use that we've already got?' As they already had a fairly gutsy four-cylinder engine, management was not about to contemplate tooling up for a replacement.

"The V4 had a toothed rubber cam belt but Alec and I went one further than that. In an attempt to produce a completely silent primary drive on an 1800 prototype we used a toothed belt there too. With broad sprockets and a nice wide belt, it was absolutely wonderful. Unbelievably quiet. Not a whisper from it. There was only one problem. It had a life of only 200 miles!"

Eric Bareham spoke of how the B-Series engine was modified for use in the 1800. "The bore was enlarged from the three inches of the 1,622cc A60 to 3.16 inches but retained the original stroke, giving 1,798cc. We retained the standard cylinder spacing and overall length of the engine but managed to install five main bearings and enlarged big ends. In place of the rather complicated arrangement of clutch and primary drive used on the A-Series front wheel drive units, we used a conventional flange-mounted flywheel with a Borg & Beck diaphragm spring clutch, followed by a shaft carrying a drive pinion. The primary drive was thus moved to the extreme end of the power unit and consisted of a train of three gears as on the A-Series. The primary gears turned out to be noisier than on the A-Series

because they were only separated from the outside air by the end cover."

Reg Korner from Cowley (who had had a brief spell at Austin in the 1930s before going to Jowett where he later engineered the Jowett Javelin and Jupiter bodies for Gerald Palmer) was seconded to Chris Kingham to do the 1800's body. "Reg was an extremely sound body engineer," said Chris, "but he didn't get on well with Issigonis. He just wasn't quick enough for Alec. I'm afraid Alec was very impatient. There were a number of excellent people who Alec thought were no good. His mind worked quicker than anybody else's and he expected a fairly immediate response. At times I had to be a peacemaker between an impatient gaffer and a competent but plodding engineer. Reg Korner was a case in point but it was undoubtedly Reg's expertise and knowledge that resulted in the amazing strength of the 1800's structure."

Ron Nicholls explained the secret behind the 1800's tremendous strength. "It had a torsional stiffness of about 13,000ft/lb per degree of distortion whereas a Ford had 5,000 or less. On a conventional car the loads go into the body at the wheel centre lines. With the 1800 the wheelbase had in effect been reduced by the combined length of the rear trailing arm and the distance from the front wheel to the centre line of the Hydrolastic suspension unit – something like three feet in total. In effect you had taken that amount off the wheelbase and instead of twisting the car through its wheelbase you were twisting the car through its wheelbase minus three feet. Yet you still had the advantage of the long wheelbase so the car handled extremely well"

All the Issigonis-designed front-wheel-drive cars handled so safely and predictably that they could be taken round corners far faster than most others. "So much so," said Gil Jones, "that a chap from Ford reckoned Issi had done a disservice to the industry by making cars that could go so quickly round bends that they were liable to produce dangerous circumstances."

As for Sir Alec's own thoughts on safety, Bernard Johnson recalled, "He always talked about 'primary safety' – designing cars not likely to have an accident in the first place. All his cars had very responsive steering and never behaved in an unpredictable way. Every one of them was stable in side winds. You could have the biggest gust of wind you like and the cars would only deviate a very small amount. With front-wheel-drive and the mass well forward, the driving wheels would stay glued to the road. In an unexpected emergency his cars would probably steer you out of it – that was his idea. He wasn't

A fleet of 1800s was taken to Garve for their introduction to the press in August 1964. The group facing the camera are Issigonis with stick, Dick Burzi, Bill Appleby and Gil Jones.

interested in 'secondary safety'. He told a group of journalists who were discussing safety, 'Put a row of carving knives along the dash just in front of their faces. That'll make them be careful.'"

Good though the 1800's body was, one serious structural fault was only just cured in time. At the press launch at Garve in Scotland, George Coates found that after a day's running the front tyres were catching on the rear of the front wheel arches. "After about three stops from 70–80mph the wheels moved backwards by about ⅜in. Barry Wood and I drove each car up to a tree, put a chain round the tree and into the front towing eyes and then backed off with a wallop to re-establish the clearance. But when you took it down the road again the same thing would happen. So the balloon went up and strengtheners were sent up from Longbridge for Barry to weld in. We put them in each car while the press were out testing others."

Bernard Johnson had seen the first instance of that same structural problem when testing the 1800 in Wales prior to the press launch. "When one of the lads had cause to take to the grass he put his brakes on but didn't slow up much before hitting a drain with the locked wheel and that was enough to do it. It pushed the wheel straight on to the wheel arch."

Pat Layton remembered the same incident. "Oh yes, Gil Jones was ready to stuff that car up the

tester until we convinced him that something unto-ward was wrong. So they started to look at it more carefully but neither testers nor engineers were heeded by Issigonis."

Eric Bailey had already warned Issigonis that the 1800 body was very weak at that point. Issi's reply? "You go back and read your books and I'll design the car."

Persuading Issigonis to alter a design was obvi-ously far from easy. "As an engineer," said Ron Boswell, "Issigonis was quite brilliant. If we said we had a problem with so and so he'd say well why don't you do this or that. You'd think, 'blimey, why didn't we think of that'. But if you were working on an idea of his and were silly enough to say, 'We've changed this a bit', his face would change and what-ever it was would be in the bin. The trick was to pretend that everything was down to him. I remem-ber a colleague saying to him, 'Sir, remember you suggested last week how we should alter this valve?' You could see that Issi hadn't a clue what this guy was talking about, but the chap carried on, 'Well we've tried your suggestion and it has solved the problem.' At that Issi was beaming. It wasn't his suggestion, we'd been working on it for weeks, but if we had said we had solved the problem with an idea of our own it would have died the death. We had to kid him on all the way."

According to Ben Benbow, "Issigonis had total disregard for the customer. The first 1800 mock-up was in Dick Burzi's studio and it had no choke or handbrake. When I questioned what the arrangement was going to be he said, 'Oh dear boy, don't worry about such things.' But look where the choke was and that awful umbrella handbrake. You had to go in search of it, didn't you? He just didn't seem to care."

Issigonis obviously hadn't forgotten his run-in with Barry Kelkin over the Austin 1100 fascia. "At the launch of the 1800," said Barry, "Issigonis pointed to the fascia and said to me, 'That's how I wanted the 1100 fascia, narrow like that.' If you look at the original 1800 fascia you'll see it is even narrower than that of the Austin 1100. There is nothing above or below the ribbon speedo. He'd got somebody else to do it and made a point of fetching me and asking why I couldn't have done the 1100 like that. I have to admit that it gave the vehicle width."

Geoffrey Iley didn't like it all. "The fascia on the first 1800 was stark to the point of, well, dare I say lunacy? With that ribbon-type speedometer the whole thing looked like a cheap washing machine. I hesitantly suggested to Alec that perhaps we could have done something a little more attractive. I said a woman getting into an 1800 in a showroom might not want to be reminded of the washing machine at home. 'I don't want bloody women driving my

The Austin 1800 fascia. "That's how I wanted the 1100 fascia, narrow like that," said Issigonis.

cars', was his reply. He was so idiosyncratic in so many ways. He was on another plane entirely."

Chris Kingham felt that people just did not see the advantages of the 1800. "It had a lot to offer and wasn't expensive. Of course trim items do sell motor cars so it probably needed a few more. The whole car was very practical but very austere. Perhaps if we had pandered more to accepted taste rather than pioneer for posterity we might have sold a few more. The cable gear change wasn't very wonderful but we were constantly striving for refinement and the cables were seen as part of that process. At one stage we tried a hydraulic arrangement which gave the most wonderfully smooth gear changes. Alec, loving novelty, said 'If we can make that work we will have the gearchange in the door pocket on the driver's side.' It was a lovely idea and meant that as you opened the door everything swung out of the way. Unfortunately you tended to get stretch in the system so it needed constant adjustment. We had it on prototypes but having failed to solve the problems we had to ditch the whole idea. All through those Issigonis years we were breaking new ground. We were never allowed to carry a design through to the next car. With Issigonis that wasn't good enough. It was actually a tremendous success story except that we were never quite able to attain the standards we were aiming for."

As road test engineer Arthur Whittaker saw it,

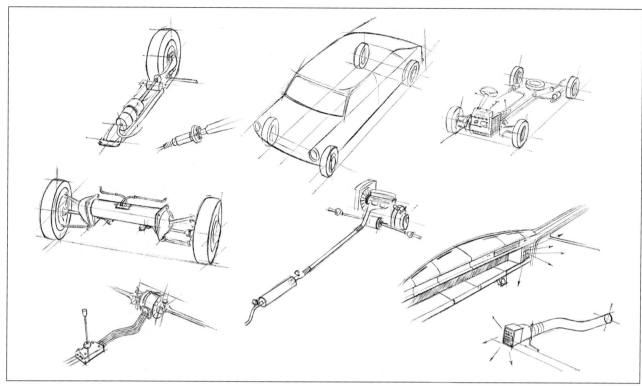

Issigonis used his own sketches in the first 1800 sales brochure. According to Aubrey Edwards, "When we launched the 1800 Issi even insisted on producing the brochure himself. Oh God it was a pig's ear of a thing. Each page looked as though it had come out of a different catalogue. I think he realised it hadn't quite worked because he backed off and we never had any more trouble from him after that."

"The cable shifts never really worked properly and you might well ask why it wasn't put right before the launch. But that's one of the things a tester always complains about. He makes report after report and no-one seems to take a blind bit of notice. Issi was a firm believer in letting the public do the testing. He'd say, 'Mmm mm. Let the public test it.' But that was a fatal mistake. Smashing guy as he was, he was a law unto himself. The 1800's popularity went down and down because of the early faults. It was a shame really."

Swiss distributor Emil Frey had no argument with the basic 1800 concept. "It was very good, thrilling even, but not enough thought had been given to reliability and finish. In those respects it was not comparable with its rivals. Over half the cars had 10–15 per cent of their retail cost taken up in pre-delivery inspection. I told Issigonis the 1800 was fine so long as we had his mechanics on hand fixing them for us."

"George Harriman was responsible for an awful lot of our difficulties," said Ted Price of Fisher &

Ludlow. "He liked to think he and Issi could run BMC between them but they couldn't. Everything they did got us deeper into the mire. I got fed up to the teeth going to policy meetings and having to say, 'But George, what about so and so.' He ordered capacity to build 4,500 1800s a week but we only ever did about 1,500–1,800 at the most. All that extra capacity had cost a fortune. I could write a book myself about the daft decisions he made."

After its launch in 1964, the Austin 1800 was voted 'Car of the Year'.

When Ron Nicholls first drove the 1800 he was extremely impressed with the spacious interior. "I even liked the looks but the fact that it didn't sell well could be put down to both its unconventional looks and a lack of refinement and reliability. People were beginning to remark that the Austin reliability of old was no longer to be taken for granted."

How true that was. Having owned an Austin 1800 in which he covered over 100,000 miles, the author believes it to have been one of the finest family saloons ever produced. But he only purchased it ten years after the initial launch. In those days it made sense, certainly for the private buyer of BMC cars, to allow quite a period of time for the design faults of each new model to be rectified. That people should think like that did not bode well for the future of BMC.

The 1800-derived Austin 3-litre of 1967 did not improve matters either. "The prototype of the 3-

The Austin 3-litre was announced at the 1967 Motor Show but the first 100 cars went to selected customers for proving and the car went into production 12 months afterwards with twin headlamps to replace the almost rectangular ones of the early cars. The show car is seen here at the premises of Clements Brothers of Bromsgrove where it was taken to check out the turntable.

litre was in the air-raid tunnels for ages," said Gil Jones. "Some wag had written 'Ron's Folly' on Dymo tape and stuck it on the front bumper." The Ron so irreverently referred to was Ron Nicholls who, although the project engineer in charge of the 3-litre, was certainly not responsible for its concept.

"The 3-litre came from Harriman", said Ron. "At 29 years of age it was my first major project. I did it in E-Cell, alongside Eric Bareham who was working on the Maxi in D-Cell. Actually, I built the forerunner of the 3-Litre while still in the experimental department before E-Cell was formed. Even that used the central section of the 1800 with a new front and back end styled by Farina with some help from Dick Burzi. It was a car that Harriman and the board had conceived and was totally at odds with Issi's philosophy. Issigonis had become a little unpopular by this time, having caused a lot of problems for a lot of people.

"The first 3-litre prototype used coil sprung front suspension and leaf springs on the rear. The body was made in Doug Adams's shop and then came through experimental without any connection with the Issigonis cell system. It was initially powered by what was known as the 'Blue Streak' six-cylinder version of the B-Series engine used in

Australia. An in-line engine and rear-wheel-drive were deemed essential by the likes of George Harriman for a large refined car. He saw the transverse engine as something that belonged to a smaller car. Self-levelling suspension was expected to improve the ride but the first levelling system produced by Armstrong was very inefficient and didn't impress anyone, so the car was dumped in the tunnels.

"It was later given to Issigonis to see how he could improve it and that was when E-Cell was set up. He and Charles Griffin felt that to compete with Ford the car had to be technically superior so they decided it needed Hydrolastic suspension. We started with an ordinary Hydrolastic system as in the 1800, but the handling wasn't good enough. So we changed to a semi-trailing rear suspension with a much-improved self-levelling system that gave superb ride and handling."

Ron Nicholls then laughingly recalled the saga that led to the car's first trial run. "The car was sat over the pit and when I said to my foreman, Maxi Oliver, 'OK Max, start it up,' the car hurtled forward, ploughed into a desk, smashed up its front end and one rear wheel dropped into the pit. It had taken six months to build so there was I close to tears and Max was wondering what the hell had happened. It was an automatic gearbox and although it was in neutral according to the lever it turned out that the inhibitor hadn't been set so the thing was actually in 'drive'. So in that few seconds we had smashed up our first pre-production vehicle, a lovely car in deep blue. Just at that very moment in walked Alec Issigonis and Charles Griffin, expecting the ride that I had promised them. I looked at them and they looked at me and we all looked at this car and they just burst out laughing with tears rolling down their cheeks. They could see I just didn't know where to put myself. Without more ado off came their jackets and we all got stuck in trying to get this damned car out of the pit. We eventually managed it, got it repaired and in a few days they had their drive. They were extremely kind about the whole business but on the run, well, there was no way in which Alec was ever going to be impressed with the car. It wasn't his car. He wasn't interested in it. He drove it up the road making funny grunts and groans with a sort of 'told you so' attitude. It was no offence to me because I was one of them."

Fred Eysenck spoke of the origin of the new C-Series engine that went into the production 3-litre. "I said to Stan Johnson, 'Why don't we produce a 3-litre engine?' He said, 'We've got one.' It was when Formula 1 was going to go to 3 litres and I was an

The Rover 3-litre. 'Roverisation' might have happened earlier! With the coming of Leyland in 1968, Michelotti was asked to re-style the 3-litre body with thoughts of using Rover's V8 engine in mind. Harry Webster actually ran a 3-litre with the Rover engine installed.

enthusiastic race watcher. I said, 'No, not that Morris Engines thing. Let's do one that people can use for performance. Let's build it square.' Much to my surprise the management agreed and before we knew where we were we were actually working on it as a production project. We started off slightly over square but unfortunately, when Morris engines got their sticky fingers on it, they returned it to the bore and stroke of the original C-Series to try and save money. We might as well have not produced it at all because although the cylinder head was of improved design and there were seven main bearings, it was just a very slight modernisation of the existing engine. It was also used in the MGC."

The 3-litre was launched at the 1967 Motor Show but production had barely got properly underway when the merger with Leyland took place. The merger brought Harry Webster from Standard-Triumph to Longbridge as director of engineering in place of Issigonis. According to Harry, "The 3-litre was a beautiful ride but oh, that bloody engine. I had a three litre and I thought it was a wonderful car but I'd put a 3½-litre Rover V8 engine into mine. That saved 2cwt and I ran it about for years. Using the V8 engine would have helped us to standardise on engines within the organisation."

Ray Bates, who became Harry's deputy at Longbridge, did a lot of work on the 3-litre. "It was something of a nightmare because we were always having trouble with the self-levelling and the power steering. There were leakages everywhere. I drove Harry's car with the Rover V8 in it and it was pretty damn quick. It was Harry's personal transport for some time but was rather unreliable."

According to Chris Kingham, "The 3-litre was

An ADO 61, 3-litre prototype on test in France. Ron Nicholls recalled they were aiming to produce a car for Europe and so spent a great deal of time attempting to perfect the ride on French roads with their heavy cambers and considerable undulations.

Almost there. The production 3-litre sported twin headlamps, as per this prototype which is seen outside Dick Burzi's studio. This specimen still lacks the front quarter lights of the production car.

received quite well initially. Like the 1800, it was torsionally very stiff and handled and steered well. But after the Leyland merger we had to decide which cars were going to be dropped. Harry Webster said he saw the 3-litre as a very high class touring car for Europe because its specification enabled it to cruise at high speeds in comfort. Charles Griffin and I had done all our ride and handling development on French roads and Harry Webster also took it over to France and confirmed it to be exceptional as a long-distance tourer. In the event we simply had far too many models and as it didn't have much of a reputation in the market place it got the chop."

Charles Griffin was adamant that the car should never have been built at all. "Neither Issi nor I wanted it. BMC was not democratically organised at all. The chairman made all the decisions. He would say we are going to make a 3-litre motor car and that was that, although in this instance I think he had the support of the sales department. I had to be responsible for it and make it work as well as we could but it wasn't a sensible car. The company at the time was well into front-wheel-drive motor cars so we shouldn't have been messing about driving the rear end of the 3-litre. It only offered the same interior as the 1800 and had lost most of its advantages."

21

The decline and fall of BMC

"Wilson and Benn decided Stokes was the bloke and with their assistance Stokes somehow took us over."

BERNARD JOHNSON

Although the British Motor Corporation may well have failed to reap many of the benefits that could have followed on from its formation, it does also seem that many of the elements that brought about its eventual demise were already in place well before its creation.

"Just after the war," said Roy Hall, then involved in CKD engineering, "we didn't seem to worry too much about what the public wanted. We just said 'we'll make motor cars'. We knew we could sell them so we were not too worried about how much they cost to make. We didn't even worry about

Little and Large 1951 style. Bob Grice, then chief of the road test department, obliges the cameraman taking press release photographs by parking a pre-production A30 alongside a Sheerline Saloon.

warranty costs either, not until it was too late. If the labour force got a bit uppity and asked for more money, we just paid up to keep the tracks running. That was the sort of attitude we adopted and it sowed the seeds of future problems."

As Joe Edwards saw it, "The British motor industry had the world at its feet at the end of the war. Austin was way ahead of anyone else in Europe. We were producing cars of all sizes from the Sheerline down to the A30 and pushing them through the door to a car-starved market. So what went wrong? Well, it pains me because I saw it all happen. As soon as those cars went over the doorstep they went up anything from £300 to £500 in value. People just couldn't get cars. If we had had management with the right financial understanding the company

could have accumulated millions for development and expansion in the years to come. But we didn't. Anything on the home market was ridiculously under-priced. Len Lord was not a finance man.

"Neither he nor George Harriman took a serious interest in training management. We had all just grown with the thing. I had come out of the bloody toolroom for heaven's sake. They happened to like the colour of my eyes or whatever but nobody gave me any management training. I had to learn the hard way. When I was running BMC there were 123,000 people working for me. Had I been trained for it? No. I must have been deficient in many areas. Not only that, but we had no depth of design background. Dick Burzi was a charming chap but if the truth is to be told, he was a one-week Italian designer. Len Lord used to say, 'That's rubbish

"We were squandering money on unproductive items such as the multistorey car park," said Bill Davis. Opened in September 1961 with such headlines as 'Austin Expands Upwards – the world's largest multistorey car park is completed'. The idea was to house the 3,000 or so newly produced cars that were usually parked on the Longbridge site and thus make room for a second car assembly building – CAB 2 – to increase Longbridge's output ability from 8,000 cars a week to 10,500. When the car park was built, Albert Green, superintendent of CAB 1, said, "I'll fill that bugger in a week." He did too.

Burzi. Tear the bloody thing up. I'll show you what to do.' I saw him do that time and time again. So we missed the money and had no real design programme at all."

Bill Davis, a BMC director in the 1960s, spoke in a similar vein. "The company was run by a long sequence of ex-production engineers; Len Lord, George Harriman, Joe Edwards and myself. Perhaps we weren't sufficiently commercially orientated. Our prices were certainly too low. The Mini should have been £10 dearer at least. We should have had more assistance in formulating product policies, market research and so on. We were so concerned with turning out the present generation of vehicles that too little thought was given to the future. We were squandering money on un-productive items such as the multistorey car park."

Successive post-war governments certainly have to share some of the blame for the demise of BMC. A decision to dispense social justice by spreading the motor industry around the country meant BMC was forced to build its trucks at Bathgate in Scotland. That led to a tremendous increase in costs and enormous difficulties in procuring the right labour locally. Successive governments also used the industry as an economic regulator by constantly fiddling with purchase tax.

The basic responsibility for many of the ills cited

above, other than those of political origin, must be laid fairly and squarely at the feet of Len Lord, but after his retirement, the message from all levels of employees at BMC was that things got worse, not better.

"We never used to see Harriman walking about the factory as Lord used to," remembers Barry Brecknell. "He seemed to hide himself away and allowed his lesser lieutenants to do that job. The leadership faded and the momentum was lost."

Alf Dolphin agrees. "Sir George didn't take the same interest in what was going on and it was under him that things began to go wrong. He would talk to the men of 'emoluments'. If he'd said 'wages' they would have known what he meant. I think that helped put the trades unions' backs up. He had given them the impression he was a bit of a playboy. Dick Etheridge would stand in Cofton Park and ask the men, 'Where do you think the lord of the manor is now?', meaning Harriman. 'He is basking in the sunshine at Monte Carlo.'"

After the Second World War the trades unions had begun to flex their muscles with increasing regularity but it has to be said that management was partly responsible for the build up of an 'us and them' mentality. In 1956, for example, 6,000 men were dismissed at BMC, 3,000 of them at 'The Austin', without any real consultation. Such actions quite naturally angered the men, their shop stewards and the works committee.

Members of the management were falling out amongst themselves too. After that strike, Joe Edwards, then BMC's director of manufacturing, found himself confronting Len Lord rather than the unions. "Lord wanted me to take over labour relations but I wasn't having that. He then accused me of wanting his job. I said, 'I don't want your bloody job and I slammed the door on my way out. That's when the staff cried in front of me, when I told them I was leaving. Imagine that the men should cry in front of you. Len Lord wasn't daft but he was pig-headed, he really was. He had an enormous inferiority complex."

But Mike Sheehan, later an industrial relations manager at Longbridge, felt that Lord's proposal made sense. "Joe was well-liked at Longbridge so it was a great shame that he didn't take on the industrial relations job. Lord had sensed that it needed someone of Joe's calibre to take on what was going to be a totally new industrial relations scene. Joe didn't see it as a career move but if he could have brought his depth of thinking and his warmth for people into that job we might have seen real progress."

Sir Leonard Lord and Joe Edwards are seen here going over Longbridge production figures in the 1950s but it was each other they seemingly were never quite able to figure out.

Whatever the rights and wrongs of the Lord/Edwards confrontation, industrial relations continued to deteriorate until it was undoubtedly a case of the tail wagging the dog. By the mid-1960s a few militant shop stewards had virtually wrested control, not only from management, but from the unions themselves. They would simply walk through the shops shouting "Everyone out!" and out the men came, very often not even knowing why.

"It wasn't all through malice," said Paddy O'Reilly. "But even simple disagreements could get very complicated. If the men lost money through adverse circumstances the foreman could give them an hour or so on a 'pink ticket'. That became a fiddle. If a man had to put a bit of grease on a 'blank' in the press shop, or wipe some oil off, it would slow them down. So if it wasn't on the 'layouts' as an agreed part of the job they would want a pink ticket. Of course, a man might have to perform 200 operations like that an hour on the big presses, bloody hard graft, make no mistake, so it became one long battle from morning to night. On the inner door panels of the A35, every time a shipment of material arrived the bloody steel blanks were always oily. It used to cause suction when the blokes tried to slide them off the pile to put them in the rolling machine, so they had a legitimate claim to a pink ticket because it certainly slowed them down.

"I tried everything to get this oil reduced. I went to the chief material controller and asked him to get the suppliers to reduce the oil but he said he wasn't taking that responsibility in case they went rusty. So

I took it on myself and wrote to the steel company saying I didn't want them oiled. We waited with baited breath as the men took the first shipment of dry blanks up to the press. I'd primed the rate-fixer and sure enough, they went down to him for their pink ticket. He was able to say there was no oil on them so I thought I'd done a good job there. Two days later, when we set the draw dies up to press the panels, the shop stewards came down with four men off the job wanting a pink ticket. Why? Because the blanks were so dry they couldn't draw them without having to put tallow on them. They had a legitimate claim too, damn it. What we had gained on the swings we lost on the roundabouts. We all saw the funny side of that one."

Ron Savage, who had 'a baptism of fire' as a rate-fixer in 1958/59, found the men in the paint shop to be some of the most militant. "They gave me Trentham paint shop just as the Mini was about to go into production. The aggro was something awful

Greasing 'blanks' in the press shop. If operations which slowed the men down were not an agreed part of the job, it could lead to legitimate demands for 'pink tickets' which allowed them extra time on the job. If the demands were not met then industrial strife ensued.

but the men in there had a rotten job. The bodies were dipped in red primer and hung on the line. The first job was to 'wet flat' them by sluicing them with water and rubbing them with wet and dry paper. Then they were 'tagged and blown dry'. A tag rag is a sticky piece of mutton cloth that removes any fluff. Then they were primed again, flatted again, tagged again and so on – then into colour and the final finish and baking. The men were soaking wet all day and amongst paint fumes all day. A pretty horrible state to be in. There were separate gangs doing the A35, A40 Farina and the Cambridge. Imagine trying to settle piecework prices with 40 or 50 of those blokes. I think the management should have grasped the nettle then, in 1959/60, because you had to barter and argue for ages to get every single piece-work price fixed. In earlier years, the rate-fixer would just time a job and say 'That has taken you two minutes so that is your time' and that was it; but not in 1959.

"There was nothing wrong with piecework really," continued Ron, "It was payment by results. If you set a fair time, a man working at a steady pace earned a normal living. If he wanted to bust his gut he could earn more. But the management at Longbridge wanted production at any cost and that

was where they lost control. Most of the hassle took place when introducing a new model. That was the only chance for the men to get improved rates because of an agreement that no piecework price would be altered unless the means or method of production was altered. So we'd spend weeks and months arguing about the piecework rates. There was a procedure for settling disputes. The foreman would talk to the shop steward and if they disagreed it would go to the superintendent and then to the general superintendent and so on. That would lead to a plant conference but all that would achieve was, 'We want more,' and 'We are not going to give you more.' Unresolved problems went to a monthly conference at York where all the Engineering Federation issues in the country were negotiated. Senior trade union officials like Scanlon would be there, so the director of the company and his personnel people would trek up to York each month with a whole sackful of these piecework prices. It was a bit of a jolly for some of these Engineering Federation people, living at York for three or four days, wining and dining. The poor local director was thinking, 'Christ, I've come to settle this problem and these people don't really want to know.'

"Some shop stewards were genuinely interested

The men in the paint shop were among some of the most militant but, "The men were soaking wet all day … and amongst paint fumes all day. A pretty horrible state to be in." – Ron Savage.

in furthering the interests of others. But there were also those who, having failed to make their way up the management tree, had decided to make it up the trade union tree and achieve just as much power. Some did it to make a bob or two on the side, jollying off to the TUC meetings etc, and there were those who simply wanted an idle life. While they were in the office arguing they weren't doing any work. The average rank and file trade unionist would have been sickened if they had seen how their money was being spent at York and elsewhere. Having said all that, without the trade unions we'd still have women down the coal mines and little boys going up chimneys. But the balance of power had swung too far one way. Later on, under Thatcher, things probably went too far in the other direction. It is very difficult to hit it right."

Les Farmer made the point that management was not averse to taking advantage of any industrial unrest. "The strikes weren't always caused by the men. I've known occasions when we had bodies outside on the field and, with winter coming up, we didn't want them lying about so a three-day strike in the body shop helped clear the stocks. I don't say the management caused them but a stoppage sometimes suited management quite nicely. There was always a little bit of politics in these things."

Politics were certainly about to play a great part in the whole future of the British motor industry. In 1965, BMC took over Pressed Steel. As a result, Joe Edwards (sacked by Lord in 1956 and immediately appointed as managing director of Pressed Steel) returned to Longbridge as MD of BMC with Harriman as his executive chairman. In July 1966, BMC merged with Jaguar to form British Motor Holdings, or BMH.

Much greater ructions were about to follow. Joe Edwards described the state of play when he became managing director of BMC in 1966. "Technically, BMC was way ahead of anyone but most other aspects had been badly neglected. On my return to Longbridge I found that George Harriman spent all his time downstairs in the styling studio talking to Alec Issigonis – all the time – didn't do anything else. That's how he ran the company. Apparently that's what he had been doing while I had been away and the place had just disintegrated. I immediately reduced the overmanning considerably, put a new buyer in, got a styling man in and was just moving into the area of labour relations and getting a hold of the model programme and costings when Harriman dropped a bombshell.

"He told me he had been talking to Donald Stokes about a possible merger with Leyland. He warned me about Stokes and Harold Wilson, saying Stokes had become the man of the moment because he had sold a few buses to Cuba. That was the first I knew of what had been going on. I said to George, 'If that's what you have been doing chum, I'm not very happy.' He said, 'Well, will you come over and see Stokes?' I agreed. So we got into an 1100 and sneaked into Stokes's place at Coventry. I sat there – innocent Joe – but the discussion didn't interest me. I thought, 'I'm not bloody well having this'. At our next board meeting I said I wanted them all to know that such a merger was not for me. 'Don't count me in on any of this.' They knew that when Joe said something it wasn't bullshit and of course it came to pass. After the merger I resigned. The Wilson government had handed Stokes the thing on a plate. Bloody right they did – Harold Wilson and Tony Benn."

Geoffrey Rose was one of many who were sorry to see the resultant departure of Joe Edwards. "It was sad that he and Stokes couldn't get on because if Joe had been in charge and Stokes had looked after marketing and sales I think it might have been a different story."

A merger between Leyland and BMC had been on the cards for some time. Prime Minister Harold Wilson and his Minister of Technology, Tony Benn, both felt that government intervention was essential if the British motor industry was to be put back on its feet. The original plan would have meant a takeover of Leyland by BMC. After much dithering, partly caused in the later stages by Joe Edwards's total opposition to working under Donald Stokes, the BMC position was so weakened that Stokes then held the whip hand. What came to pass was, in effect, a take over of BMH by Leyland.

Geoffrey Iley felt that if Joe Edwards had got back into the BMC driving seat some five years earlier then history might have been very different. "Joe was a 'people' man. Harriman was a divide and rule man. I've heard it said that he would never have more than one of his senior henchmen in his office at a time so that he could play one against the other. He and Alec Issigonis formed an unholy alliance as the boss and his chief engineer. As far as they were concerned, the less the sales or any other department knew about their plans the less they would be able to influence anything. Product planning as an activity just didn't happen at BMC. During the Harriman years, there was a group of young Turks – Geoffrey Rose, Mike Sheehan, myself and a few others – who used to meet from time to time and discuss what the hell we could do to meet our production schedules. We knew that we needed

Industrial strife would lead to stoppages, fewer cars being built, or those that were built being short of components. This stockpile of cars at Longbridge in 1963 was largely due to window shortages. When the multistorey car park was full, distributors had all the cars they could cope with and every spare bit of land at 'The Austin' was full (as above), they had to look elsewhere … hence these cars with taped up windows at Wythal aerodrome. "On the

way home I used to pass the airfield at Wythal," said Geoffrey Rose. "It was an Air Ministry aerodrome so, off the cuff, I rang up the squadron leader and to my delight he said, 'All right old boy, we can accommodate them.' So we had this wonderful outlet for 7,000 cars only about three of four miles from the factory." "That's when I learned that you get 750 cars to an acre," said Geoffrey Iley.

professional help. We knew we didn't have the skills that they had at Ford to make a better fist of things. Our manufacturing plants were spread all over the place and many had become old-fashioned. We went to see George Harriman but were virtually patted on the head and told we were 'doing just fine, chaps'."

By 1967, the BMC range of cars had become an almost absurd mixture of two different design schools: one at the very cutting-edge of technology and another, which by comparison, was almost archaic. This was hardly the way to reap the benefits of mass production. What would Sir Stafford Cripps have made of it all? With such a belt and braces approach, retaining old models after introducing their intended replacements, BMC themselves seemed to be saying, "we'd better just hang on to these old models in case the new ones aren't a success." Perhaps they had a point. The early problems of the front-wheel-drive cars certainly stretched customer loyalty to the limits and fleet managers were getting very concerned at the number of days they were off the road for repairs.

Even Alex Moulton, one who much preferred to give his attention to the future rather than look back with recriminations, agreed that BMC had erred. "I'm certain that the cars weren't well enough developed and any faults which did appear, in the gearboxes and transmissions and so on, weren't dealt with quickly enough."

Ron Nicholls wondered if Issigonis was simply demanding more than Longbridge could offer. "He was very intolerant of others but perhaps some of our engineers with conventional thoughts just weren't able to provide what he wanted. Some certainly weren't good enough. Gearbox design was never really on top of things. It may be a little harsh to put it like that but that's how it seemed to me. Perhaps the technology just wasn't there. Remember, he was asking for giant leaps forward."

Pat Layton of the experimental department was another who recalled how Issigonis would regularly ask for the seemingly impossible. "He was certainly arrogant but if he had allowed himself to be swayed he wouldn't have developed the things he did. I heard a draughtsman say to him, 'This won't work you know.' 'That'll work', said Issi. 'No,' said the chap, 'it can't possibly work because …' 'It'll work', said Issi. 'Do you know why it will work? Because I have said so. Do it.' So the chap had to find a way of doing it. People were tearing their hair out trying to cope with his demands."

"I was very fed up with being subservient to Alec, charming as he was," said Duncan Stuart. "I could see the Mini was not going to make any money and I went to see Harriman at about the time they turned down our V4 engines for the 1100 and 1800. I said, 'You know we are doing all this research but you don't use any of it so why don't you put the whole of my research and development department on cost-cutting the Mini? We could easily take £20 out of the production cost.' He said, 'That's a good idea. Talk to Alec.' I replied, 'Surely it is you who should talk to Alec?' He answered, 'If Alec is in favour I'll support you.' In effect he was telling me that Alec was running the company. I'm sure that's where things went wrong, because the gearbox itself was a disaster and the problems of the synchros, and the water and so on, could all have been avoided really. It must have been towards the end of '62 when I put that proposition. It was a great shame he didn't take it up because the benefits would have carried through into the 1100, 1800 and so on. To divorce all our research work from any product planning strategy was almost criminal. We had about a hundred people in East Works, a complete drawing office with test beds and a road test department. We spent a fortune but never saw our work used commercially. It was a crying shame. We did all the early research work in perfecting rubber cam belts but then let people like Ford gain all the benefits."

Whether or not his cars made money for BMC, Issigonis will surely go down in history as the man who did more than any other to change the very parameters of car design in the second half of the 20th century.

It was unfortunate, however, that BMC did not manage to harness his genius without letting him stray into realms that were beyond his ken, and perhaps even more unfortunate that British Leyland, who were about to become his new masters, consigned him, in effect, to the scrapheap.

To lumber Issigonis with all the ills of BMC would certainly be a gross injustice, so perhaps we should let Harold Musgrove (an Austin ex-apprentice who in later years became chairman and MD of Austin-Rover) put BMC's final days into perspective. "It wasn't just Issigonis who did what he wanted under Harriman. Production did what they wanted, sales and marketing did what they wanted, and the unions did what they wanted. There was no co-ordination, no strategy. It wasn't just that we lost our way, we were all going in different directions."

Hence the gradual deterioration of BMC and the eventual takeover by Leyland in 1968 to form the British Leyland Motor Corporation, or BLMC. It was in the midst of all this turmoil that the subject of the next chapter, the Austin Maxi, was born.

22

Enter Leyland and the Maxi

"Nya Stora Hundkojan fran BMC" – A new dog kennel from BMC

The development period of the Maxi was far from straightforward; encompassing as it did the mergers of BMC and Pressed Steel, and the eventual merger of BMH and Leyland.

"Harriman came into Dick Burzi's styling studio one day," said Sid Goble, "and told us, 'I want you to make a smaller car out of the 1800 but using the same doors.' So Fred Boubier and I went straight into a full-size drawing. No styling had been done on it at all. All we were given was the width and the wheelbase and we put the doors of the 1800 on the drawing and worked round those. There were no tailgates on production cars in those days but when we drew the Maxi with a boot lid like the Mini we found that the sloping roof made it too shallow to accommodate a reasonable boot lid. It was Boubier

and I who decided to create a tailgate by joining the boot lid to the backlight. Believe it or not, we decided on that ourselves and approval came afterwards. We just couldn't get the proportions right any other way. So that was the start of the Maxi."

"Work began about 1965," said Eric Bareham, then BMC's assistant chief designer of engines and transmissions. "Issi dragged me off my perch in the main drawing office and bunged me in the office next to his. The first prototype was a one-off that Sir Alec had done. He was proposing an 1,100cc engine in a car weighing 2,000lb. I didn't think much of that idea so went to East Works R&D to see what they had in the way of engines. Ted Payne said, 'We've got a belt-driven OHC engine. It's one of our 1,300cc engines but I've opened it up to 1,450cc

This early Maxi prototype of June 1965 was, "a cobble-up that we built in the body shop using an 1800 body cut through the middle and reduced in width and length but using the same doors," said Godfrey Coates. The white sheet is being shaken during the exposure by men standing behind it to try to get rid of the creases and thus leave a less-distracting background.

as an exercise. You can have that if you like.' When we showed it to Sir Alec he said, 'Mmm, all right, put it in.' The distributor was driven off the back of the camshaft and came perilously close to the master cylinder. We had installed it but had only driven it very gingerly around the block when Alec came in with a bloke from the *Daily Telegraph* and drove off in the thing. He tried to turn round in the dual carriageway outside the works, no doubt in top gear, so the engine went bang, bang, bang and knocked the distributor off. Out he got, said, 'Oh jolly hard luck,' sort of thing, and left us to get the wreck home. Old Ted Payne produced a skew-driven distributor and it was all right after that."

"The design of the much-maligned Maxi was quite radical," said Ron Nicholls. "A five-door car was something very new. The Maxi was aimed at a changing market – a more family-orientated market – people with more leisure, taking camping and caravanning holidays. The Maxi was offered to fit that sort of bill. A new 'get up and go' age, if you like. You could even make a bed out of the seats. It was received with a great deal of enthusiasm because there was nothing else like it. The criticisms came later.

"The early prototypes had a very short nose. Issi started with his usual concept of the smallest exterior package and didn't want it 'any longer than *this* or any wider than *that*.' But the bonnet did eventu-

"Become a five-car family. For the price of a single Maxi," ran the Austin advertising, "Family Saloon, Estate Car, School Bus, Removal Van and Overnight Camper – if you want more than just another car, take a long look at the features of the versatile Maxi at your local Austin showroom."

ally take an increase in length of about 3 inches, mainly so that you could get at things. I remember viewing it with admiration. I thought this is a car that I would like to own, an ideal car for the family to carry the luggage and pull the caravan but without being too big. Although a first-class concept, it was appallingly executed. You can't defend that aspect. Perhaps Eric and Issi weren't the right combination. Eric did exactly what Issi told him but I think somebody like Chris Kingham, Jack Daniels or myself, who knew him better, might have said, 'Heh, can we rethink this one a bit?'. Mind you, it wouldn't have been easy. When I told Issi I thought he was barking up the wrong tree about something on the Maxi he said, 'Mmm look, this is my tree and I'm barking up it. You go and find your own tree to bark up. Mmm?'"

Pat Layton offered further insight into life under Issigonis. "Two chaps from Dunlop arrived one day and Issi said, 'Ah, Mr Dunlop, I'm bringing my Maxi over to your rolling road this afternoon.' This chap said, 'But you can't. We have got another client's car on it.' Issi insisted, 'Well, take it off.' The chap replied, 'I can't. It's all set up.' 'Who do you work for?' asked Issi, and then rang this fella's boss and said, 'Ah, Issigonis here. I'm bringing my Maxi over this afternoon to put it on your rolling road – yes, this afternoon, yes. Why? Well have you ever driven a steam locomotive on a cobbled high street? That's what my Maxi is like and I must improve it. See you this afternoon.' That was that. If he was determined to do anything no-one could stop him. But that was part of his genius."

The design of the Maxi's E-Series engine was not of Eric Bareham's choosing. "Issigonis wanted the thing as short as possible. He said the siamesed cylinders worked on the 1,275cc A-Series engine so we'll do that again. We tried all sorts of configurations for an OHC engine. He didn't think belt-driven camshafts were sufficiently proven at the time so they were out. The extreme shortness between the bores meant that the whole cylinder head was horribly crowded. It is amazing it did as well as it did. The valve size was strictly limited. In fact, we had to angle them slightly towards each other to make more room for them, as per the old Hornet from my days at Wolseley.

"Funnily enough we didn't get any valve trouble. There was a bit of sinkage during the early bench tests. The valves would rotate and screw themselves into the head but they gave no trouble in production. It just seemed to cure itself and no-one knew why – just like the bearing troubles that you get on test-bed running that don't repeat themselves in production. Mind you, production does bring its own problems when people leave the choke out to hang their handbag on for example."

John Barnett in engine development spoke of the E-Series engine's development period. "Any problem that was going the E-Series had it. The overriding specification was based on the six-cylinder transverse engine, the 2200, which was to be built on the same transfer machines and had to fit the 'Landcrab' body with the radiator at one side. So the whole thing was squashed up to get it in transversely. When it actually came to putting the six-cylinder engine in the 'Landcrab', [this was the nickname given to the Issigonis-designed 1800/2200 series of cars] the radiator was moved to the front of the car with an electric fan so we were stuck with a very short engine with its attendant technical difficulties for a reason that was no longer valid.

"We had all sorts of problems with bore finish, high oil consumption, pistons picking up, valve seat sinkage, skew gear wear and gasket leakage. We tested four new engines a day until we got the spec sorted out. After those tests we had something of a redesign and by September 1967 we had quite a few engines running about, first in ADO 16s and 17s (Austin 1100 and 1800) and later in ADO 14 Maxi prototypes. In the Spring of 1968 we completed the first series of tests on the German autobahns, with four vehicles. We ran the engines for 631,000 road miles and 6,600 hours on the test bed and simply worked our way through the problems."

In the previous chapter, Joe Edwards made mention of appointing a new stylist after BMC merged with Pressed Steel. "Joe was certainly pretty go-ahead," said Sid Goble. "In fact in late 1967, without our knowledge at Longbridge, he'd got a hold of a lot of Ford people and set up a styling department at Pressed Steel with Roy Haynes in charge as a sort of *fait accompli*. Roy was quite a catch in those days having just produced Ford's Mk II Cortina. He enticed quite a few Ford men to join him at Pressed Steel, including Harris Mann as his chief stylist on exteriors, Vic Hammond on interiors, and Vic Horner as his modelling manager.

Barry Kelkin remembered that reorganisation. "Pressed Steel also took charge of all body engineering. As body engineers we remained at Longbridge but answered to Ken Osbourne at Pressed Steel."

The first that Andy Duthie, then a clay modeller at Pressed Steel, saw of the Maxi was a mockup that had come from Farina. "It must have been late '67 when it arrived from Italy with a very peaky snout on the leading edge of the bonnet. When Roy Haynes joined us he straightened that out using a

grille that he brought from Ford. He also put that horrible Ford Cortina-like bumper on it. The original Maxi fascia was just like a big Airfix kit, a horrible plastic fascia which thankfully was soon changed. I think Roy was trying to out-Ford Ford at the time."

Vic Horner was also involved in the attempt to improve the looks of the Maxi when he arrived from Ford. "Roy Haynes wasn't happy with the general design but it had gone a bit too far down the line to do very much about it. After altering the front we also made the rear lamps more integral with the body, more like those on Roy's Cortina."

Harris Mann has never forgotten his first sight of the original Maxi. "The Issigonis philosophy was to skin over the mechanicals as closely as possible, so the front end had been pruned down to the bare minimum. It was such a shock coming from Ford, where we had already done the Capri, to see the Maxi sitting there at Cowley. A booted version of the Maxi was virtually ready for production as well and was a very strange looker indeed. If Roy Haynes had had his way he would have cancelled them both."

In the end it was neither Roy Haynes nor even Issigonis who determined the final specification of

The Maxi's E-Series engine. Wesley Hunt, who worked under Eric Bareham on the engine, recalled, "The Australians were asking for engines with more power so Geoff Cooper suggested we resort to overhead camshafts. Issigonis was in charge so we went to see him and he said: 'Wesley, we'd better put something down on paper.' So, under Issigonis's supervision, Eric Bareham thrashed out the E-Series overhead camshaft engine but it was really through Australia that it was done."

the Maxi because the merger with Leyland took place before the car was ready for production. The resultant departure of Joe Edwards saw Donald Stokes taking overall charge and bringing in George Turnbull from Standard-Triumph as managing director of Austin-Morris. An ailing Harriman was certainly no match for the ebullient and irrepressible Stokes and was shunted into an honorary president's role. The talents of Issigonis were about to be sidelined too.

"Harriman wasn't very well," said Barry Kelkin, "and seemed quite resigned to unload everything on to Stokes. When Stokes took over he said, 'Oh we'll soon put a stop to this Issigonis bloke.' But you know Issigonis had learnt a lot by then. He had come to realise that there was more to making mass-produced cars, especially innovative mass-produced cars, than a few drawings on the back of a fag packet. He was getting to the stage where I think he could have been harnessed when Stokes came along. It was a shame really."

Harry Webster, chief engineer of Standard-Triumph, was appointed by Stokes as technical director of the Austin-Morris division of BLMC in place of Issigonis. "I was instructed by Stokes to try and get some cohesion into the whole group. Austin and Morris might have been joined together but it was still a case of never the twain shall meet. They

Farina's mock-up for the Maxi had this 'very peaky snout' at the front end which Roy Haynes later straightened out.

still had two of everything. It was an impossible remit to try and get them all singing from the same piece of music but it would have been futile to let them go on as they were. I realised that Charles Griffin was the mainspring there. My first move was to give him as much control as I could and sideline Issigonis by putting him into a separate organisation called Forward Research."

According to Sid Goble, the deposing of Issigonis was fairly traumatic. "Issi had been away and when he came back he found Webster installed in his office. He came to Dick Burzi, almost in tears. The great man had been humiliated. He no longer had an office and didn't know what to do about it. Dick had a room where he kept old styling models so he cleared those out and put Issigonis in there."

The combined genius of Issigonis and Moulton had undoubtedly put Longbridge at the forefront of design but the men from Leyland did not see it that way. According to Ray Bates, appointed in 1969 as Webster's technical manager, "Stokes said he moved Harry Webster to Longbridge to try to get some of the Triumph flair into Austin design. You see, Leyland had previously taken over Standard-Triumph and the senior men at Leyland had got to know the Triumph people before they knew anyone at Austin. Webster had done the Spitfires and TRs and so on, so it wasn't surprising that Stokes should choose him for the job. Mind you, most of the 'flair' had actually come from Michelotti.

"Although Issi was a fountain of ideas he was not

a man who could embrace anyone else's. He knew what he wanted and bugger everybody else. He would have been a very difficult man to harness. I think it was more as a matter of kindness and consideration that he was set aside in his own area with his own group of people. I tried desperately hard to have a rapport with Issigonis but I didn't succeed. I think that the gulf had already been created and he was seen as being in the way of progress as far as product-planning was concerned.

"I was appointed as Harry's technical manager, but Charles Griffin was his director of engineering and I was rather left on my own and ignored. I certainly wasn't very well received. I drove a Triumph Herald so they regarded me as a rear-wheel-drive man, not an Austin man, so I was no bloody good. They really didn't like me parking the Herald outside the Longbridge design block. Getting to know Charles Griffin was quite difficult but as I did get to know him I got to like him more and more. Charles was a true engineer, not a man who would delegate responsibility and sit in his office. He was a hands-on man and I warmed greatly to his ability and generosity."

Gil Jones, then in charge of the Longbridge

Two Maxi prototypes were tested in Portugal in the summer of 1968. The hatchback is seen here being followed by a Maxi saloon. By this time, both the front and rear styling had been reworked by Roy Haynes from Ford, hence the Cortina-like grille and bumpers.

experimental department, spoke of Harry Webster delaying the launch of the Maxi so that they could, amongst other things, modify the gearbox. "Stokes accused Issigonis and Griffin of pulling the wool over his eyes about the car's readiness for production. Anyway, it was my lot to tell Webster that the gearbox was no good and face the consequences. When he got on to Issi and asked,'What's all this about the gearbox being no good?', Issi and Charlie came back to me with the same question – as though they didn't already know. Even when it came to the launch in Estoril in Portugal it was still a poor gearchange, particularly when the gearbox was cold."

Bernard Johnson, then Gil's deputy, took up the story. "It fell to Harry Webster to try to perfect the Issigonis design. We had plenty of trouble with it but you have to remember it was a very bold venture. A new OHC E-Series engine and a new, trendsetting five-speed gearbox. As for the five-door body, only Renault had done that before with the 16. The things wrong with it were beyond the development engineering. I mean, you couldn't do anything with that cable gearchange. We didn't like it and we said so but Issigonis said 'just carry on with it'. Eventually we put a rod change on but the whole gearbox under the E-Series engine wasn't really big enough. The distance between the shafts was too small, which meant the synchro cones were also too small."

Godfrey Coates, the son of George Coates, spent

Were they trying to keep the proposed saloon version of the Maxi a secret? In every photograph where Maxi saloon and hatchback appeared together the saloon was always almost completely hidden behind the hatchback. By looking through the window of this hatchback on test in Portugal we can just make out the four-light saloon's rear side window.

some 45 years in Longbridge's experimental body shop. Godfrey accompanied both four and five-door Maxi prototypes to Portugal in August 1968. "During the dust tests at Estremoz one of the gearboxes packed up so we had to have the engine out in a field. The lads jacked the car up on both sides and after draining the Hydrolastic fluid, they took off the wheels and lower suspension arms. After that

For a better idea of what a saloon version of the Maxi would have been like we have to resort to this Cowley clay model. Note that it is badged as a Morris.

they lowered the car on to the ground and undid the rest of the engine mounts. Then they used the two side jacks to lift the body off the engine. After changing the gearbox they slid the whole thing back underneath and did everything in reverse order. That was our only spare gearbox and when the other car hit a large boulder the sump took a nasty bash in the middle and the oil ran out. By a fluke I had some Araldite in my tool box and we came all the way back to England with the gearbox stuck together with that."

After subjecting the Maxi to that hot and dusty Portuguese summer it was taken on a winter trip to the Arctic Circle. "It was in the days before alternators," said Brian Taylor, "and in snowy conditions at minus 22 degrees Celsius you needed the heater, the heated rear screen and the headlights on all the time. The battery regularly went flat so it was decided the car needed an alternator."

Throughout the development programme many attempts were made to improve gear selection but as Brian Taylor pointed out, "It was fairly obvious that the Maxi gearbox was going to be unacceptable."

This time, of course, it was not Issigonis who passed the car as fit for production. He had already been sidelined. The 'sign-off' of the BLMC Maxi was undertaken by Stan Dews on 15 November 1968. At that time, a four-door booted version was still being considered for production, with its own proposed 'sign-off' date of 15 February 1969.

At the hatchback 'sign-off' it was suggested that careful quality control would allow the gearbox to function satisfactorily. It was also agreed that the electrics and heating system would be tested for

After the heat of a Portuguese summer, preproduction Maxis were subjected to an Arctic trip in the middle of winter. As a result, all production Maxis would be equipped with an alternator and be unofficially announced to the Swedes as 'a new dog kennel from BMC'.

cold climate conditions on another trip to Sweden and Finland in January 1969. "We stayed a night in Gothenburg," said Brian Taylor, "and when we came back from the Arctic Circle two weeks later the local press was waiting for us. They had taken photographs of the Maxi on the way up and had them in the papers and wanted our comments. Of course we all had to keep quiet."

The Swedes had certainly taken a good look, even under the bonnet. A fully detailed description of the car appeared in the Swedish equivalent of the *Sunday Express* of 19 January 1969 under the heading, 'Nya Stora Hundkojan fran BMC, (A new dog kennel from BMC), Hundkoja (doghouse or kennel) being the Swedish nickname for the Mini. The test team were certainly in the doghouse on their return to Longbridge because that report from Sweden had preceded them.

After its launch in 1969, the Maxi was built at Cowley where Eric Lord was then director of quality control. "I put the first cars through a vigorous road-test procedure and found the gearbox a disaster. The cable change and the synchromesh were not man enough for the job. I told George Turnbull (who Stokes had appointed as MD at Longbridge) that it would kill the car. Gil Jones suggested that if we adjusted it properly we wouldn't get any trouble, but we didn't have highly skilled road-test mechan-

ics on the production line. We even pre-stretched the cables and then readjusted them but it was still no good. George Turnbull eventually took my point and, although we had to keep producing it, he gave instructions for the design of a rod change. Of course that took 12 months and we had made a hell of a lot of motor cars by that time. A lot of people said they would never buy another because they couldn't get the damn thing in gear. The distributors and dealers had a rough ride with that. All they could do was to keep adjusting the thing."

Charles Griffin would not have produced the Maxi at all. "We should have used the 1100 layout and developed that into a Maxi-sized car. We produced the Mini in '59, the 1100 in '62, the 1800 in '64 and the Maxi in '65 and '66 and the components of each were almost totally different. If you developed one you didn't get spin-off for the others. The Maxi had hardly any carry-over apart from the doors. The E-Series engine and everything else was new, just as the 1100 had little carry-over from the Mini. The error really was making the 1800 and the Maxi, both with different components. Neither was a high volume car so it was a great waste of machining capacity. If we were going to make the two they should have been commonly tooled."

Like all the Issigonis-designed front-wheel-drive cars, the Maxi had excellent road manners. With its high fifth gear it cruised very happily too. The Maxi 1750 of 1970, with its increased power and rod-operated gearbox, was certainly a great improvement on the original. It had, and still has, some ardent devotees, but it would seem that Eric Lord was right. The Maxi was another car which never really

Following the 1,500cc car's launch in 1969, complaints about lack of power and that dreadful cable gear-change saw an immediate start on the design of a rod-operated gear change and an optional, 1,750cc engine. The Maxi 1750 launched in 1970 was a much-improved car.

recovered from the bad publicity of its early days. Between 1969 and 1981 only some 471,000 were produced – the equivalent of two years' production had the original forecast been realised. A trendsetter it may have been, but the 1100/1300 range, launched almost a decade earlier, still managed to outsell it by three or four to one.

BLMC's early plans to reorganise the Austin-Morris dealerships were put in the hands of Filmer Paradise, a flamboyant, cigar-smoking American, who was appointed by Stokes as Austin-Morris director of sales in November 1968. Although 1969, the year of the Maxi's launch, saw him planning a drastic reduction in the number of retail outlets, he assured *Motor*, "We're not about to make gifts to our competitors of capable merchandisers of automobiles." Behind the scenes he was making decisions that would result in exactly that.

"One ex-BLMC director recalled, "I personally heard him declare, 'We don't want the rats and mice of the industry representing us. If the bastards can't sell 150 cars a year, cancel their franchises right now. Let them fold up their tents and disappear into the night.' So he sent his minions out to get rid of all the small local dealers. Almost overnight there was

this massive blood-letting of small dealers. The very people who had fostered great marque loyalty in their own communities were suddenly told their services were no longer required. These people were also the pillars of their local communities throughout the country and, after being so badly treated, were naturally declaring at their local pub or golf club that they had thrown in the towel with British Leyland, that they had had enough of all the crap cars they were sending them anyway and had now signed up with Datsun or some other foreign producer. Having been axed overnight by Filmer Paradise, instead of 'folding up their tents and disappearing into the night' these ex-Austin and Morris stalwarts were now extolling the virtues of Datsun or Renault. Our market share plummeted. I saw all that and shed tears over it. It was destruction from within."

BLMC decided to retain separate Austin and Morris dealerships and proposed that these dealerships would in future market two distinct products. Austins, it was said, with their front-wheel-drive layout would be more technically advanced. A more conventionally engineered Morris range would be retained in order to compete with the products of General Motors and Ford. Although there had been thoughts of marketing that booted Maxi prototype as a Morris, the first and, as it turned out, the only Morris car that would conform to BLMC's new marketing strategy was the Morris Marina, the subject of the next chapter.

23

In reverse gear – the Austin Marina

"That's not a car. Anyone could make that."

ISSIGONIS

Yes, the *Austin* Marina. Although styled at Cowley, the Morris Marina of 1971 was 'engineered' at Longbridge and one little-known version was even sold in the USA as the Austin Marina.

The decision to build a rear-wheel-drive car that utilised Morris Minor mechanical parts is generally attributed to Harry Webster. As technical director after the Leyland merger, there is no doubt that Harry did 'father' the Marina but things were not quite as simple as that.

Way before the Leyland merger, concern was being expressed that BMC was not catering for the more conservative section of the market. There were both private and fleet buyers who were still

very wary about front-wheel-drive cars, seeing them as too complicated by half, as well as less reliable and more difficult and costly to service. It was being suggested that perhaps Ford's policy of producing less technically advanced products and offering what the public perceived as 'more car for the money', should be looked at more carefully.

We have already seen how, by 1967, Joe Edwards had brought a whole host of people to BMC/BMH from Ford. His aim was not only to come to grips with BMC's wayward finances but also to import something of Ford's discipline and expertise into product-planning by appointing the likes of Roy Haynes.

"I am not a stylist, although everybody identifies me as one," said Roy Haynes, "I am a highly trained

Confusingly, this is an Austin Marina, not a Morris Marina.

product strategist. Ford spent a fortune on me."

Haynes's work on the Cortina Mk II had brought him into the limelight. "I was heavily into cost cutting and if you were good at cost control you shone in the eyes of Ford management. They had no interest in producing anything that was not going to make money. During the development of the Cortina a tight rein was kept on costs. If we wanted something which was going to cost a bit more, more glass for example, we had to pay for it by chiselling money out of something else – using cheaper bumpers or metalised plastic tail lamps and all that sort of thing."

When Roy was taken on by Joe Edwards as director of styling for BMH, George Harriman did not want him to be in conflict with Dick Burzi or Alec Issigonis at Longbridge. "So I was sent down to Pressed Steel at Cowley," said Roy, "to run things from there. Under Joe Edwards, Pressed Steel was probably the most efficient and well-organised company in the whole group and I think Joe's idea was to make the corporate headquarters of the BMH group at Cowley.

"I knew where Ford were going and was shocked to find that BMH had no answers. So, I began work on the BMH model strategy. It wasn't really my brief to do that because I was only responsible for the Austin-Morris division, but at that time they had 26 different body shells on the production line and I could see that we couldn't invest in all those without going broke. I produced a ten-year plan that

would have drastically reduced costs by having only five basic platforms."

"When I got to Cowley," said Vic Horner, "Roy already had his ten-year plan covering the whole range of vehicles. Stokes and Webster weren't on the scene then but when they did arrive Roy submitted it to them. It was a good plan and quite adventurous so perhaps no-one would bite the bullet on it. It was such a diverse company that had come together that they were difficult days with a lot of in-fighting. I went to a meeting with Harry Webster, Charlie Griffin and Stan Dews and they just seemed to be setting Roy up really and he couldn't take it. It was a shame because he had a lot of ability."

Roy aimed to simplify the A and B class cars (the Mini and 1100) by creating a Mini the same width as the 1100 and thereby using common mechanical parts, with the Mini retaining its small wheels and shorter wheelbase.

BMH had no C class car, except the Farina A60/Morris Oxford, in a class which accounted for 60 per cent of the world's motor cars, so Haynes's immediate priority was to plan a C class replacement. Thus began the programme, later designated as ADO 28, which came to fruition as the Marina, a car meant to fall between the Cortina and Escort in size.

"The quickest way to get a sub-Cortina car," said Haynes, "was to use rear-wheel-drive. There was a lobby for front-wheel drive but the Cofton Hackett engine plant wasn't ready so there was a shortage of fwd power units. Not only that, warranty costs on the fwd units were crippling the company. The rear-wheel-drive Marina was, if you like, a retrenching move."

Roy Haynes, the Cortina-Marina man, who was head-hunted from Ford by Joe Edwards, is seen here with both of his creations.

ADO 28. Haynes expected his fastback coupé (seen here as a full-size model) to appeal to the more youthful driver. Note the front grille design being proposed by Haynes. "I certainly wasn't responsible for that plank-like bit of metal they stuck across the grilles of some of the production versions," said Roy.

As Harris Mann remembered it: "Prior to the Leyland merger Roy had put up a good case that with front-wheel-drive and Hydrolastic suspension the costs went sky high. The 1100 was much more costly to produce than the equivalent Anglia or Escort. If we were to get the company into a profitable position we needed a car which was cost-

effective rather than technically advanced. BMC had been run by engineers who knew nothing about cost-effectiveness. Inventive engineers, certainly, but the profits were very small even though they were churning out great numbers of cars."

Haynes planned to make the ADO 28 coupé as different as possible from the saloon, expecting the

This Roy Haynes's full-size mock-up for the four-door ADO 28 Marina saloon, is badged as an Austin. Using the front doors of the two-door coupé on the four-door version saved £0.75 million. The money thus saved was spent on producing different rear ends for coupé and saloon. "It was Ford thinking really," said Roy.

fastback to appeal to the under 35s and the saloon to the family man. "The Marina was the first car ever," said Roy, "where the front doors of the two door car were also used on the four door version. The £0.75 million we saved on tooling was spent on the completely different sheet metal for the rear of the cars. It was Ford thinking, really. The success of Ford was based on cost control. The 'body in white' weight target of the Mk II Cortina was 480lb. Pressed Steel had never made a body down to that weight but they responded magnificently and under the direction of Harry Barber produced a Marina body that was lighter still. It was the lightest, cheapest body that they ever produced."

Norman Biggs recalled starting on the Marina clay models at the beginning of 1968. "Roy Haynes and Harris Mann did most of the exterior styling and Vic Hammond the interior. There was a lot of night working because I think Roy was rather keen to make his presence felt as director of styling."

Roy Haynes was also advocating what he called his Condor programme: the use of the basic ADO 28 floorpan, stretched in length and width, to produce MG and Jaguar versions. "The Condor had a wider track and different power units and styling but it was based on the Marina," said Roy. "We built a clay model of one Condor which was a Jaguar. When the Leyland merger came the only thing I could do was to take the Condor programme to the product committee of Austin-Morris and present it to them. They were aghast that we had even thought about it. It went beyond the bounds of their

Haynes's ADO 68 Condor proposal was for a well-styled four-seat sports coupé. It was based on an ADO 28 floorpan which had been stretched in length and width but clothed in different sheet metal and fitted with different running gear to produce either MG or Jaguar versions. "We could have had an MG to match the Toyota Celica," said Roy, "and a Jaguar to match the Datsun 240Z – easy meat and lovely money."

thinking. They didn't really know what to do with their programme on a corporate basis.

"I asked Syd Enever, the chief engineer of MG, if he could make an MG out of it. 'Sure,' he replied, 'All I would want are two brackets on the underpan for a Panhard rod to stabilise the rear axle. Apart from that, we'll modify the front spring rates and all the rest of it, but we can build it all right.' So I styled two cars, an MG and a Jaguar, and just as I was doing that we merged with Leyland. When Stokes came on board he criticised me bitterly. Joe Edwards phoned me one day and said, 'I'm bringing Donald Stokes down and I want you to run through your plans with him.' Joe, of course, had handed in his resignation almost as soon as the merger took place. Stokes didn't really turn my plan down, he just ignored it. He was a fairly pompous sort of individual and came into the studio with all his hirelings behind him and when he came up to this car and asked what it was, I said, 'It is a Jaguar, sir. Well, actually it is ADO 28.' He said, 'What?' I explained, 'This car has got an ADO 28 floorpan and screen. It is using ADO 28 inner door panels and all I have done is to hang on some new sheet metal.' From the basic Marina I had got the guys really going and we were getting into Jaguars, Triumphs and Rovers. The hidden cost of floorpans is enormous. Cutting their numbers down and using common bulkheads would have saved millions. It was an exciting period for me and it was a tragedy that we never carried on with it. The arrival on the scene of the Leyland people was just devastating."

Norman Biggs did not think the Leyland management understood Roy Haynes's plan. "It was on the wall of Roy's office at Cowley along with the plans for facelifts and replacements. I don't believe Stokes knew what he was looking at. At Ford everyone would want to know the forward plans for at least that long but I don't believe that Austin-Morris or Standard-Triumph had ever done that before."

Returning to the Marina, Roy Haynes recalled that when Harry Webster arrived as the new director of engineering he proposed restyling the Morris Minor and using Morris Minor parts and also instructed Michelotti to build a car on a Morris Minor platform.

"Haynes was hopping mad that Webster had brought in Michelotti." said Vic Hammond. "When I went round to his house one Sunday morning he had a full-size print of Michelotti's Marina on the floor of his lounge and he was stamping all over it – hopping mad he was!"

Hammond light-heartedly described an August 1968 viewing of the clay models for the Marina: "There was George Turnbull, Harry Webster and

Harry Webster was championing this Michelotti proposal for the Marina but the main board chose that of Roy Haynes.

about a hundred others. Haynes had designed the car and all this mob had come to approve it. Unknown to us Harry Webster had got his mate Michelotti to do one as well and there was also one from Farina. Farina's looked like a bloody goldfish bowl and Michelotti's was all covered in junk."

Harry Webster's version of the same episode exposes something of the tensions and diametrically opposed opinions of the day. "There were to be three models. One by Farina, one by Michelotti and supposedly one by Haynes. Stokes wanted them all to the same specification and colour. Michelotti stuck to that but Haynes did a prototype style really tarted up and the main board came from London and chose Haynes's. I thought Michelotti's was best

but the main board voted for Haynes. Farina's was fantastic but too heavy and too costly to produce – so much glass and the panel work was complicated."

Roy Haynes chuckled. "Yes, I think we had half of British Leyland there. We won because our package was better, giving more room for people and luggage. Farina's would have been too expensive to make. It was only after Webster arrived that any animosity developed over which mechanical parts to use for the Marina. Syd Enever asked me if I realised that they were going to spend £1.9 million retooling the Triumph gearbox for it. When I went, 'Wow', he said, 'They must be out of their minds.' He put the drawings of the Triumph box on my table and said, 'Look at the distance between those

It was generally agreed that this somewhat sleeker offering from Farina would have been too expensive to produce.

two shafts and the size of the bearings. You can't put the horsepower into that box that you can put into the B-Series. If we spent three quarters of a million putting synchromesh on the B-Series first gear then that box would never cause anybody any trouble.' Harry Webster wouldn't listen. The Marina could have sold a lot better if it had been engineered better. The front suspension was a mess and we were in trouble with the Triumph gearbox from the word go with horrendous reports in *Which?* magazine.

"In my view it was the Leyland merger which destroyed the British Motor Corporation. It was criminal. They began selling off parts of the company to finance what was in effect a bottomless bucket, rather than cash in on our strengths and formulate an integrated model strategy. With all the BMH and Leyland outlets throughout the world we had a great marketing opportunity and could have had Ford by the short and curlies. Toyota, Datsun and Honda, built their future on the US market. If Leyland had taken what I was offering we could have had an MG to match the Toyota Celica and a Jaguar to match the Datsun 240Z – easy meat and lovely money."

According to Andy Duthie, "The basis of Roy's plan was good but perhaps he was too headstrong and volatile. Engineering was still seen as the leader of design, not styling, and Roy was trying to break that mould. We thought 'great' but then we got into the Leyland thing which was a crying shame. Roy had just had this kingdom handed to him and could see it under threat from Webster."

As Vic Hammond remembered it: "About a month after the viewing of ADO 28 Roy called us all together to say he was leaving. He had had an up-and-downer with Webster."

It pained Roy Haynes to look back on his decision to leave BLMC. "It meant relinquishing my lifetime's ambition to see a British automotive company develop into an aggressive market leader worldwide. But there was no point in staying. My philosophy was totally at odds with Webster and Stokes. In one newspaper feature Stokes said he had disagreed with me because I wanted to have too much standardisation – one bodyshell for the whole of British Leyland – and then make it into an Austin, Morris, Jaguar or Rover. This was simply not so. My plan was to sink the hidden engineering costs over about four or five different model ranges. My policy would not have reduced the 'brand identity' of the individual cars – just the opposite. It increased the possibility of developing brand identity by reducing investment in hidden areas of manufacturing. It would undoubtedly have led to redeployment of labour and I think that was the real crunch at the time. But as we have seen, there was no escaping it in the end."

Alan Webb at Longbridge saw the coming of the Marina from a different angle. Just prior to the official takeover by Leyland he was taken out of C-Cell. "I finished up in an office already occupied by Jack Daniels. There was a lot of politics involved at the start of BLMC and I think I was put up there so that Charlie Griffin could say to Stokes that he already had someone working on a conventionally driven car. Stokes wasn't enamoured of fwd and Hydrolastic suspension. He thought it too costly. I was simply told to do a medium sized, conventionally suspended rwd vehicle. Then one Friday Charlie Griffin asked Eric Bailey and me for a rush job. We went in on the Sunday morning and literally took my quarter scale as it was, the track, the wheelbase, the engine, everything that was relevant to the chassis, and Eric superimposed on top of that some seat positions, steering wheel position and so on. Then Eric did an outline to represent the body shape and on Monday that was sent to Farina. In my opinion that was the start of the Marina from the Longbridge end. After that I left Jack Daniel's office and went down into the main design office and, with about half a dozen senior layout people, started putting down a layout for the Marina. We never did do a full-size layout as we did with ADO16. It was all done on separate drawing boards, front suspension on one piece of paper and the rear on another."

When the cells were disbanded after the formation of British Leyland, Ron Nicholls became the chief development engineer for BLMC, with the Marina as his first project. "I had great difficulty in dropping my allegiance to Issigonis and front-wheel-drive," remarked Ron. "The Marina came about because Harry Webster and his product planners looked at the Morris Minor and said, 'this is a great car, highly successful and has brought in a lot of money. Let's do it again.' Other than that, anything connected with Alec Issigonis was frowned on. That was conveyed to me very forcibly. Harry Webster had me in his office and made it obvious that if I continued the way that I was going – he didn't explain it – but said he would fire me. It almost got to the point of him being hysterical if the name Issigonis was mentioned. There was I, trying to promote the continued development of front-wheel-drive cars, so all he could hear was my championing of Sir Alec's cars. I hadn't anything else to talk about. That's what I'd been working on, but he didn't like it. That he came very close to firing me there is no question."

"The idea," said Ray Bates, "was that there were two market sectors to attack, one with advanced technology and front-wheel-drive cars, the other with cheaper Ford-like rear-wheel-drive cars. With hindsight the Marina was definitely going backwards but it was conceived with thoughts of taking on Ford. It was also designed to be head on with the Vauxhall Viva at Viva prices and had it been held to that it probably would have been very successful. As a 1300 it was not a bad package, but it didn't have the suspension or tyres for the performance of the 1800 engine and ended up over-priced."

As Charles Griffin saw it: "When Stokes and Webster arrived I was director of engineering and Webster came as the technical director. They were days of confusion really because the planning committee was largely Leyland people and they supported whatever Stokes wanted. I remember very distinctly Harry Webster saying how the Morris Minor design with its torsion bar suspension was still modern, so why didn't we update it a bit. But we would never have produced the Marina."

Fred Coultas had a similar tale to tell. "We had entered a period where there was a lack of direction. It is easy to blame all sorts of things but it was a strange time when, as engineers, we weren't really sure what we were supposed to be doing. None of the products I was involved in was I ashamed of in any way. For instance it was my team which did the Marina chassis. Nobody in their right mind would have used lever-arm shock absorbers or those Morris Minor trunnions but it was an evolution of the Morris Minor and we were given that as one of the constraints. We had got to make it work. It took us seven or eight years to get rid of those lever-arm shocks. No engineer would have decided to go that route, but we had to."

"I look at the Marina," said Roy Haynes, "and think we were absolutely bang on target with that package size, but it was spoilt by its engineering. It was also less successful than it might have been because they let the reins go and the costs went down the tube."

The Marina did not impress Stan Johnson, a senior Longbridge engine designer. "The Leyland men had arrived with a very aristocratic approach but even by 1971 we realised they weren't up to much. The Marina, for example, was going backwards."

Dave Smith recalled the prototype Marina being in the next shop and the then deposed Issigonis asking him to take him in to see it. "He was quite shy like that but he just wanted somebody to go in with him. When he saw the Minor's trunnions he said. 'Mmm. Dear boy, we stopped using those

because they were no good and now they have put them back on. Mmm.'"

When Arthur Whitaker asked Sir Alec what he thought of the Marina Issigonis replied, "That's not a car. Anyone could make that." You can see, of course, what Issigonis was getting at. But it could also be argued that had Issigonis not promulgated the disastrous policy of 'Let the public test them' in relation to his otherwise ingenious and revolutionary front-wheel-drive cars, then anyone suggesting the retrenching moves that led to the Marina would have been laughed out of court. In the event it was the problems of BMC's early front-wheel-drive cars that made simple cars like the Cortina and Marina seem such sensible propositions. By 1970, 'Vehicle in Warranty' costs were averaging £5 for every Mini, £12.50 for every 1100 and nearly £17 for every 1800. Perhaps Issigonis had more of a hand than he thought in the design of that Morris Marina.

At least Eric Lord did manage to head off one howler. "I was at a pre-launch presentation of the Marina when up came an image of the car on the moors somewhere with sheep grazing in the background. That was fine but the caption read, 'Beauty with brains behind it'. I said to a fellow director, 'They are pulling our legs aren't they? That's a bloody sheep in the background. Beauty with the sheep's brains behind it?' They had printed thousands of brochures with that on so I said, 'You'll have to bale those and cut out that sheep or we'll be the laughing stock of the industry.' They had to get Nuffield Press to work day and night to reprint all those catalogues."

Although never a knock-out, the Marina and its final version, the Ital, did manage to soldier on for some 12 years from 1971 until 1984 and despite stiff competition from the Cortina, Escort, Viva and Avenger, not to mention the ever increasing imports, it was British Leyland's best seller, over one million being sold in all.

The Ital was so-named because of its revamp by Ital Design. Although originally built at Cowley, Ital production took place at Longbridge from 1982 onwards in order to make room for the Maestro at Cowley. This meant that when Ital production ceased in 1984 the death knell for the Morris name was rung at Longbridge. Len Lord could not have planned it better. Had he still been in charge he would no doubt have been pilloried for allowing the Morris name to suffer such indignities but in any case, as we shall see later, it was the ghost of William Morris who would get the last laugh, the Austin name eventually suffering an equally ignominious death at Cowley.

The new Morris Marina, beauty with brains behind it.

Above: This first Marina brochure (reprinted without the sheep that originally stood behind the car) still claimed the car had "Beauty with brains behind it". Perhaps Issigonis would have gone along with the original brochure which gave the impression the car had been designed by a flock of sheep.

Below: The Marina was produced at Cowley from 1971 to 1980. It was powered by either the 1,300cc A-Series engine or the 1,800cc B-Series engine which was replaced by the 1,700cc OHC O-Series in 1978. In 1980, after a restyle by Ital Design, it became the Morris Ital seen here which had the option of a 2-litre O-Series engine. After a total production of 1.2 million Marinas and Itals, 1984 saw the demise of the Morris name. Ironically, the last Morris car was built at Longbridge.

24

Aggro and Diablo –
the Allegro and Princess

"Then Lord Stokes came and gave us the square wheel."

BARRY KELKIN

That quartic steering wheel certainly did not do the Allegro any favours. Those designing the Allegro, were of course, on a hiding to nothing. Only a very remarkable car could have come through with flying colours as a replacement for the Issigonis 1100/1300.

"The 1100 was still a high volume seller," said Barry Kelkin. "Something like 5,500 a week – phenomenal – but we'd been up to 8,000 a week so the figures were obviously dropping. Harry Webster asked Michelotti to do a facelift. After it arrived at Longbridge we got as far as discussing the tooling costs, which wouldn't have been that great, but eventually Harry said, 'I don't think we want to be associated with an old model. We ought to do a new one. The lads at Cowley have a few things in the melting pot so perhaps we'd better look at those.' That's when Harry chose the Allegro designed by Harris Mann. The 1100 could have easily been updated but it was obvious that Webster didn't want to perpetuate anything that Issigonis had produced. He thought the Allegro was the best thing since sliced bread. I remember him saying, 'It is a pretty little car.' I felt it hadn't enough character to sell in the same volume as the 1100 but I must admit I began to quite like it as it got nearer to production. It was reasonable to drive so I thought well, perhaps it will be all right."

Charles Griffin, speaking in 1990, admitted that the original 1100/1300 was a dreadful 'rot-box'. "The cavities produced by placing the subframe into confined spaces just filled up with mud. We'd already designed totally new subframes specially mounted to give less vibration and better sound insulation. They rode superbly and we had it all tooled for production when Stokes came and it was stopped. The 1100 was still holding about 13.6 per cent of the total market. On its own it was as good as the total production is now."

For a former Triumph man, Ray Bates was generous in his praise for Griffin's proposed 1100/1300 update. "When I arrived at Longbridge Charlie and his team had already designed a very refined version of the 1100/1300. It was brilliant. Unfortunately the cost accountants decided it was far too expensive to make and said we ought to design a cheaper version, the car which turned out to be the Allegro. The Allegro definitely began as a cost-cutting exercise but throwing out the subframes and mounting the Allegro's suspension directly to the body meant that all the work done to isolate road noise was thrown away."

"I very much wanted to use subframes when we installed the Hydragas suspension on the Allegro," said Alex Moulton. "It was a mistake to put it directly into the structure as happened with the Allegro, but that was the effect of the Triumph culture coming in."

Ron Nicholls said that Stokes and Webster wanted to drop Hydrolastic and Hydragas suspensions completely to try to save money. "There isn't any question of that. They wanted nothing remotely connected with Issigonis but Moulton won the fight to retain his suspension because of the contracts already made with Dunlop. Hydragas gave better ride and handling and more sophisticated damping than Hydrolastic. But costs were going up and up and so they took the subframes off. Compromising the design like that may well have been one of the reasons why it didn't sell. It made it much less refined."

This early Harris Mann rendering for ADO 67, the Allegro, was based on reskinning the Issigonis 1100 and looks as though it could have been quite a sleek car.

"Those who argued against the development of the 1100 with modified subframes," said Charles Griffin, "were saying that what the 1100 wanted was more space in front of the engine for a radiator, more space in the boot and elimination of the subframes to produce a larger car without any increase in weight. That was the argument for the Allegro. But they didn't take account of the fundamental problem of the inter-coupled type of suspension with high units of load going into the car's structure. Allegro wasn't a fair swap for the 1100 in my opinion."

Much of the 'blame' for the Allegro has fallen on the shoulders of Harris Mann but he quite reasonably pointed out that the Allegro was a mere caricature of his original concept. "We started the 1100 replacement at Pressed Steel, Cowley. I played around with a clay model, not an official programme to start with, but when the final package was created many of the good points of the 1100

This glassfibre model of the Allegro shows the lines as agreed for production. The car had already suffered from engineering decisions regarding the engine and heater. It was about to suffer still further. "That accepted model is completely different to the production car," said Harris Mann, "they did a lot of things at Cowley when they tooled it up. They put 'overcrown' on all the body panels and made the doors belly out instead of retaining a nice smooth line through the car."

were lost. I had designed a completely new car by simply reskinning the 1100 but new requirements kept coming through. They had spent so much money developing a heater for the Marina that we had to use that. It was a very deep heater indeed compared to what was in the 1100, so that began to change the whole package. Then they decided to use the Maxi engine, one of the tallest engines on the market, with its long stroke and OHC as well as SU carbs and air cleaners. Gradually the whole frontal aspect of the 1100 was completely destroyed and the original concept went by the board. Although the Allegro was meant to be an advance on the 1100 by providing more luggage space, better seats, better heating, more engine options, trying to offer that little bit more of everything, it wasn't anything like as successful. The improvements sounded good on paper but took away the original character."

"After the Leyland merger," said Barry Kelkin, "it became obvious that Harry Webster was determined to bring control of body-engineering back to Longbridge. We knew the days of the Pressed Steel styling studio were numbered. He would call them 'bloody Pressed Steel' and summoned people like Harry Barber and Ken Osbourne up from Cowley to give them the third degree. I worked for them, knew and respected them, so it was terribly embarrassing at times. Webster's sole purpose seemed to be to take the Pressed Steel people apart. I remember him telling me, 'We are having no more nonsense from that Pressed Steel gang down at Cowley. We'll break that lot up.'"

According to Harris Mann, "We were asked to move to Longbridge when the clay model of the Allegro had just been approved. That's when Roy Haynes had his almighty blow up with Harry Webster. He was told he had to go to Longbridge, so he pulled out."

As Vic Hammond saw it, "After Roy went, Webster said, 'Right you lot. If you want a job you go to Longbridge, otherwise you bugger off.' That is certainly was what was intimated, make no mistake."

Harris Mann described his own arrival at Longbridge as, "Unbelievable. It really was. Poor old Dick Burzi and Sid Goble had been told nothing. They were flabbergasted when we all trooped in. Burzi was naturally rather put out and retired soon after. I thought I had better make my peace with Issigonis but when I introduced myself to him he asked, 'Are you an engineer?' I said, 'No, I'm a designer.' He replied, 'Well designers are engineers.' I said, 'Well it's not the case where I came from.' He was obviously putting me in my place, telling me

not to get any fancy ideas. We really didn't have anything to say to each other after that. He just got on doing his own thing in a spare room."

Longbridge men were not happy when they realised just what sort of car was going to replace the 1100. "Imagine having given Issigonis the shove," said Fred Eysenck, "and then producing the Allegro – incredible. I can still hear Harry Webster's voice as he tried to make the case for that bloody silly quartic steering wheel."

Bernard Johnson joked, "We called it the poor man's power steering. The idea certainly didn't come from the engineers. We didn't like it because as you let the wheel feed back through your fingers it created a most uncomfortable effect but we could not persuade them to see sense."

Whoever first dubbed the car, 'the All-Aggro Allegro' was not far off the mark. As well as being expected to replace the class-leading 1100/1300 on its introduction in 1973, it was also chosen to act as the guinea pig for the introduction of the 'measured day' at Longbridge.

In 1970/71, 60 per cent of all industrial disputes at Longbridge had centred around the piecework method of payment. Production so lost was getting more serious year by year; 20,000 vehicles and 17,000 engines in 1968/69 rising to 40,000 vehicles and 90,000 engines by 1970/71.

"Some days there were three or four separate

The Allegro interior. "Then Lord Stokes came and gave us the square wheel."

strikes," said Ron Savage, industrial relations manager. "Measured daywork was meant to cut out the argy bargy: the men would get a fair wage and the management would get a fair day's work. Initially, of course, production plummeted. If we suffered a breakdown or a shortage of supplies, inevitable in a big company, the blokes would say, 'Well, there's nothing coming down the track and the silly buggers are going to pay us no matter what, so we'll just sit here and wait.' The foremen, by and large, were people who had little or no training in man management. They were good at their job, but not man managers. They were all mates. I mean, if Fred came from Stourbridge in the car of a chap who worked on the track, he wasn't likely to give him a bollocking, was he?"

Chief rate-fixer, Bill Chance, much preferred piecework. "When they changed over to day work an average bloke was earning £36 a week. They had

The 'All-aggro Allegro' got off to a bad start, being built at Longbridge in the troubled days caused by the introduction of measured daywork.

to offer them £47 to accept day work. If anybody had told me I could have played about with £11 a man a week, I could have doubled the output with piecework. We all know what happened over the next two or three years: output went down and down and they would have gone bankrupt if the government hadn't stepped in and bailed 'em out."

With the Allegro about to go into production, Paddy O'Reilly, who had just been promoted to superintendent status, was put in charge of building the Allegro bodies. "To cap it all I was told that I had to introduce measured daywork at the same time. On measured daywork you might have to do perhaps 30 particular tasks an hour. It was down on paper exactly what each man had to do. When the men got wise to that, if there was any deviation whatsoever from what was on that bit of paper they would stop work. The foreman would ask, 'Why the bloody hell have you stopped?' 'Ah, well, it says I've got to pick those pressings up from here but the labourer has dropped them over there; now that ain't what I'm supposed to do.' If a gang on the track under piecework found themselves a man short

through sickness they just worked that much harder and shared his money. On measured daywork they wouldn't even start work. 'We are a man short.' 'OK,' the foreman would say, 'Carry on and I'll get you a sickness relief man.' 'No. Our job description says we should have eight men. Get us the eight and we'll start.' It was a bloody nightmare. No use the foreman saying, 'Well carry on then and instead of doing 40 an hour only do 35 the first hour while I find someone,' because they would say, 'Who says we can manage 35 with seven men?' So the foreman had an argument on his hands before he could even go and get someone. I was dead against this measured day but I had to bring it in. In the finish, the Allegro build was held up as a shining light of how a job should be done on measured daywork but it nearly bloody killed me in the process.

Having seen this January 1970 sketch by Harris Mann, Donald Stokes decided he would like it developed as a new 1800. The mock-up below it was then developed from the sketch but was considered a little too dramatic, particularly at the front, so work began on its refinement.

"There was everything wrong with the Allegro to start with. They advertised it as the lead-free model but we used to put more lead into it than enough. It was a bad design. They said they couldn't make the roof in one panel but we made the Sheerline roof in one, we made the A30 roof in one and they could have done the Allegro too. We used to have to weld them, lead-load them and then clean it up – a big gang of blokes on unnecessary operations. The Allegro boot aperture was always too big and the boot lid was too small. You had to create a gap all the way round. I can drive behind Allegros today and tell you whether it was made on the night shift or day shift. The boot lid was set to the left by the day shift and to the right by the night shift. It was two years into Allegro build before Ray Butterworth made a device to clamp the wings in before welding them so that the boot fitted nicely."

Assembling Allegros in CAB 2, Barry Brecknell was also having problems. "We just couldn't tie the screen aperture down to a production tolerance. The screens would burst because they were too tight. Dozens of them. The men couldn't get them

RECORD 6 21 8 70 71

The proposed frontal treatments for the Austin and Morris versions of 'Diablo', or ADO 71, had got very near to the production versions by October 1971.

seated and sealed within their own work areas. They would eventually get 'em in but maybe ten stations up the track."

Trying to look at the Allegro's sales performance in as kindly a light as possible, Anders Clausager remarked that while the Allegro on its own did not compare with the 1100/1300 in terms of sales, if you add up the Marina and the Allegro sales you will get figures that are much closer to the 1100/1300 range. "Yes, it had taken two cars to produce those sales but having the two cars did give the advantage of being able to offer the customer two very different products in the marketplace. We must remember also, that from 1970 onwards there was a dramatic rise in imports (both European and Japanese) so all home market sales fell considerably."

All the more need of course, for the Allegro to have been better than it was but the next question was whether BLMC would make a better fist of ADO 71, their proposed replacement for the Issigonis 1800.

In overall charge of body engineering for 'Diablo', as the ADO 71 project was sometimes referred to in its development period, was former Rootes man, Tom Penny. "The ADO 71 Princess was the British Leyland car that I had most influence on but I didn't get all my own way because I wanted to make it into a five-door vehicle."

So did Harris Mann. "Stokes had seen one of my sketches and said he wanted it as a new 1800. The sketch was the basis for an initial car that didn't quite come off. It was a little bit too dramatic, too over-featured in a lot of ways, so we set about refining it.

"Replacing the 1800 was a little more straightforward than the work on the Allegro. Being a larger car, it could take the different engine options more easily. The fact that it had a larger heater than the old 1800 and a taller engine didn't seem to harm the project at all. I originally sketched it out as a five-door car but they turned it down in case it took sales away from the Maxi. It was a strange way of looking at things – hard to believe then and just as hard to believe now.

"We tried to produce an interior that was much less austere than Issi's 1800 and more in tune with competitive vehicles. I was a lot happier with the Princess than the Allegro. We were evolving something new, setting a different trend from everything else but, like everything that breaks the mould, people either love or hate it. They were frustrating times because there was never any money in the kitty. It was more and more a case of looking in the parts bin to make up the next model. For a while after its launch there was a waiting list for the 'wedge' but as time went on the reliability and quality was so poor that it was let down. I still like to think that it was an inspiration to other designers and helped to develop the spacious wedge shape of several family cars that followed it."

The high tail certainly gave the car a cavernous boot and, according to Sid Goble, "The new wedge shape fitted in well with all the new European and American regulations which we had to consider – sightlines and so on. Instead of roofs sloping down at the back they were tending to go up due to the influence of the regulations. A low bonnet gave you good sightlines at the front. You could have a higher tail, giving more luggage space, because you don't need a very low sightline at the back. My boss, Jim Puddephat, had been in packaging at Ford and had all the regulations at his fingertips."

Harris Mann's wedged-shaped 1800 replacement was launched in March 1975 as the 18–22 Series, with Austin, Morris and Wolseley variants. Leyland had thus abandoned their idea of producing two distinct Austin and Morris product ranges. Indeed, after a few months, all the 18–22 models were to be sold under the Princess badge, a decision which saw the disappearance of one of the oldest names in motoring, a name put on the road by Herbert Austin, that of Wolseley.

At its launch, the 18–22 Series used either the four-cylinder 1,800cc B-Series engine or the six-cylinder 2,200cc E-Series engine. But adapting the B-Series engine to conform to existing American and proposed European emission regulations saw it lose some 25 per cent of its power and 10 per cent of its torque. To solve the problem, new 1.7 and 2-litre OHC O-Series engines replaced the 1800 B-Series in the updated Princess 2 of 1978.

"We were looking for a bigger engine than the

The new 18–22 Series was launched in Austin, Morris and Wolseley versions in the spring of 1975 but, three months later, in a move that hardly inspired confidence in the buying public, it was decided to sell all variants under a Princess badge. When Aubrey Edwards in the Austin publicity department was told of that decision he could not believe it. "I'm not sure if they realised that in doing so they had consigned Wolseley, one of the greatest names in British motoring history, to the scrap heap."

1800," said John Barnett, then head of engine development at Longbridge. "We couldn't get more than 1,748cc out of the four-cylinder E-Series. We knew the B-Series would stretch to 2 litres, having already built experimental B-Series engines of that capacity. So it was agreed we would do a redesign which became the single OHC O-Series. It was done in 1.7 and 2 litre forms, single and twin carb, in-line and transverse – all things to all men. In effect we made a gradual transformation of the push-rod B-Series into a belt-driven single OHC with an alloy head, the O-Series.

Barrie Parkes, who later took over from John Barnett added, "Although we wanted a high-performance engine we were limited in what we could do. We had to use basically the same crank because we had to retain the existing 1800 transmission for the transverse installation. So the engine was built up around the 1800 crank which was adapted at the front to take the camshaft pulley and oil pump drive. We were stuck with a B-Series type layout of siamesed bores giving a lot of cooling and distortion problems. We were getting cracking of the walls of the crankcase on the prototype so we had to stiffen the crankcase around the main bearing housing. To cure instability of the crank in its housings we

increased the counterweights of the 'B' crank. In production the O-Series engine barely changed until we developed it into the twin OHC M-Series that went into the Rover 800."

Ron Nicholls thought the O-Series always struggled to be a good engine. "Under Appleby and Bareham the 'A' and 'B' were tremendous engines. They were as good as anything in Europe. They gave superb fuel consumption figures. But poor old British Leyland was always short of money to do a new engine. It was always a development of what we already had and I think that was the main problem with the O-Series."

As for the styling of the Princess and Allegro, if Farina had had his way there would have been very different replacements for BMC's 1800 and 1100 and perhaps even the Mini. At the 1967 Turin show Farina unveiled a stunning aerodynamic saloon based on the BMC 1800's mechanical parts. He also

produced a proposal for the 1100 along similar lines. The 1,800cc version ended up at Longbridge as a running prototype which was given the nickname of 'Yellow Peril'.

"With hindsight," said Harris Mann, "the Farina Aerodynamica was probably the path to have taken. It was trundled out on quite a few occasions but somehow or other it was never developed. Looking at the pictures now it was certainly a nice car which makes it difficult to say why that route was never taken. Of course, Webster was a great fan of Michelotti and if there was anyone to be favoured as far as Harry Webster was concerned it was Michelotti rather than Farina."

Ray Bates's comments reinforce that idea. "With hindsight I can see that we had the technology to have made a killing by concentrating on front-wheel-drive cars only. Especially if we had gone forward with the Aerodynamica type of styling.

Farina's BMC 1800 Aerodynamica of 1967. Building both 1800 and 1100 versions of Aerodynamica could have put BMC/BLMC way ahead in both styling and technology and would surely have cost no more in design and development costs than the Marina, Allegro and Princess.

This 1800 Aerodynamica was broken up but the BMC 1100 Berlina Aerodynamica still sits in the Pininfarina design and research centre near Turin.

Harris Mann had initially envisaged ADO 71 as a five-door car but was told it might take sales away from the Maxi. It was only when the Princess was completely reworked to produce the hatchbacked Austin Ambassador of 1982/84 that the load-carrying capabilities of the design were fully developed. Allowing Harris Mann and Tom Penny to have their way in the first place would have saved a lot of money in the long run, and would almost certainly have improved sales.

Perhaps if Aerodynamica had come from Michelotti it would have gone forward."

Charles Griffin pointed out that when Aerodynamica came along in 1967. "The place was actually falling down around our ears so there simply wasn't the money. Of course, Roy Haynes was in charge of styling then and he didn't seem very keen on it."

"Yes, I was asked to deliberate on it," said Roy, "and suggested it might be something way down the road but that it wasn't an answer to our immediate problems."

Ron Nicholls remembered the motorised version of Aerodynamica. "I think it could have been a very nice car but politics were pulling the company in all directions. We would have had to change the styling a little because there were areas that would have been impossible to press. You could never productionise Farina's stuff without making lots of changes."

It would certainly seem that Farina's proposals had a great deal of promise. BMC had already solved most of the initial problems inherent in the front-wheel-drive configuration. All the 1800 lacked was style, all the 1100 required was further refinement to the subframes and suspension, along with extra luggage carrying capacity. The Aerodynamica's styling was in keeping with these needs.

Was the problem really lack of funds? The money was found to produce the Marina, Allegro and Diablo so why not 1100 and 1800 Aerodynamicas instead? It seems that the perceived need to attack Ford with the Marina, a project very dear to the heart of the then chief stylist, Roy Haynes, was the main reason. But if Michelotti had been the stylist of the 1100/1800 Aerodynamicas, might not Harry Webster have been tempted to choose that route instead of plumping for the Allegro and Diablo?

"The logical thing," said Alex Moulton, "would have been to use new 1100 subframes equipped with Hydragas and with a new Pininfarina body on it – anything other than what happened with the Allegro. But we did the best we could within the constraints imposed."

Could not 1,100/1,300cc and 1,800cc versions of Aerodynamica have put BLMC way ahead in both technology and styling, kept the 1100/1300 at the top of the charts, and given the 1800 concept a chance to really shine? We shall never know. What we do know is that by the time the 18–22 Series was launched in March 1975, BLMC had suffered financial collapse. A month or two later it ceased to exist and was nationalised and renamed British Leyland.

25

Interlude of hope and glory – the Mini-Metro

"They couldn't make up their minds whether they wanted a big small car or a small big car."

VIC HAMMOND

The Metro's tortuous development period eventually gave birth to a worthy car, albeit one that side-stepped the original intention of replacing the Mini. In 40 years of the Mini, only Issigonis ever

The bodyshell of this 9X prototype was built in Body Experimental by Ron Dovey. After the Leyland takeover Issigonis kept the car at his own home so that it could not be scrapped and it is now at the Heritage Centre at Gaydon. The numberplate shown was taken off Sir Alec's Maxi to add realism to the photograph.

managed to hatch a proposal that might have upstaged and replaced it.

"Stokes said the cupboard was bare when he arrived," claimed Rodney Bull, an engineer who worked with Issigonis in the latter's final years at Longbridge, "but 9X was already sitting there, a completely new Mini with a completely new power unit. It still needed much development but had originally been timed to appear at the 1971 motor show. There were even plans for a four-door, six-

cylinder version that could have replaced the 1100/1300 range."

In true Issigonis style, a mere update of the existing Mini had not crossed his mind. If he was to devise the ultimate small car package he required a purpose-built engine and transmission along with a new body. The power unit he fathered for 9X was much slimmer than the A-Series, taking up only 15 per cent of the vehicle's length, whereas the Mini's power unit took 25 per cent. Although slightly shorter than the Mini, 9X provided considerably more legroom for its occupants.

"Don't forget we are talking of some 13 years before the arrival of Metro," said Fred Eysenck, who worked on the design of the 9X engine in 1967. "It was a lightweight engine with a belt-driven single overhead camshaft, still with an in-sump gearbox but we had got rid of the idler gear, the drive from the crankshaft primary gear being directly on to the layshaft. The power unit was 140lb lighter than the A-Series unit and produced something like 57bhp per litre with a single carb, with potential for more."

"The single OHC 9X engines were built in four-cylinder versions of 847cc and 1,000cc and six-cylinder versions of 1,270cc and 1,500cc," recalled John Barnett. "They had a compression ratio of 10:1 and had an aluminium cylinder head and transmission case but a cast iron block. Issigonis saw the small six-cylinder engines as a means of achieving even further refinement."

The great man himself showing the 9X to be much roomier than the Mini. Note the Mini-like door bins, door catch release and sliding windows.

How the 1100/1300 replacement would have looked if based on the 9X. This extended version of the 9X could have used the 1,270cc or 1,500cc six-cylinder versions of the 9X engine.

John Sheppard, who engineered the 9X bodyshell, attributed the outside shape to Fred Boubier and Sid Goble but this mock-up of their design was produced by Farina.

John Sheppard engineered the body shell. "It was a wonderful little car. Fred Boubier and Sid Goble put up all the outside shapes. To simplify construction we eliminated the subframes and produced a car with 40 per cent less parts than the Mini. We also went for more orthodox suspension: MacPherson strut front suspension and a trailing arm and torsion bars at the rear. It was about 2½in wider than the Mini but 260lb lighter."

"By this time, Alec Issigonis and Alex Moulton were getting to the end of their working relationship," said Ron Nicholls. "They were barely being civil to each other but I think it was Issi who did the falling out. He decided that the costs of the Moulton suspensions were too high and sought a cheaper alternative. By 9X it had got through to Issi that costs did matter. The 9X engine was of rather complicated construction and probably one step ahead of the existing technology, so there might have been problems in building it under production conditions."

As Ray Bates saw it. "We were losing so much money a week we had no hope of doing 9X. A spanking new engine? No chance. We had to look at what we already had and how to improve it. That was the story of our lives. There was never any money to do anything at British Leyland."

"After Leyland took over," said Dennis Harold, "George Turnbull saw the 9X prototype, and after a drive in it, he said he thought it was absolutely marvellous and wanted to know why he hadn't been told about it. But when they told him it was an Issigonis project he said, 'Ah yes. Well it's a nice little vehicle', and just walked away."

Dave Smith, who worked on the 9X engines, experienced Issigonis's own reaction to the sidelin-ing of the 9X project. "I asked Sir Alec if he thought it was personalities and politics that were holding 9X back and he said, 'Oh no, dear boy, no, no, no.' But a few weeks later he said, 'Dear boy, you were right.' I'm afraid Harry Webster had won the day."

Joe Edwards was much more outspoken: "It was Donald (Stokes) that turned down 9X, Alec's proposed new Mini. He said it was rubbish but he didn't bloody well know. He was only a truck sales-man."

It is understandable that Longbridge men should want to blame 'that bloody crew from Triumph' for every possible ill that ensued after the Leyland merger. Politics did undoubtedly play its part in the 9X saga as well as in the sidelining of Issigonis, but it was not quite as simple as a Webster/Stokes alliance against Issigonis. The Mini itself was still selling well and it could justifiably be argued that there was a much greater need to update the mid-range cars. Hence the decision to produce the Marina, Allegro and the 18–22 Series before deciding what to do about the Mini. According to Vic Hammond, "It wasn't until about 1972 that Stokes's lot decided we needed a new Mini but they couldn't make up their minds whether they wanted a big small car or a small big car."

That uncertainty was confirmed by Doug Adams. "Webster said to me one day, 'I want you to put two inches into a Mini.' I'd got back to the shop but hadn't begun work on it when he came back to me and said, 'I think we'll have it four inches wider.' The next day he added, 'I think we'll go the whole hog and have it six inches wider.' So we put six inches into a Mini Clubman and used that car for years around the works."

A clay model of one of many variations on the ADO 74 'Super-Mini' theme of 1972/74. In the background are proposals for ADO 73, the Marina II of 1975.

Ray Bates also worked on wider-bodied, more barrel-shaped Minis. "New outer skin panels and curved side glasses provided a more roomy interior but the work was always low-key because we were being told that the Mini would never manage to comply with the changing safety regulations."

A project known as ADO 74 began in the spring of 1972 with the styling department producing several full-size clay models. By then the day of the supermini had already dawned so all proposed dimensions were being compared with those of the Renault 5, Datsun Cherry and Fiat 127. As a result, ADO 74 was nearly 18 inches longer than the Mini. Its proposed SOHC 1,100/1,300cc transverse engine and five-speed front-wheel-drive transmission had the cylinder block steeply inclined to the rear of the vehicle to improve packaging. Suspension was by

This ADO 16 bodyshell was 'cut and shut' to produce a 'simulator' using the ADO 74 underpan and running gear.

MacPherson strut at the front with trailing arms and coil springs to the rear.

An ADO 16 (1100/1300) bodyshell, shortened by 3½in, was mated with the proposed ADO 74 understructure to produce a prototype that was used as a simulator to evaluate the ride and handling of the new suspension. The project was abandoned in 1974 when Harry Webster left Longbridge just prior to the financial collapse of BLMC.

In the years following the Leyland takeover, Donald Stokes simply did not manage to deliver what was expected of him. His enterprising sale of Leyland buses to Cuba in the mid-1960s had seen him caricatured as a swashbuckling cavalier of a super-salesman, just the type to inspire a dramatic recovery in the motor industry. Sadly it wasn't to be. In the political and industrial climate then prevailing, the cards were certainly stacked against Stokes making any great headway but there are many who thought he was simply not up to the job.

According to Eric Lord, "When Leyland appeared we all got swept up into different heaps and a disaster unfolded; countless idiots arrived, professional windbags. Centralisation became the order of the day with Stokes trying to break down the loyalty to individual marques, saying we belonged to Leyland now, but that was the equivalent of trying to force Austin, Morris and Wolseley men to change their faith."

Austin men were certainly far from happy to see the Austin name being purged from the Longbridge scene. The massive illuminated Austin sign at the end of the car assembly buildings was assigned letter by letter to skips, as was the fine 'Austin of England' sign and the 'Flying As' that adorned the side of CAB 1. The pride that such emblems had engendered in Austin men must surely have been dented when they saw them removed.

"Under Harriman," said Howard Dancox of East Works R&D department, "there had been far too little in the way of financial controls but under Leyland the pendulum swung too far in the opposite direction. It wasn't long before you almost needed a sanction committee to blow your nose. Most of those in financial control were young graduates. You had to justify everything to snotty-nosed little kids who hadn't a clue."

Eric Holbeche also took badly to the ever-increasing bureaucracy under Leyland. "A rash of new office blocks appeared all over the place, with all new furniture, carpeting, and staff. You then found yourself answering to people who had never been inside a bloody factory in their life. They just worked in these office blocks making decisions. Stokes had a lot to answer for."

When Donald Stokes became Lord Stokes in 1969, Filmer Paradise, then just about to start axing the small dealerships, declared that everyone realised Stokes to be, "One of the great ones."

Everyone?

Not Joe Edwards, who recalled, "A lot of people at Longbridge hated Stokes's guts and I put him wise about that. The whole thing was a crime. He hadn't got a clue."

Not Bill Chance. "Stokes was about as good to Longbridge as that kettle," he said, pointing to a kettle on his hearth. "If they made him a lord for what he did they should have crowned me King for what I had to put up with as a rate-fixer."

Donald Stokes himself poured fuel on such fires by perhaps being a little too honest, admitting to people like Ted Price, MD of Fisher & Ludlow, that he was neither a production man nor an engineer. "Stokes hadn't got a clue," said Price, "As I took him round the factory he admitted he knew nothing about it."

By 1974, BLMC was in such financial straits that the government asked the chairman of the National Enterprise Board, Lord Ryder, to investigate the situation. The ensuing Ryder Report led to the nationalisation of the company as British Leyland Ltd, with Stokes suffering a similar fate to Harriman, being virtually 'kicked upstairs' as non-executive president. Ryder also proposed that vast sums of money be made available to help make BL competitive again.

According to Mike Sheehan, "Ryder proposed a joint management council, which first met in 1975, with almost equal numbers of trade unionists and managers running the place. Quite frankly it was disastrous. However good these men were, and they were not all Red Robbos, (a reference to Derek Robinson, the militant convenor of shop stewards at Longbridge) even union officials would agree that they were not in a position to look at the managerial problems and give joint responses. Even when we did agree on an expansion plan or rationalisation plan, the unions didn't have anything like the authority to see them through. To put it bluntly, no-one knew how to handle the industry. It was totally and utterly out of control. Some advances had been made with standard daywork but there was no real concept of 'just-in-time delivery' or 'built-in quality' Thoughts of making motor cars to compete with Japanese or Continental models were a million miles away."

In the immediate post-Ryder days British Leyland

The only 'Austin of England' badge to be seen in this photograph, taken outside CAB 1 at Longbridge in 1981, is on the boot of the author's Austin A35. The fastenings of the original sign, taken down in the Stokes era, can still be seen on the wall above the top windows. (The original 'Austin of England' script is clearly seen in the photograph of the viewing platform for the Golden Jubilee celebrations in Chapter 16.)

became something of a joke. On radio and television, in the papers and the local pub, 'Leyland-bashing' became a national pastime. Industrial disputes became even more commonplace, 'build-quality' of the cars suffered considerably and customers took their business elsewhere, mainly to Japanese and other imports. As North Sea oil came on stream from 1975 onwards the situation was exacerbated by a strong pound making it even more difficult to export.

By late 1977 it was clear that Ryder's objectives

were not achievable. The Stokes era had failed to produce a range of cars that could take on the competition and had also failed to sort out the hotchpotch of inefficient plants. Stokes, it seems, was just too nice a guy to partake in the necessary shedding of labour; a much 'tougher cookie' was required. Hence the appointment of Michael Edwardes.

Prior to his appointment, he had watched with both fascination and horror as the Leyland saga unfolded: "I think the Leyland merger was a big mistake. Wilson and Benn were on a 'bigger the better' sort of tack. Looking on as an outsider at the time, I was not in favour of that. Merging the whole of British Leyland was a very dodgy thing to do. If you do a thing like that you have got to be prepared to use the axe. They had failed to do that."

When Edwardes took over in late 1977, he would have much preferred to have tackled an Allegro/Marina replacement as his initial priority but development of project ADO 88, the car that would

The massive illuminated Austin sign at the Longbridge works. The pride that such emblems must have engendered in Austin men must surely have been dented when they saw them removed by British Leyland.

After Harry Webster left Longbridge in 1974, the tight packaging requirements for ADO 88 were set by Charles Griffin, who was said to expect his cars to be bigger inside than outside!

eventually become the Metro, was too far down the road for there to be any hope of doing so. Fully engineered prototypes were already being put through their paces in mid 1977 and the plans for a factory to build it were already drawn up.

According to Harris Mann, "It was when Charlie Griffin took over from Webster in 1974 that we got cracking on ADO 88, an Issigonis type of package

that at one stage was a very plain Fiat Panda-like car."

"The way ahead seemed to become clearer under Charles Griffin," said Ray Bates. "He really began to drive ADO 88 forward." Charles Griffin himself recalled ADO 88 as his final project as director of advanced engineering. "Yes, I was very heavy handed with the styling chaps on that. I wanted the biggest interior in the smallest exterior possible."

Leyland had acquired Rover in 1967 and in 1975,

The tight packaging requirements saw ADO 88 develop at one stage into a very boxy, Fiat Panda-like car.

when Rover stylist David Bache was put in overall charge of styling for 'Leyland Cars', he gave the ADO 88 package to Farina to see what he could make of it. Farina's offering was deemed too fussy and too costly to produce. Harris Mann was then asked to further develop his own schemes and a revised model was agreed upon in early 1976. A very large spanner was thrown in the works in 1977 when, at several 'clinics', only a few participants picked the finally agreed ADO 88 model as their first choice when comparing it with competitors' cars such as the Fiat 127 or Ford Fiesta.

"They thought ADO 88 was a good package," said Harris Mann, "but felt it was too austere and slab-sided with too upright a rear end. It didn't have any curvature in the bodyside because it was restricted by engineering requirements. We couldn't change Charlie's package. After the clinics we were asked to try and address the criticisms by putting more shape into it."

Rex Fleming (ex Rootes) then ran Longbridge styling. "The brief was to put a bit more section into ADO 88, a bit more width. The roof, the windscreen, scuttle and everything remained the same but David Bache negotiated a little bit of give on the dimensions."

"The project became designated LC 8 (LC standing for Leyland Cars) just about the time I retired in

By 1975, ADO 88 had already assumed a basic Metro-like character but after being panned at 'clinics' at a very late stage, it had to undergo urgent modifications before emerging as LC8 – the Metro as launched.

1978," said Charles Griffin. "As it turned out the Metro was the nearest you could get to a replacement for the 1100. If you get a tape measure out you will find it was an 1100. It had everything the 1100 had but was much lighter. I was already lobbying for that sort of motor car with John Barber before the collapse of Leyland. That poor Metro had to go through a traumatic gestation period. It certainly grew out of travail."

Although the restyled LC 8 retained the same space-efficient package fought for by Charles Griffin, including the Hydragas suspension that allowed a relatively roomy load area, almost every exterior body panel was altered to give slightly more width, a rounder look and more lively stance. The final model was approved by Ray Horrocks in 1977, just before the arrival of Michael Edwardes.

When Charles Griffin retired, Ray Bates became director of engineering for Austin-Morris. "So I picked up on LC 8. The vitality of Michael Edwardes had produced a new sense of purpose. We had been through the Leyland Cars bit with about eight different managing directors and at last we could see where we were going. It was a very rewarding experience. It was as if a cloud had been lifted. We could now identify with what was going on. It was a superb time. If the Metro didn't succeed we knew we would all be out of a job but I had the finest possible team of engineers: Ron Nicholls, Fred Coultas, Bernard Johnson, John Barnett, Barrie Parkes, and others. They all worked like idiots getting Metro fit for production. We would take the prototypes to Gaydon about ten at night,

knock hell out of them around the Warwickshire lanes and return to Gaydon about 1.30 in the morning. After a quick debrief, Harold Musgrove (then manufacturing director of Austin-Morris) would say, 'Right. We'll have a meeting in my office at eight in the morning.' Quite often the chaps worked through the night. Believe me, they played a blinder. There was a great spirit, a war-time spirit."

Bernard Johnson saw those days in much the same light but laughingly recalled, "It's a terrible story really. I mean we had built 24 ADO 88's before the decision to go to LC 8. So only two years before production we'd got these 24 cars that we weren't going to produce. I'd been establishing the new Gaydon proving facilities when they asked me to do the Metro. I went down to the workshops and said to the fellas, 'We'll do it as we did in the old days, build the cars, test them, and if they don't work we'll make them work and tell 'em what needs changing. We did that using the 24 ADO 88's. Then

An OHC A-Series engine built in 1975. A 970cc version gave 59bhp @ 6,750rpm (40bhp @ 5,100rpm) and 51lb/ft of torque @ 5,250rpm. (51lb/ft @ 2,600rpm). The 1,275cc OHC version gave 84bhp @ 6,750rpm (59bhp @ 5,300rpm) and 80ft/lb @ 4,500rpm (69lb/ft at 3,000rpm). The figures in brackets give output for the standard 998cc and 1,275cc A-Series engines. Although the OHC engines were of substantially improved performance it was decided to take the A-Plus OHV route.

we built six LC8 Metros and tested those in Germany, Finland and Canada."

John Barnett spoke of developing the Metro's engine. "We produced some overhead-cam versions of the A-Series in 1975 which were excellent engines with substantially improved performance. But the standard A-Series had the advantage of producing excellent torque at remarkably low rpm and was also very economical on fuel. It was still holding its own with anything on the market. It was always just good enough to make the case for replacing it very difficult, particularly when we were so short of money. There had been a great proliferation of A-Series engines: 848cc, 948cc, 970cc, 997cc, 998cc, 1,070cc, 1,098cc and 1,275cc. After exhaustive tests we decided we could cover all applications with the 998cc and 1,275cc versions. So we developed those into the 1-litre and 1.3-litre A-Plus engines for the Metro."

"In developing the A-Plus engine," said Barrie Parkes, "we raised the compression ratio, improved the induction manifolds, reduced the weight of the pistons and modified the con rods and valve gear. We filled in the centre panel above the centre main bearing and added ribbing to the block to improve the stiffness and reduce noise. We improved the combustion chamber slightly and significantly improved the efficiency of the exhaust system."

Although a great deal of the 'sense of purpose', spoken about by Ray Bates, was inspired from the top by Michael Edwardes, much of it, it seems, was instilled at shop floor level, eyeball to eyeball with the workers, by Harold Musgrove.

"From 1978 onwards he really started cracking the whip," said Harris Mann. "He was determined to have Metro spot on. He was quite a swine in some ways but he didn't half stir the place up. People had become very complacent, had totally ignored the threat from Japan, but he dynamited the place. He chased up everything on the prototypes. 'I don't like that. Get it redone.' If someone said, 'We can't redo it' it would be a case of, 'Get the bloody thing done.' Looking back, he really did a hell of a lot, but he was definitely a man to agree with. He bawled people out all the time but ensured that ADO 88 had an extraordinary amount of work carried out on it in a very short space of time to turn it into LC8."

Not everyone liked Musgrove's approach. "Musgrove was a nasty man," said one senior designer. "Getting the Metro into production he would say, 'I want that done by tomorrow morning.' You might start to question it and he'd say, 'You've got all night.' He would say, 'If you are not going to piss in the same pot you might as well bugger off.' He was horrible. He really was. He destroyed people. I was just thankful I wasn't working directly for him."

Although others talk of Musgrove in a similar vein, most Longbridge men appreciate what he achieved. "It was a necessary stance at the time," said Barry Kelkin. "Someone had to do the pedalling."

Sir Michael Edwardes, in agreeing with that point of view, recalled, "Yes, Harold Musgrove had pretty heavy boots but he was a tough chap dealing with tough guys. He undoubtedly inspired respect and perhaps sometimes fear, but you don't necessarily have to like someone to respect their ability. Speaking in general terms of making appointments, I might well think, 'I don't like the bastard but he is the right chap for the job.'"

"You couldn't criticise Harold for his commitment to the company," said Ron Savage. "He was out of this world. A real shop floor man who knew the business and whatever he did, right or wrong, it was done with the benefit of the company in mind."

Longbridge 1980. Some of the men behind the Metro who feature in this account are, from left to right, stylist David Bache and sales director Tony Ball with Ray Bates, director of engineering, sixth from the left, to the rear of the car. To the right of the car are, Tony Gilroy, director of manufacture and Harold Musgrove, then chairman and managing director of Austin-Morris.

Tony Ball saw Musgrove's confrontational approach as a deliberate ploy. "There were meetings where Harold would crucify people. Strong men would be almost reduced to tears and people would tremble in his presence. He would thump the table and wag his finger and give them the sharp end of his tongue like there was no tomorrow. Then he would come out and put his arm around me and say 'Do you think I was tough enough in there?' It was not exactly an act but it was a deliberate management style and the mask dropped immediately afterwards."

As Harold Musgrove himself saw it, "I was certainly very determined but I hope in a very positive way. Oh yes I fell out with some people but I believe that I and a number of others did save the company at that stage. In any case, if you don't get the respect of people you can shout as much as you bloody like but they won't come with you. The men at Longbridge were marvellous. I used to have meetings with all the employees, giving them a talk for ten minutes wherever they worked and showing them the new cars. They never leaked anything. I found them totally trustworthy. Every bloody one of them."

Tony Ball, of Mini-launch fame and who by this time was chairman of BL's Europe & Overseas Marketing Co., was asked by Michael Edwardes to mastermind the launch of the Metro. "Knocking BL and knocking Britain had become a national pastime," said Ball. "We were working against a

background of Michael Edwardes facing up to 'Red Robbo' – a watershed in British industrial history. When Michael Edwardes sacked him for opposing the recovery plan it could have led to a general strike but Edwardes had managed to get across with sincerity the logic of what we were doing, to the people who mattered, the people on the shop floor, by going direct to them at home over the heads of all the mass meetings in Cofton Park. We had to surmount all that by saying, 'This is our financial position and these are the new models we are bringing along'; involving them before launch time so that there was a progressive build up of a 'we are in this together' attitude, saying, 'If we don't get this car right you can say goodbye to the industry.' We were doing all this against the background of factory closures, economising, rationalising and so on. Not an easy task. We also had to keep our dealer network happy until the car was ready. The dealers were terribly disillusioned and I had the task of persuading them that this new car would be the salvation of the company. I addressed them at Wembley Arena and felt almost like Billy Graham trying to inspire faith that there was a future if they stuck with us.

"We also had to persuade the public that something pretty wonderful was about to happen. I progressively released titbits of information about the Metro over the twelve months prior to its launch so that the country started to talk about it but nobody knew quite the whole story. We had the whole of the press moving in our direction, actually wanting us to succeed, as opposed to sticking knives into us and saying the quicker you go down the plughole the better. Our advertising campaign deliberately and unashamedly pulled at the patriotic heart strings of the nation. 'We don't want you to buy British just because it is British. We want you to buy British because it is now the best. This car represents all that Britain stands for, particularly the quality of being able to fight back when our backs are against the wall.' We devised a series of advertisements based on repelling an invasion, using the White Cliffs of Dover. Working with Ray Horrocks, Harold Musgrove and Sir Michael Edwardes was almost like being a member of Churchill's war cabinet. I felt very proud to be part of that team.

"The Metro launch was one of the most dramatic ever. We held it on board a cruise liner so that we could bring the whole of the dealer network together. We had hidden the cars away inside the bulkheads of the ship and after I had summarised the hard work, creativity, love and care poured into this car by hundreds of people, we launched it through the bulkheads to the tune of 'Land of Hope

and Glory'. Hard-bitten people from the motor industry and journalism were weeping openly. It was a truly emotional moment. Here was tangible evidence that at last somebody was providing what the company and the country needed."

For Austin men, the 1980 launch of the Metro was of added significance, bringing as it did, the restoration of the Austin name to a BL car. This was a deliberate reversal of Stokes's previous attempts to bludgeon great names like Austin, Morris and Rover into a uniform Leyland identity. According to Sir Michael Edwardes, "When I took on the job I already knew what the management at British Leyland were up to. The process of killing off the old brands had already started. They were thinking of using the Leyland name across everything, even Jaguar. Austin was a very strong name so naming the new car the Austin Metro made total sense."

That decision certainly suited Harold Musgrove, then chairman of BL's Light/Medium Cars Group. In the year Metro was launched, the author received a letter from him which ran: "To those of us closely associated with Austin and Longbridge, where I started work as an apprentice in 1945, this [the restoration of the Austin name] gave an important impetus. We were confident that there was scope to re-establish the Austin name, because we knew that the Austin skills of product design and manufacturing remained a powerful force. It was symbolic that Metro was launched in the 75th year of car making at Longbridge. Metro represents everything that is world-renowned about Austin engineering: unparalleled use of interior space, coupled with astonishing economy and refinement. It brings the company into a new era, following the pioneering work of Herbert Austin and the era dominated by the genius of Issigonis. This new era is one of new technology and greater productivity, supporting advanced product design. The Longbridge factory now houses some of the finest manufacturing technology anywhere in the world. It is our job to use it to international standards of efficiency. It has often been said, and rightly so, that the recovery of BL Cars must be product-led. I am confident that over the next few years, with Metro as the start, our new product range will be absolutely right. But Longbridge in particular has to act as a pointer for the whole of British industry. It must be living proof that we can compete in every respect; on product, on quality and on operating efficiency. In doing so, Austin men will be writing a new chapter, perhaps even the finest chapter, in the company's long history."

Stirring stuff.

26

The end of the line for Austin – Maestro and Montego

*"I couldn't believe my eyes. The car's whole stance and proportion was wrong
… To find a car that was two decades out in its thinking was just mind-boggling."*

ROY AXE

After the wonderful 'go for it' attitude of the Metro's pre-production days, the Maestro and Montego story comes as a dreadful anticlimax.

"We did our Maestro proposal at Longbridge," said Rex Fleming, "and Ian Beech produced an alternative version in the Rover styling studio at Solihull for David Bache. At a viewing of both cars we couldn't believe it when David Bache said he thought Ian Beech's model was the right route to take and that Harris Mann's was completely wrong. Here was the boss of styling supposedly presenting two cars to management but completely dumping on one of them. If he didn't damn well like it he

Harris Mann's 1977 sketch of what eventually became the LM 10/11 Maestro/Montego project; LM standing for BLMC's Light/Medium Cars.

shouldn't have been showing it. In fact, the shape of the panels on Harris Mann's car would have given it a more solid, better quality look. The production Maestro was a good package and had a big interior so it must have failed on its appearance or desirability."

"As far as we were concerned we were doing a Maxi replacement," said Ian Beech. "Maestro was supposed to be a car in the Longbridge mould, a functional, sensible, family holdall. Initially there was no talk of any MG or performance derivatives. We were planning to get two cars out of one – Maestro and Montego – a hatchback and a notchback. We knew they were working on another version at Longbridge. We all had the same package but were working separately. Longbridge was famous for big interiors. I wanted to create more

This Harris Mann full-size clay model lost out to the Ian Beech/David Bache proposal. Rex Fleming thought the shape of the panels gave Mann's proposal a more solid, better quality look. Note the LC 10 designation that was used prior to the formation of Leyland's Light/Medium Cars division.

tumblehome by curving the side glazing but I was hampered by the stipulated specific distances from head to sideglass. Several people at Rover and Longbridge did schemes but David liked mine so I got to do full-size clay models, both the hatchback and a booted version using the same front end. Roger Tucker also did a notchback and a hatchback at Longbridge.

"At the Longbridge viewing they selected my hatchback and Roger Tucker's notchback. The product-planning folk wanted the bigger look for the notchback, to seemingly offer a lot of car for the money, as per Ford. Because of its faceted corners

A prototype of the Ian Beech Maestro from the Rover studio at Solihull. "The side fluting on Ian Beech's Maestro was always regretted," said Ray Bates. "Anyone trying to restyle or face-lift it was completely stumped." "The Bache studio had designed the Maestro on the Land Rover and Range Rover principle," said Harris Mann, "with great big gaps between the panels. Bache thought that with big gaps and sloppy fits it would all go together easily. But whether you have tight gaps or wide gaps, if it won't fit it won't fit."

my notchback didn't look as big. They liked my passenger cabin so decided to add Tucker's front and rear ends to my passenger cabin to produce the Montego. Montego was then developed at Longbridge and we took my Maestro away to Solihull to develop the exterior. It was a long grind. It came to a standstill at one stage because of the flap to get the Metro up and running. In fact the Maestro had to tread water for so long that it lost some of its freshness.

"Crisp cars were considered modern when I started on the Maestro in 1976 but it ended up with even more of a folded-paper look than it was meant to. Apparently the body engineers liked the sharp features I had given it so they decided to emphasise them a little. It took ages to get the Maestro into production and once in production it wasn't replaced as soon as it should have been. It meant the Maestro was always out of phase with the current trends. David Bache didn't have a lot of input but he was very good at looking at a design and picking out anything not quite right. If I were doing the Maestro now I would want more form in it but the stipulated package didn't give me a lot of

Ian Beech also produced this proposal for the LM 11 Montego saloon or 'notchback'. Management decided they wanted a 'bigger look' and aimed to get it by grafting on the front and rear of Roger Tucker's 'notchback' to Ian's passenger compartment. Roy Axe was never shown Ian's 'notchback' but when he saw it in the 1990s he thought it might have made a better car than the actual Montego.

"This glassfibre model of a high performance version of the Maestro was produced before we knew it was to be an MG", said Ian Beech.

leeway. Even Harris's proposal was quite flat-sided, without any real shoulder on the waist line."

Harris Mann recalled the task of trying to amalgamate the passenger compartment of Ian Beech's Maestro with the front and rear ends of Roger Tucker's proposed notchback to produce the Montego. "David Bache insisted on offering Musgrove these American type schemes for the rear end – little opera windows and so on. We told him Musgrove didn't want anything like that but he insisted we do them for a presentation. When Musgrove walked in he completely blew his top and

walked out again. David was a very free and easy character. I don't think he liked Longbridge. He certainly didn't spend very much time with us. We were told after each viewing what was required for the next one. There might be a month between the viewings but David would rarely visit us. He would come into a meeting with Harold Musgrove and others, a styling review meeting with everyone there on time except David, the very person who should be making the presentation.

He would arrive completely cold, without having discussed things with us, and try to bluff his way through. This got up Musgrove's nose. If Musgrove said, 'I don't like so-and-so, would you please redo it', David would continue, 'But I still think we should …' In the end Musgrove would explode in four-letter words and lay into him quite freely in front of everyone. He didn't bother to take him into a corner for a quiet word, he just laid it on the line there and then. David came in for a hell of a lot of Musgrove abuse over a short period of time until at one viewing Musgrove just told him to get out. 'You're fired,' he said."

The departure of David Bache saw Musgrove appoint Roy Axe (ex-Rootes and Chrysler) as chief stylist of BL. Roy took the job on after being impressed with the way Musgrove clearly had his heart and soul into reviving BL's fortunes. "Initially I thought I'd made the biggest mistake of my life. I was ushered into a room and stood in front of this object and asked, 'What do you think of that?' It was the Maestro. I couldn't believe my eyes. The car's whole stance and proportion was wrong. The spiky lines and all the facets and scollops made the

The first, hand-built Montego prototype. An earlier mock-up had been built by cutting and carving a Maestro. The marriage of two designers proposals to produce the Montego gave considerable problems …

surfaces look hollow and weak. Design was moving into more rounded forms and this car was back in the old folded-paper era. Its proportions were peculiar too. Its front wheels were almost under the A-pillar, producing an enormous front overhang, and there was virtually no rear overhang so the car had a very awkward stance. The sill was very high off the ground and looked even higher because of the way it sloped under. In short it was a complete shambles. I thought so and said so. The interior was even worse. The fascia panel was like a wet codfish, all floppy. It was engineering of the fifties not of the eighties. To find a car that was two decades out in its thinking was just mind-boggling. When I said, 'We have got to start again,' it was made clear to me that the car was only four months off production so there was nothing anybody could do.

"A few days later I was shown the Montego. That shook me even more. I was absolutely appalled. Roger Tucker's front and rear ends had already been grafted on. Once again I suggested starting from scratch but it was made crystal clear to me in words that only Harold would use that it was not an option. I simply had to improve it as much as I could. I went along with that but, in retrospect, it was not the right decision. We changed the bumpers, the lamp configuration at front and rear, the bonnet and the rear screen. The wraparound window was something I wanted to get rid of altogether, but just couldn't manage it, so we raised its base to strengthen the side view. But look at the proportional problems we had with that front wheel-arch being hard against the door-opening line. The wheel was so far back on that car it was just unbelievable. We lived with that and the enormous ground clearance for the rest of the car's life. They had effectively produced a platform and then perched the people on top of it. The result was a very high car, but with no more than normal head-

… particularly at the rear end. Roy Axe wanted to get rid of the wrap-around rear window altogether but had to settle for raising its base to strengthen the side view.

room because the floor was so high. Proportionally the car was a disaster all along the line. The engineers had been running the operation and they provided the styling people with the package and there wasn't really any opportunity to go back and say this is in the wrong place or that is in the wrong place. Nowadays the package is created by both sides working together.

"The car was 20 years old when it came out. I ought to have stopped it, but Ray Horrocks (then MD of BL) would have had to go back to the government and tell them they had just screwed up in a big way and needed x more millions. He wasn't in the mood to do that. But it was a car that should never have happened like that. It really shouldn't. The company had invested millions in automated equipment to make this antiquated machine. It was tragic. Incidentally, it drove quite well. The old O-Series engine wasn't that wonderful but I mean Ford weren't making particularly brilliant engines at the time. So it wasn't an unpleasant car to drive but things fell off it all the time. It was unreliable."

Even Harold Musgrove later regretted having let Maestro/Montego proceed in the form it did. "Looking back I feel we should have said it just wasn't good enough and stopped it. But I don't think we had the luxury of that being a possibility and to be perfectly frank it was infinitely better than the Princess or Allegro. But in market research it never managed to come first in any category – top in nothing. If Roy Axe had been responsible for it from the beginning it would have been an entirely different car."

As for the 'engineering' of Maestro/Montego, Ray Bates recalled, "Maestro began in 'advanced engineering' under Spen King. There was no way Spen was going to go down the subframe and Hydragas route with Maestro and Montego. He said it wasn't cost-effective, so it was back to conventional suspension. In any case we were dealing with up to 2-litre engines with end-on gearboxes, making it a very wide motor car. You hadn't really got room for subframes with that configuration. At one stage Spen had to allow an increase in track on the Maestro because we couldn't package the gearbox and suspension and get acceptable turning circles. The excellent interior roominess of Maestro was partly due to the width requirements of the transmission."

Bernard Johnson's last job at Longbridge was as chief development engineer for Maestro and Montego. "That meant I had worked on the whole of the post-war Austin range. The first Maestro prototypes had either 1,300cc A-Series engines with in-sump gearboxes or the 1,700cc O-Series with an end-on LT80 gearbox – a hefty lump. Then we put in 1,500cc and 1,750cc E-Series engines and quietly bought a Volkswagen gearbox and used a wooden backplate to bolt it on to the E Series engine and found it fitted in a treat. The E-Series 1,500 was overvalved, so it didn't pull at the bottom end – right? The 1,750 was undervalved, because it used all the same stuff, so that didn't breathe at the top end – right? So we decided to amalgamate the 1,500 and 1,750 'E' into the 1600 and called it the R-Series. As a 1,600cc unit it was just right, definitely the best version of the E-Series. That went a treat in the Maestro and that is how the Maestro was born. It meant making a special crank for the end-on gearbox because the E-series had the gearbox in the sump. I was nattering with the engine blokes in the office one day when someone suggested making crankshafts for the 1,300 A-Series to take the Volkswagen gearbox as well and so get rid of the in-sump box. I got them to make three cranks: 'Don't say anything to anyone, just make 'em and see what it's like.' Before we got round to fitting them management said, 'This E-Series with the Volkswagen gearbox is rather good and VW have agreed to do a deal, so how long to do an A-series?' 'Oh,' I said, 'about three weeks,' knowing that we'd done it already. They said, 'Impossible.' So we just got the crank and slung it in, cut a backplate out of a bit of boiler plate and they had it in three weeks. Even now they don't know we had made it all unauthorised. There was no real problem with the Maestro. It wasn't a complicated car."

The car might not have been complicated but the politics certainly were. "In early 1979," said Ray Bates, "a survey showed that if we were to engineer Metro and Maestro properly, then only 20 per cent of our design manpower could be available for other vehicles. Basically, we needed 1,360 people to achieve the product plan instead of 1,072. We had a ratio of engineers per product line of 140 at Austin-Morris whereas Ford had 600 and Daimler Benz had 1,200. So I told Harold Musgrove that we just didn't have the manpower at Austin-Morris to do

On a high. Prince Philip presents Ray Bates with the Design Council award won by the Metro in 1981. The euphoria created by the success of Metro did not last long. "We had just worked our backsides off on Metro," said Ray Bates, "… and then we got this kick in the teeth … 'Sorry, we are going to merge you with Rover-Triumph' … I was absolutely devastated."

Maestro. We were two years away from production and didn't have a gearbox for it. We had just worked ourselves to a frazzle on the Metro and here we were again trying to scrape the barrel with a shortage of engineers, poor facilities and very little money. Unfortunately, my memos to Harold Musgrove virtually did me out of my job by prompting the integration of Austin-Morris engineering with that of Rover-Triumph, and the whole lot to be run by Joe Farnham. So we had just worked our backsides off on Metro, thought we had done a great job and then got this kick in the teeth. 'Sorry. We are going to merge you with Rover-Triumph.' It meant that at the end of 1980 I had the annoyance of Joe Farnham being appointed over me. By that time I had been converted to front-wheel drive and here was a man coming from Chrysler as our supremo, who knew bugger-all about front-wheel-drive, to take over LC10 (Maestro). When the reorganisation took place Maestro came under light/medium cars as the LM10 project and Joe put himself in the driving seat by destroying the organisation I had created with all the wonderful chaps in the Austin-Morris team that had worked on the Metro. That highly successful team was just fragmented. Suddenly we had a new man, a new structure and different people working on two sites.

"All the enthusiasm and momentum we had built up with Metro was destroyed. Metro was a tremendous success story. We worked all the hours God sent during the day and would then go testing at Gaydon until two in the morning and be back at work at eight. The Austin-Morris engineers were superb. They gave their all. Musgrove promised us the biggest party ever. He said we were all going to get drunk but we never had it. We had just come off this high, having won several awards, and people were riding on the crest of a wave. People were saying we had won the war, had done a bloody good job. So we had just said to ourselves, 'Right let's get on with the next one chaps' – Maestro – when we suffered this reorganisation and all the enthusiasm was just dissipated immediately. I was shattered. I wanted to strengthen the team not pull it apart. The bitter pill was to be told by Harold Musgrove that Metro was not really a success because it had only been produced by panic engineering. He said the new organisation would be more professional. I was absolutely devastated.

"As Maestro and Montego came towards production they had to be engineered in this new organisation amidst general turmoil and bitterness. So the conditions were far from ideal. I suppose it must be admitted that the Montego was quite a sensible

A 1986 Austin Montego Mayfair Estate. In 1987, the Austin name was removed from the cars but the Maestro and Montego continued in production until 1994. The estate version of the Montego carried on slightly longer than the others. Many people, although obviously not enough, were sorry to see the demise of this particularly spacious load carrier.

motor car. We did have trouble with the carburettor and automatic choke, trying to mate modern electronics to an old carburettor, and the quality was suspect at times, but the upmarket version, certainly, wasn't a bad car. It had good handling, lots of room and a boot which would carry anything. You could just keep putting things in there. Both Maestro and Montego were excellent towing vehicles too."

Worthy, roomy cars though they might have been, Maestro and Montego did not provide too many thrills and certainly never managed to compete with what Ford and Vauxhall were offering, particularly from the fleet buyers' point of view. Had they been a real success then the Austin name, which had been restored with Metro, might well have gone from strength to strength. But Musgrove's hopes of an Austin revival were not to be. In 1987 the Austin name was removed from Metro, Maestro and Montego. Although production of these cars continued into the mid-1990s, the company's future, it seemed, lay in going upmarket.

A more upmarket image would be fostered by gradually introducing the Rover name across the complete range of cars. Although the Metro eventually became the Rover 100, and continued in production until early 1988, neither the Maestro nor the Montego, other than a few Montegos sold quietly on the Continent, was deemed worthy enough to carry the Rover badge. Indeed, as described in the next chapter, the first all-new car carrying the Rover name to be built at 'The Austin' would in truth, be a Honda,

So which car was the last Austin? Not an easy question to answer. No-one seems to know exactly which car was the last to leave either Longbridge or Cowley sporting an Austin badge in 1987. That being so, perhaps we should award the honour to the last Montego estate, built in 1994, which was signed by the Cowley workforce and is now in the BMIHT collection at Gaydon. That car was built, let it be noted, at Cowley, so the last car to be introduced as an Austin thus suffered similar indignities to those of the last Morris.

One could argue, however, that the last Austin, even though it might not bear an Austin badge, had not yet been built at the time of writing. Why? Because as of January 2000, a batch of Maestros in kit form, originally intended for Bulgaria, was still being assembled and sold by Trans European Trading of Ledbury. So, take your pick.

27

To Rover via Honda and on to BMW

"Why English no do exercises in morning? Good for body, good for mind, good for soul."

JAPANESE TECHNICIAN WORKING ON THE ROVER 800

The Michael Edwardes era saw not only the introduction of the Metro, Maestro and Montego but also a much-needed reappraisal of both industrial relations and production methods: out went 'Robbo' and in came the robots. Concerted efforts were also made to improve the quality of the product. Although all this was achieved against almost impossible odds, the most far-reaching decision of that era, the link-up with Honda, came about

In 1984, this Honda Ballade-derived, Triumph Acclaim replacement was announced as the Rover 200. It was blatant badge-engineering but the Rover name and the assurance of Japanese quality led to people buying them in large numbers.

by dire necessity rather than by choice.

When the newly arrived Michael Edwardes took stock in 1977 what bothered him most was the length of time it was going to take to produce a new mid-range model. As we have seen, the Metro project was so well advanced compared with that of Maestro that although he would have liked to, he could not switch the order of their proposed launches. But the Allegro and Marina, which in Edwardes's words, didn't exactly set the world on fire when they were launched, were now facing very strong competition so he had to find someone else's creation to fill the gap in the medium sector. Hence the tie-up with Honda to produce the Triumph

Acclaim of 1981, a barely modified Honda Ballade.

Interestingly enough, the situation could have spawned renewed links with Nissan but, as Sir Michael Edwardes put it, "I did meet the chairman of Nissan in the Dorchester for lunch and we talked about past technical tie-ups, but the next thing was that I was reading in the press that we were talking about a technical tie-up. He had gone public, so that killed it. In any case, Honda made an ideal partner. That was a real coup."

Tony Ball was involved with that initial link-up with Honda in 1979 and agreed that, "Honda represented an ideal partner. They not only had a vehicle that we could use to fill a gap in our range but we also realised that we would be able to use their engineering skills and their quality standards as an example on our own assembly lines."

In 1984 the Triumph Acclaim's replacement became the first Rover 200, produced by modifying the Honda Ballade replacement and badging it as a Rover. Designed in Japan, it was nevertheless announced as 'A Car Bred to be Rover'. As the first Rover to come off the production lines at 'The Austin' it represented badge-engineering at its blatant best. It did make sound economics, however. The Rover name and the Japanese assurance of quality meant people were happy to buy them in large numbers. Incidentally, the Acclaim had been badged as a Triumph because the original intention had been to produce it at Canley, the decision to

produce it at Cowley being an afterthought. The later decision to concentrate on the Austin and Rover names meant the Acclaim was the last Triumph produced.

The first fully fledged Honda/Austin-Rover design project was agreed in November 1981 as project XX, which became the Rover 800.

When Roy Axe was appointed as director of design in 1982, designs for the XX were just beginning to appear on paper. "We made a model before Honda arrived for the first meeting and they were rather taken aback that we had done it. Although they felt it needed considerable modification, the main features, particularly the wrap-round effect of the glasswork, the thin pillar at the back and the contrasting lower colour were carried right through to the final car. After that meeting a Honda team came over to us and we built the clay models for the Legend and 800 side by side at Canley."

Ian Beech worked on those models under Roy Axe and Gordon Sked. "It was a shame we couldn't just develop our initial model," said Ian. "We had aimed at an elegant looking car that retained something of a likeness to the Rover SD1. The aerodynamics people had asked for the whole car, including the glasshouse, to be tapered towards the rear. Honda wanted it to look a much larger car so we had to compromise by taking out the taper, removing some of the tumblehome and squaring up the corners somewhat. It rather spoilt the car and although without Honda we wouldn't have had a car at all, it did always seem that we had to compromise more than they did because they were in the stronger position."

Wind tunnel testing of the XX clay model for the first fully fledged Honda/Austin-Rover design project. The end result was the Rover 800 of 1986.

When Honda arrived on the scene they were rather taken aback to find that Roy Axe and his team had already produced this stylish mock-up for the Rover 800, the main features of which would be carried through to the production car.

Although the design responsibility for the XX rested with Honda, Ron Nicholls was involved in the development of the chassis for the Rover 800 version. "Basically the suspension of the Rover 800 was Japanese but we had the responsibility for its development. In those days Honda didn't quite trust us and rightly so. They were apprehensive as to how effectively we would do the work. It took several years to gain their confidence."

"Just before its launch there was a problem on the 800's gearbox," recalled Pat Layton, "and the Japanese came to rectify them in the workshops of our new proving ground at Gaydon. I told the shop stewards that I wasn't interested in demarcation or anything like that. 'We are going to be pulling gearboxes out and they'll be rectified and modified. You'll do some, they'll do some. We all know of the Japanese reputation for efficiency and output so I want you to at least equal it. Not only that, you'll be polite. The Japanese are a very polite people.' 'Ah don't worry about it. Leave it with us,' they said. Well, they all worked away feverishly but the Japanese used to do their exercises before they started work. One of them who could speak a bit of English asked one of our guys, 'Why English no do exercises in morning? Good for body, good for mind, good for soul.' Without thinking about it, this chap came out with several expletives to indicate that he had already changed three gearboxes while they

had been 'effing' about out there. Fortunately the Japanese engineer didn't understand his Brummie accent but we did actually change more gearboxes than they did. The lads rose to the challenge."

Since 1952, however, things had obviously gone full circle. Yutaka Kume's 'technical void' had opened up here in Britain. It was now the turn of the Japanese to show us how to build quality motor cars. Roy Axe spoke of Honda producing a sea change in Austin-Rover's attitude to quality. "Austin-Rover were not aware of how far they had fallen behind in design. I asked Harold Musgrove why he had hired me and he said he had a world-class manufacturing operation that could do anything but that his problem was producing something that looked good. That was not quite the case. Certainly they had spent millions on automated machinery for Metro, Maestro and Montego but it was essentially making 20-year-old cars. When the alignment with Honda came along, if Austin-Rover hadn't been so proud of its own capabilities, of supposedly being a manufacturing genius, they could have embraced Honda there and then and said, 'We have just goofed again with the Montego so please show us how to do it.' Honda would have been only too pleased to do so. Although the 800 was greatly enhanced by Honda's approach to it, Austin-Rover were still determined they were going to do it their way. They would only make common the areas that had to be common. The 800's doors gave monumental problems from the day it came out. With Honda having already designed the body, our guys were then told to seal our own doors, a lunatic way of doing it. Harold beat hell out of the

Under Japanese influence, Rover 800 prototypes gradually developed the flatter sides and somewhat fussier general appearance of the car that made it into production – the Rover Sterling is the model shown here.

sealing guys but they hadn't a cat in hell's chance. When Honda designed their Legend they designed the doors and seals as one and had no problems at all. We could have followed Honda's procedures but pride got in the way."

The arrival of a new chairman, Graham Day, in May 1986, was an event of some significance in that Mrs Thatcher saw Day's appointment as a prelude to getting the company into shape for privatisation. Almost immediately, under his leadership, Austin-Rover became known as the Rover Group and Day declared his intention of taking the company upmarket, beginning with the launch of the Rover 800 in July 1986.

"I was saying we were not ready for privatisation," said Harold Musgrove, "Not yet. And we weren't. There were no hard feelings but I disagreed with Day's strategy. I disagreed with getting rid of the Austin name entirely. I would have kept it for the Metro and its replacement, the volume car side. Of course Graham Day didn't want to pursue the volume car side but if you are going to have a motor industry you have got to have a volume car. At least that's how it seemed to me."

Apparently, research had indicated that the Austin name, particularly in the younger age groups, had become devalued. "If people don't want the Austin name on the boot," said Day, "then we'll take it off."

"The use of the Rover name was already being

heavily debated when Graham Day arrived," said Roy Axe. "The whole idea was to develop a corporate identity with a single name. Rover was researched consistently as our strongest name and the most appropriate to use in moving upmarket. By the time the Graham Day era dawned it was clear to everybody that confrontational management was getting us nowhere. There were all kinds of problems and Harold was swept away. It was George Simpson who moved us towards a much more co-operative management approach which enabled Rover to swallow its pride and say, 'We will ask Honda how they do it.' For project YY, the second Rover 200 of 1989, Honda held our hand through all the design stages right up to production – everything. It was then a case of, 'Just show us, Honda, and we'll embrace it.' A very open approach like that. That all happened under Graham Day, George Simpson and John Towers but in my view that is something that could have been done in 1983. Rover couldn't afford to engineer the YY Rover 200 in any case so it was agreed that, although it would be jointly styled between Honda and ourselves, the engineering, including the body engineering, would all be done by Honda. That's why that particular Rover 200 was so good – because Honda did it. We did all the styling sketches back here in England but it was taken over to Japan for modelling."

Ron Nicholls saw further advantages flowing from the co-operation with Honda. "For years I had been a voice in the wilderness saying we must reduce costs by improving our production efficiency not by skimping on the engineering. The finance men couldn't see any further than their noses. They regularly spoilt the job for the sake of a few pence. I was able to use Honda to fight management. It was quite a serious business. I was doing battle with the American engineering director, Joe Farnham, and the chairman at the time, Harold Musgrove. Run by finance men the cheaper solution was chosen every time. After Honda arrived on the scene we could say that for the ideal solution we must have so and so and Honda would back us up. Honda never once asked how much does it cost. They looked for the appropriate engineering and then brought the price down by purchasing agreements or manufacturing processes but never once prostituted engineering.

"I was in Japan for seven months on the YY – Rover 200 project," said Ron, "Roy Axe came each month because he had his styling boys out there under Geoff Upex and they were working alongside Honda stylists. One of the benefits to Honda was getting the European styling for a car they wished to market over here. All the engineers and designers were in one office and the styling studio producing the clay models was next door. You looked out of your window and you could see it all happening. Everybody involved was in that building. The stylists would come in and say look I want the bonnet line to be this high or there might be problems with wheel travel or whatever but they would be solved there and then. We started in January and finished at

According to Roy Axe, "For project YY, the second Rover 200 of 1989, Honda held our hand all through the design stages." This car would also benefit greatly from Longbridge's superb new K-Series engine.

the beginning of May and had prototypes built five months later. In eleven months we had prototype cars undergoing testing."

Until that joint YY programme, Austin-Rover could not understand how Honda managed to beat them through every design stage. The secret, it turned out, was a process known as 'parallel engineering'.

"Honda programmed two years and made it every time," said Rex Fleming, "On the 800 we both started at exactly the same point and went through what we thought was a similar process, but by the time we had just about got our drawings out of engineering they had bloody cars. It was difficult getting to grips with it. It turned out that they do a set of skin lines which they give to 'manufacturing' and 'manufacturing' then make that car. Whilst doing so, they alter anything necessary to ensure a quality product without ever referring back to 'design'. At Rover they referred back to 'design' for every single thing that needed moving. Then they would model it again, look at it, argue about it, make a new drawing of it, send it back to 'manufacturing', to 'engineering', backwards and forwards. It all cost time and money. We would go through the whole bloody process again and again."

It was the team spirit of the Japanese which impressed Vic Horner. "They worked long hours so that they didn't let their team mates down. In England you still had a bit of the, 'I can't stop on tonight' sort of thing. Harold Musgrove had started tightening up the discipline prior to the Japanese coming, ensuring people paid attention to quality

and making suppliers responsible for quality. But after the Japanese came we ran Total Quality Management meetings and courses. It gradually got through to everybody that they had to think about the customer. That was all because of the Japanese."

"Their design and fit of panels was so meticulous," said Ron Savage, "that we didn't get the production problems that we had had previously. Their fixation on quality and their determination to 'get it right first time' made that period an education."

Ray Bates pointed out that the Austin-Rover/Honda collaboration was not all one-way traffic. "There is no doubt they taught us a lot about quality and attention to detail, but they failed miserably in terms of ride and handling. We spent an awful lot of time improving their suspensions. Their gearboxes comprehensively failed our tests in reverse gear and we did a great deal for their interiors, including their demist and ventilation systems."

One superb British contribution to the Longbridge-built Rover 200/400 was the twin overhead-camshaft version of the Longbridge-designed all-aluminium K-Series engine. That the K-Series

Harold Musgrove, then chairman and chief executive of Austin-Rover, waves off Class 47 locomotive No 47337, on 24 April 1986, it having just been named Herbert Austin *to commemorate the 80th anniversary of the first car built at Longbridge.*

The reintroduction of the traditional Rover grille on the revised Rover 800 in 1991, and its use on all subsequent models, seemed to set the seal on 'Roverisation' by strengthening brand identity. "When we launched the original 800 the SD1 style front represented a recognisable Rover face but after several other manufacturers moved in the same direction – Renault for one – it lost character. That was when the move back towards the grille really took off." – Roy Axe.

actually went into production was largely due to Harold Musgrove. "In '83/84, the government wanted us to use a Japanese engine," remembered Harold. "Although getting the money out of the government was a major battle I got great support from Norman Tebbit. It was he who persuaded Mrs Thatcher to let us have the money for the K-Series."

Roy Axe felt it was this second Rover 200 Series of 1989 which satisfied people that Longbridge-built cars could once more be relied upon. "Rover did very well out of it. Unfortunately Honda found the joint exercise an awful hassle and said they would never do that again. 'We will do Honda's car and

you can make it into a Rover.' With the Rover 600 that's exactly what they did. Rover was presented with a *fait accompli* in terms of the middle part of the car. It worked remarkably well on the 600 but much less well on the 400 which followed it."

Deciding to reintroduce a Rover grille on the cars seems to have been a successful move. "For even the first Rover 800 that did pass through our minds," said Roy Axe, "but Rover had thrown tradition aside with the 2000 and SD1 and had anyone gone to that management committee and suggested we put an old upright grille on the front they would have been laughed at. It would have given everyone the chance to say, 'here they go, the same old game again', especially after the Vanden Plas Allegro. So we simply adopted the SD1 look."

In 1988, Rover Group was finally privatised by being sold to British Aerospace. On purchasing Rover Group, BAe agreed not to close down or sell Austin-Rover or Land Rover within five years. It was hardly surprising that Roland Smith, the BAe chairman, called it the 'deal of the decade'. Just as Rover Group had managed to conjure up a trading profit, Aerospace was effectively being handed many millions of pounds to take the company off the nation's hands.

There were understandable headlines in the press such as, 'Going for a Song' and claims that the company had been grossly undervalued, but Mrs Thatcher was delighted to be ridding the national purse of what she saw as a bottomless pit that had been fed billions of pounds to seemingly no avail for many years.

Privatisation was one thing, selling out to a foreign company was quite another. That's what came about in 1994 when the Rover Group was purchased by German car maker BMW. Although this was undoubtedly a sad day for British motoring enthusiasts, let us not forget that Herbert Austin himself almost sold out to General Motors in the 1920s.

It was at least satisfying to note that in 1928, by buying out the Dixi motor cycle firm, BMW had ensured that the first car they ever built was the Austin Seven that had previously been built under licence by Dixi. (See colour section.)

Discussing the BMW takeover, soon after it took place, Tony Ball declared, "I would have preferred to see the company remain in British hands but although we no longer have a British-owned motor industry we do at least have the world's motor industry in Britain. The world has decided that Britain is the place to build motorcars and I'm delighted about that. We are now the springboard of the motor industry into Europe."

Certainly there were those who hoped that as a member of the newly designated BMW Group, Rover could have a brighter future ahead than ever before. Perhaps Harold Musgrove's 'finest chapter in the company's long history' was yet to be written, albeit with Longbridge under its new rather soulless title of BMW Plant No. 32, and as a manufacturer of BMW Group cars bearing the names of Rover, MG and Mini? In January 2000, Longbridge was turning out the Mini, the MGF and the Rover 25 and 45, and was already preparing for the new Mini.

But January 2000, (when the manuscript of this book was delivered to the publishers) was proving a very difficult time to make forecasts about the future of either the Longbridge plant or even the BMW Group itself. Pundits were queuing up to declare that BMW's acquisition of Rover was an act of folly which would inevitably lead to such a drain on their resources that we would eventually see BMW losing its independence to Ford, General Motors or Volkswagen. As for the Longbridge plant, in February 1999, Neil Collins, city editor of the *Daily Telegraph,* declared: "If car plants are to be treated as centres to generate wealth, rather than branches of social security, Longbridge should be closed." He went on to say, "Closing Longbridge would not guarantee BMW's independence; but keeping it open would almost certainly end it."

An interview with BMW Group's spokesman, Vin Hammersley, at Longbridge in early January

January 2000. Q-gate at 'The Austin'. The frontage of the reception building had changed very little since the 1950s, but the factory was newly designated as BMW Plant No 32.

2000 furnished a much more hopeful outlook. "Believe me, BMW are here to stay. They bought Rover to give them the volume of production that would allow them to remain independent. BMW executives as well as the Quandt family [the controlling shareholders] have been absolutely unambiguous in their statements about wishing to remain an independent company. Of late, BMW has been the largest inward investor in the UK. They are investing £1.7 billion in the Longbridge site alone over the next few years. A separate £400 million has already been committed on this site to build the new Mini. CAB 2 has been completely swept away to allow the construction of the new Mini facility. With Longbridge currently undergoing its most radical restructuring in its entire history there is bound to be a fall in output and a considerable lag until we see the benefits coming through. BMW understand this and doesn't expect to see a profit until at least 2002. Up to now we have been working in antiquated buildings. Even the 'new' West Works was built in 1976 – almost a quarter of a century ago. We have just pulled down the water tower and No 1 shop that was part of the White & Pikes printing works of 1894 that Herbert Austin purchased for the original factory, and the old Mini is still being built in almost the same manner as it was nearly half a century ago.

"This year we have seen productivity at Longbridge rise from about 30 cars per man per year to about 50 cars per man. The scrapping of the old Mini and the introduction of the new one will give a further significant rise in productivity too. The men here have voted for all the necessary changes in working practices. When we need more cars they work for free and the extra hours are banked so that at quieter times of the year they still get paid. But all the press carping has been very damaging commercially. Even after all that investment, BMW has not received one iota of praise. We intend to be the largest niche manufacturers in the world."

BMW spokesman, Hammersley went on to declare, "The new Mini will be a global car. You won't be disappointed. It will exude Mini-ness. Trendy, popular and fun to drive, it will be sold throughout the world. BMW has a long-term strategy for the future and are not spending £3 billion on Rover just to see it ditched. They obviously intend to be around for a long while, well into the new millennium."

However, a day or two after the interview with Vin Hammersley, Henrich Heitmann of BMW was reported to have suggested at the Detroit Motor Show, that BMW could not rule out the closure of their UK subsidiary, Rover, because he feared they

January 2000. The new face of Rover. Here we see the Longbridge-built Rover 25 and 45, along with the Rover 75, then being built at Cowley – all with a new and unifying frontal treatment.

might not have the time they needed to re-establish the Rover name.

Uncertainty such as this meant that sales of all Rovers, even the new Rover 75, arguably the finest Rover ever, and well-acclaimed by the press, were not going well. The strength of the pound was hitting all exports and a growing reluctance of the British public to pay over the odds for cars that could be bought much more cheaply on the Continent found Rover Group costing BMW an estimated £2 million a day.

Naturally this led to further uncertainty and disquiet, not only in those employed at Longbridge but also in the BMW boardroom where calls to ditch the 'English Patient' were being heard with ever-increasing regularity.

It was mid-March 2000, however, before the actual bombshell was dropped, with BMW announcing that it was handing over Rover and Longbridge to Alchemy, a venture capital company. Jon Moulton, head of Alchemy, declared that "the badly tarnished Rover name" would be replaced by that of The MG Car Company which would concentrate on building a state-of-the-art range of cars worthy of the MG's sporting heritage. Moulton was also reported as saying that the days of mass-production at Longbridge were over and that the new MGs, with an aluminium chassis and composite bodywork would be produced at the rate of no more than 100,000 cars a year by a considerably reduced workforce.

The British Government, the unions and the workforce were all up in arms at the way BMW had handled the situation. Stephen Byers, Secretary of Trade, was furious at the secret way in which BMW had arranged the deal and had thus ditched a previously agreed plan whereby the Government would provide £152 million of aid to assist redevelopment at Longbridge.

Moulton insisted that there was no viable alternative to his proposals but the British Government pleaded with BMW to think again and at least allow further time for the big names in car production to consider a late bid for Rover and Longbridge.

In splitting up Rover, BMW had agreed to sell Land Rover to Ford. BMW would retain the new Mini but produce that at Cowley. Having removed the glittering prospect of the new Mini from Longbridge's portfolio it was hardly surprising that little interest was being shown in the plant. As it turned out, even the negotiations between Alchemy and BMW broke down and this left only one slim hope of avoiding the total closure of Longbridge – a bid from the Phoenix consortium, headed by ex-Rover boss John Towers, who had gained the backing of both the unions and the Government after claiming to have plans to maintain mass production of Rovers at Longbridge. BMW were sceptical but they offered Rover and Longbridge to Phoenix,

July 2000. Kevin Howe, chief executive of Rover Group, with a Rover 75 saloon.

along with a considerable loan, for the nominal sum of £10, with the proviso that the deal would be off and Longbridge would be closed within a month unless Phoenix provided evidence of appropriate funding of their own – something Phoenix only managed to do at the 11th hour on 9 May 2000.

But in these days of a high pound, serious overproduction in the industry and a clamouring for lower car prices in Britain, even those who dearly wanted John Towers and his team to succeed in saving Rover and Longbridge, were finding it hard to see how they could do so where BMW had failed so publicly and miserably.

An interview with Kevin Howe, chief executive of the new Rover Group, in July 2000, painted the picture as he saw it, albeit at that time with a necessarily broad brush.

"Yes, people are asking 'How can we succeed where BMW failed?' Well, for a lot of reasons. You see with BMW we were there to satisfy their corporate strategy. They wanted Rover as part of their portfolio for the volume market because all the forecasts of growth in the industry were in the sectors in which BMW didn't operate. We were serving BMW needs more than specifically Rover needs.

"Now we can plan purely for the good of Rover Group. BMW wanted Rover to operate in a different sector of the market to them by offering something of a comfortable, almost carpet-slippered type of image whilst BMW would provide a sporty, dynamic and more aggressive product. We intend

The yet-to-be-launched Rover 75 Estate Car which will be built at Longbridge from 2001.

holding on to everything that is good about Rover, a quality and comfort type of profile, which is an important part of our customer base, but we think we can complement that by offering the addition of some sportier products. Whether they will be MGs or not is still in the melting pot but rest-assured we are talking of much more than a badge and that we are going to enter territory that was previously closed to us because of BMW policy.

"We have a connection with Lola and will be looking to use their performance expertise to develop our vehicles. We still make MGs so we have a fair bit of knowledge there ourselves but the added specialist capabilities from Lola will be a source we can tap into. Our new man in charge of product development is Rob Oldacre, who has had experience at Rover, Rolls-Royce and Cosworth. His underlying strengths are chassis, performance engines and power train. We have also acquired the services of Peter Stevens as our product design director. He is renowned for his styling work at the RCA as well as his work for McLaren, Jaguar and Lotus. So I think we are well placed to develop some interesting motor cars. We will certainly not be shaken from doing what is required to turn this business around.

"Our overheads are now significantly lower than they were under BMW. Rover Cars used to cover the costs, not only of Longbridge and Cowley, both of which were under-utilised sites, but also the cost of the sales and marketing headquarters at Bickenhill, Rover headquarters at Warwick and a large share of the cost of the design, development and test facilities at Gaydon. With everything now concentrated at Longbridge we have greatly reduced these costs.

"We are also putting together some extremely pragmatic plans, keeping our cost base low and ensuring we have an organisation capable of selling say 175–200,000 cars a year and leaving the worry of how to produce 250,000 until the demand is there.

"The head count has been reduced considerably to just under 6,000 employees and I don't expect things to change dramatically in that respect although we will have to ensure that we remain competitive. The workforce have carried themselves magnificently through very difficult times and they appear very committed to our cause.

"People don't seem to doubt our ability to survive in the short term, the doubt is all about our ability to finance future development. We are not suggesting that the company can go it alone in the long term without collaborative involvement to develop replacement vehicles. What shape that might take is still unfolding but there are people out there who are positively interested in working with us and we are confident that we will have a partner in place for when we need to launch any new model.

"In fairness to BMW they invested heavily in Land Rover at Solihull and in Rover at Cowley and had begun to invest heavily in Longbridge, but quite a few people within Rover Group felt that priority should have been given to a replacement vehicle in the lower to medium car sector.

"Anyway, massive investment has certainly gone into what is now the Rover Group business, for example in the Rover 75 and in the 75 Estate which we will be launching next year and a great deal was also invested in the Rover 75 facilities which are now being transferred to Longbridge. We will use all that investment to our advantage.

"We plan to build the Rover 25 and 45 on one track in CAB 1 from now on, both to optimise the volumes on that track and also to allow a separate track as a dedicated facility for the Rover 75. The MGF is currently built in CAB 1 on the same track as the Mini but later in the year, when production of the old Mini ceases, it will have a dedicated facility of its own.

"Moving the 75 from Cowley is a massive project but we expect to be building the 75 here again in October. In the meantime we are able to supply demand from the stocks we have at present.

"I realise there are many prospective customers who fear it may not work – people who would want to buy one of our cars but are concerned about whether Rover will survive or not. Well, I firmly believe that we can succeed in saving Rover, MG and Longbridge. Our customers and potential customers can look forward to some very positive announcements before too long. We are definitely planning to have an extremely aggressive go at this.

Over 14,000,000 cars have been built at 'The Austin' since 1905. The 10,000,000th car, a five-door Austin Metro, came off the line in September 1985. But what, in heaven's name, would Sir Herbert Austin have thought of those high-kicking Bluebell Girls from Paris? (See page 31.)

Let's hope in a few years time you will be sat here asking me how the devil we did it."

Let us hope so too, because the survival of the Longbridge factory and the livelihoods of many thousands of West Midlanders depend upon the success of these courageous plans.

As for the past, in my interviews with men of 'The Austin', most were keen to stress how proud they were to have worked there. Certainly, until the 1968 merger, they were very proud indeed.

"I can say with honesty that I couldn't wait to go to work," said Fred Smith. "You were so involved with everything. Things began to change, not so much after the formation of BMC, as when the Leyland people came. You can imagine what the old hands thought when the Austin name was taken down at the factory. They cried blood. Their pride was taken away and when you lose your pride you slowly begin to lose everything else.

"I am forever grateful that they accepted me as an engineering apprentice," said Philip Mitchell, whose apprenticeship began in 1932. "It was an exciting place because we were a self-contained factory and made practically everything we required. We were all Longbridge bred and most of the people in managerial positions were ex-apprentices so we felt part of a big team, a family. I am proud of my inden-

tures. Herbert Austin signed them himself. I remember them taking the Austin of England sign down from CAB 1. Stokes that was. You began to feel you were walking into a foreign land. You had to keep your back to the wall in those days.

Mike Sheehan, whose apprenticeship began in 1949, eventually became director and general manager of Longbridge Operations. Today, as a vice-president of the still-thriving Austin Ex-Apprentices Association, he recalls, "It was a tremendous feeling to be associated with 'The Austin'. On that site you had a Bessemer steel convertor, a forge, a foundry, an automatic shop for making nuts and bolts, a chrome plating shop, an enormous trim shop, and a saw mill. The workforce fluctuated between 20,000 and 25,000. The engineering apprentices had the enormous privilege of sampling all those activities under one roof. There were very few things in making a motor car that you did not see. Grandfathers, fathers and sons had worked there. Admittedly things started to get less happy in the 1950s when trade union activity went absolutely berserk. With the post-war expansion a tremendous amount of labour was sucked in which did not have the family ties and loyalties of the old stagers and it began to be thought of as just another car factory. Those of us in management positions were preoccupied in just trying to keep things going on a minute-to-minute basis. But by the time I retired in 1986 we had battled our way through by a very tortuous route to procure a complete transformation of the relationships between men and management; to a much happier situation where the workforce are involved in product development and are their own quality controllers and their own motivators."

In January 2000, Tony Osborne, chairman of the Austin Ex-Apprentices Association, provided up to date information on the Association's affairs. "The Association is run by a committee of 15 who all work hard for the enjoyment of the 'Old Boys' from Longbridge. Members of the Association must have completed a recognised training course at Longbridge of at least four years duration. We still have 1,500 ex-apprentices on our mailing list and 170 of us recently sat down to our 66th annual reunion dinner at the Raven Hotel in Droitwich Spa. At last year's dinner we were privileged to have Gerald Lambert, grandson of Herbert Austin, and an honorary member of the Association, as one of our speakers. The Association's calendar revolves around this dinner, traditionally held at the beginning of December. We also arrange many other activities which range from industrial visits

Epilogue – many people thought the world of their Austins. None more so than Frank Buck of York whose marble gravestone, specially commissioned in Italy, bears permanent witness to the pride of his life – a 1957 Austin A95.

connected with the motor industry to visits of historical interest relating to Longbridge. The most remarkable of these was a recent trip to East Kirby in Lincolnshire to see NX611 – *Just Jane* – one of the few surviving Lancaster bombers built at Longbridge in East Works."

Herbert Austin's greatest legacy must surely be the many thousands of jobs and livelihoods that his 'single machine' has been providing for the best part of a century. The Austin name no longer appears on cars but 'The Austin' itself lives on, still providing (in July 2000) direct employment to almost 6,000 people and indirect employment to many, many more. Is it too fanciful to hope that the year 2005 could see Rover Group producing its own new supermini with an 'Austin 100' version to celebrate 100 years of 'The Austin'? To remind us that Herbert Austin's factory is still well appreciated by men of 'The Austin' perhaps it is fitting to repeat the words of Bill Manning:

"'The Austin' was my life. We haven't a lot now but Austin gave us everything we have."

What a shame we can't allow Sir Herbert Austin to have the final word in this almost century-spanning tale. But then again, perhaps we can.

"Humph!"

Appendix

Longbridge vehicle production figures, 1906–1999

Calendar of years 1906/07 to 1955/56 run from August to July.
From 1906 to 1917/18, 5,552 cars and 2,480 trucks were produced.
For total production year by year see later table.

Production from 1918/19 to 1927/28

	7HP	HVY 12HP	16HP	20HP	Trucks
1918–1928	75,422	58,232	871	16,980	846

For total production year by year see later table

	7HP	Big 7HP	8HP	10HP	LT.12/4	LT.12/6
28/29	26,500	–	–	–	–	–
29/30	22,042	–	–	–	–	–
30/31	25,666	–	–	–	–	6,943
31/32	19,205	–	–	3,160	–	7,310
32/33	19,985	–	–	17,697	6,309	3,318
33/34	20,224	–	–	22,858	7,730	2,540
34/35	28,655	–	–	27,314	8,547	1,399
35/36	22,084	–	–	26,078	12,194	1,381
36/37	26,678	300	–	35,311	15,495	–
37/38	11,371	12,575	–	22,756	11,580	–
38/39	4,168	7,349	17,447	28,109	12,801	–
39/40	–	–	24,230	11,290	1,924	–
40/41	–	–	5,064	11,645	62	–
41/42	–	–	707	3,749	–	–
42/43	–	–	34	5,922	–	–
43/44	–	–	–	6,886	–	–
44/45	–	–	–	4,796	–	–
45/46	–	–	15,169	19,508	–	–
46/47	–	–	31,619	28,247	–	–
47/48	–	–	9,315	7,766	–	–
Totals	226,578	20,224	103,585	283,092	76,642	22,891

	14HP	*15.9HP*	*HVY 12HP*	*16HP*	*18HP*	*20HP*
28/29	–	–	8,824	8,905	–	1,689
29/30	–	–	7,009	7,448	–	1,051
30/31	–	–	3,481	6,626	–	918
31/32	–	–	2,322	4,284	–	547
32/33	–	–	2,739	2,674	–	610
33/34	–	1,547	2,844	3,270	1,486	576
34/35	–	3,049	2,471	1,858	3,293	502
35/36	–	2,095	1,122	2,431	3,072	499
36/37	6,944	–	778	–	4,054	458
37/38	3,231	–	431	–	2,390	266
38/39	3,090	–	316	–	1,678	220
39/40	19	–	478	–	853	91
40/41	–	–	44	–	–	8
Totals	**13,284**	**6,691**	**32,859**	**37,496**	**16,826**	**7,435**

Post-war	*45/46*	*46/47*	*47/48*	*48/49*	**Total**	
12HP	1,816	5,914	968	–	**8,698**	
16HP	2,270	7,003	15,157	11,004	**35,434**	

	A40 Devon	*A40 Dorset*	*A40 Sports*	*A40 Countryman*	*A40 Van*	*A40 Pick-up*
45/46	–	–	–	–	–	–
46/47	–	–	–	–	–	–
47/48	22,817	8,033	–	–	1,920	–
48/49	61,275	7,736	–	2,007	7,945	4,787
49/50	81,046	170	–	4,792	7,774	8,267
50/51	79,383	–	552	6,104	6,144	11,580
51/52	29,437	–	2,610	3,221	7,520	13,351
52/53	–	–	849	3,061	9,052	5,959
53/54	–	–	–	2,933	14,650	5,675
54/55	–	–	–	2,914	11,454	6,959
55/56	–	–	–	1,466	11,369	4,698
56/57	–	–	–	89	414	542
Totals	**273,958**	**15,939**	**4,011**	**26,587**	**78,242**	**61,818**

	A70 Hampshire	*A70 Hampshire Countryman*	*A70 Pick-up*	*A70 Hereford*	*Hereford Countryman*	*A70 Coupé*
48/49	5,636	–	–	–	–	–
49/50	19,833	336	2,805	–	–	–
50/51	8,891	565	7,245	4,927	34	–
51/52	–	–	6,966	15,585	680	236
52/53	–	–	1,832	15,912	470	30
53/54	–	–	1,459	10,446	301	–
54/55	–	–	127	1,770	30	–
Totals	**34,360**	**901**	**20,434**	**48,640**	**1,515**	**266**

	A90 Atlantic	A40 Somerset	Somerset Coupé	A30
48/49	405	–	–	–
49/50	2,694	–	–	–
50/51	2,553	–	–	–
51/52	2,093	38,131	28	309
52/53	236	54,812	4,296	18,436
53/54	–	71,117	2,908	48,659
54/55	–	2,003	11	75,065
55/56	–	–	–	75,244
56/57	–	–	–	5,214
Totals	**7,981**	**166,063**	**7,243**	**222,927**

Note: working from the actual production registers a total of 223,264 A30s was identified.

	A40 Cambridge	A50 Cambridge	A90 Westminster	A95 Westminster	A105	Austin-Healey 100
52/53	–	–	–	–	–	94
53/54	6	–	–	–	–	4,424
54/55	10,938	49,779	8,353	–	–	5,348
55/56	17,469	56,664	16,161	–	841	4,748
56/57	1,869	8,424	1,018	9,751	2,319	5,541
57/58	384	–	–	13,280	2,545	1,512
58/59	–	–	–	5,034	1,065	–
Totals	**30,666**	**114,867**	**25,532**	**28,065**	**6,770**	**21,667**

	A35	A40 Farina	A55 Cambridge	A60 Cambridge	A99 Westminster	A110 Westminster
56/57	57,102	–	37,504	–	–	–
57/58	81,930	112	82,884	–	–	–
58/59	63,916	37,632	65,775	–	365	–
59/60	27,622	76,562	88,674	–	6,962	–
60/61	34,568	63,830	59,429	–	5,750	–
61/62	24,599	54,463	24,269	37,514	333	4,333
62/63	22,268	50,140	790	55,151	–	3,790
63/64	15,040	29,596	–	48,484	–	2,977
64/65	9,082	21,540	–	21,986	–	5,428
65/66	8,485	14,061	–	11,508	–	1,926
66/67	5,450	11,752	–	1,031	–	–
67/68	3,773	4,376	–	–	–	–
Totals	**353,835**	**364,064**	**359,325**	**175,674**	**13,410**	**18,454**

Note: from the actual production registers a total of 354,607 A35s was identified.
Note: see later table for further A55, A60 and A99 production at Cowley for 1958/68.

Other non-Austin production at Longbridge – 1953/68

	Nash Metro	*Wolseley 1500*	*Wolseley 1200*	*Riley 1.5*	*Morris 1200*	*Lancer*
53/54	9,448	–	–	–	–	–
54/55	9,480	–	–	–	–	–
55/56	6,094	–	–	–	–	–
56/57	16,133	1,955	320	–	–	–
57/58	18,731	21,730	–	2,981	5,424	6,108
58/59	17,854	14,148	–	9,420	144	420
59/60	21,878	13,903	–	8,185	–	–
60/61	4,759	16,696	–	5,952	–	–
61/62	–	12,845	–	4,421	–	–
62/63	–	10,135	–	3,884	–	–
63/64	–	8,115	–	2,834	–	–
64/65	–	3,837	–	1,741	–	–
65/66	–	30	–	–	–	–
Totals	**104,377**	**103,394**	**320**	**39,418**	**5,568**	**6,528**

Austin 25HP Sheerline saloon and chassis

46/47	**47/48**	**48/49**	**49/50**	**50/51**	**51/52**	**52/53**	**53/54**	**54/55**	**55/56**		
1	147	1,775	3,166	2,388	2,494	227	322	697	388		
								Total	**11,605**		

Austin 25HP Princess saloon, limo and chassis

56/57	**57/58**	**58/59**	**59/60**	**60/61**	**61/62**	**62/63**	**63/64**	**64/65**	**65/66**	**66/67**	**67/68**
241	335	246	432	495	353	192	307	296	308	189	121
									Total	**3,515**	

Between 1938 and 1963 779,084 trucks were built at Longbridge. Truck production then moved to Bathgate in Scotland.

The above figure includes 12,991 Austin Champs built 1952–55 and 6,418 Austin Gipsys built at Longbridge between 1958 and 1960.

A further 14,790 Austin Gipsys were built at the old Wolseley factory at Adderley Park between 1960 and 1968 making a total of 21,208 Gipsys in all.

The Austin FX3 Taxi and FL1 Hire Car were built at Longbridge 1948/58

48	**48/49**	**49/50**	**50/51**	**51/52**	**52/53**	**53/54**	**54/55**	**55/56**	**56/57**	**57/58**
22	745	1,681	2,191	1,473	335	1,285	2,134	1,118	1,426	1,347
									Total	**13,737**

The Austin FX4 Taxi and FL2 Hire Car were built at Longbridge 1958/1960

58/59	**59/60**
216	1,480
Total	**1,696**

FX4/FL2 Production moved to Adderley Park from 1960/61 to 1970/71.

60/61	**61/62**	**62/63**	**63/64**	**64/65**	**65/66**	**66/67**	**67/68**	**68/69**	**69/70**	**70/71**
1,365	738	1,309	1,282	1,530	1,423	1,158	1,943	1,468	2,272	1,591
									Total	**16,079**

Carbodies of Coventry, who had always produced the FX4/FL2 bodies, took over complete production in 1970/71.

Austin FX4/FL2 built by Carbodies

					15 months					
70/71	**71/72**	**72/73**	**73/74**	**74/75**	**75/76**	**1977**	**1978**	**1979**	**1980**	**1981**
1100	2833	2397	2312	2082	3122	2687	2422	2439	2007	2049

Total   25,450

Total Austin FX4/FL2 approx 43,225

Austin-badged or Austin-derived cars built at Cowley 1958/68

	A55 Cambridge	*A60 Cambridge*	*A99 Westminster*	*A110 Westminster*	*Princess 3-litre*	*Princess 4-litre R*
58/59	192	–	–	–	–	–
59/60	924	–	1,088	–	109	–
60/61	7,866	–	640	–	3,995	–
61/62	1,309	5,664	24	648	3,403	–
62/63	–	7,209	–	1,104	2,466	–
63/64	–	4,949	–	372	2,858	–
64/65	–	11,126	–	828	–	4,957
65/66	–	19,551	–	1,820	–	1,370
66/67	–	17,829	–	2,004	–	144
67/68	–	26,291	–	875	–	310
Totals	**10,291**	**92,619**	**1,752**	**7,651**	**12,831**	**6,781**

The Issigonis-designed FWD cars were built in a variety of locations with various badges. The annual Mini production figures were

Mini production, including Longbridge, Cowley, Seneffe and CKD.

1959	19,749	**1973**	295,186	**1987**	37,210
1960	116,677	**1974**	255,336	**1988**	36,554
1961	157,059	**1975**	200,293	**1989**	40,998
1962	216,087	**1976**	203,575	**1990**	46,045
1963	236,713	**1977**	212,323	**1991**	35,007
1964	244,359	**1978**	196,799	**1992**	26,195
1965	221,974	**1979**	165,502	**1993**	20,468
1966	213,694	**1980**	150,067	**1994**	20,417
1967	237,227	**1981**	69,986	**1995**	20,378
1968	246,066	**1982**	56,297	**1996**	15,638
1969	254,957	**1983**	49,986	**1997**	16,938
1970	278,950	**1984**	35,038	**1998**	14,311
1971	318,475	**1985**	34,974	**1999**	11,738
1972	306,937	**1986**	33,720		

Total   5,498,804

1100/1300 production figures include cars built at Longbridge, Cowley, Seneffe and CKD.
1800/2200 production figures include cars built at Longbridge, Cowley and CKD.
Austin-Healey Sprite production took place mainly at Abingdon, with a few at Cowley.
Sprite production is included in this table because the build years just about coincide!

	1100/1300	*1800/2200*	*AH Sprite*		*1100/1300*	*1800/2200*	*AH Sprite*
57/58	–	–	2,995	**66/67**	160,097	33,822	6,824
58/59	–	–	17,565	**67/68**	249,500	45,009	6,809
59/60	–	–	23,340	**68/69**	247,138	42,735	8,167
60/61	–	–	8,480	**69/70**	199,671	36,042	1,012
61/62	2,904	–	15,993	**70/71**	218,322	43,811	1,417
62/63	97,649	–	8,164	**71/72**	144,347	29,913	–
63/64	219,473	50	9,389	**72/73**	103,486	37,831	–
64/65	242,807	25,395	10,743	**73/74**	20,786	27,251	–
65/66	238,359	56,876	8,456	**74/75**	6,468	8,548	–
				Totals	2,151,007	387,283	129,354

Austin Maxi production took place at Cowley and Seneffe. Figures include CKD.
Marina/Ital production took place mainly at Cowley but the last Itals were built at Longbridge in 1982/84. Figures include CKD.
The 18-22 Series, Princess and Ambassador were built at Cowley. Figures include CKD.

	Maxi	*Marina*	*Ital*	*Allegro*	*Princess*	*Ambassador*
68/69	23,294	–	–	–	–	–
69/70	27,618	–	–	–	–	–
70/71	40,816	36,039	–	–	–	–
71/72	67,966	155,817	–	1	–	–
72/73	70,846	201,724	–	27,528	–	–
73/74	47,873	155,071	–	106,256	288	–
74/75	34,956	134,989	–	95,173	20,476	–
75/76	46,155	137,913	–	125,420	55,031	–
1977	32,479	111,636	–	95,460	47,955	–
1978	38,567	105,667	–	86,117	33,951	–
1979	27,490	96,487	–	61,415	37,128	–
1980	15,778	27,773	51,274	42,443	14,732	–
1981	12,435	–	54,970	22,908	15,381	1,254
1982	–	–	33,572	4,471	–	28,266
1983	–	–	26,753	–	–	13,905
1984	–	–	8,707	–	–	–
Totals	**486,273**	**1,163,116**	**175,276**	**667,192**	**224,942**	**43,425**

Austin Metro production took place at Longbridge, but the cars lost their Austin badge in 1987. In early 1990 it became the Rover Metro and in 1994 it became the Rover 100 which remained in production until late 1997.
Austin Maestro and Montego production took place at Cowley. Both these cars lost their Austin badges in 1987.

	Metro	Maestro	Montego		Metro	Maestro	Montego
1980	32,954	–	–	**1989**	138,751	59,938	76,560
1981	165,745	–	–	**1990**	109,605	38,762	50,728
1982	174,666	2,282	–	**1991**	81,422	18,450	23,892
1983	180,763	101,195	–	**1992**	79,600	10,226	12,881
1984	150,917	84,553	58,833	**1993**	79,677	7,178	15,292
1985	174,666	88,849	95,874	**1994**	76,821	4,043	14,542
1986	158,546	63,721	70,623	**1995**	81,782	–	–
1987	161,285	58,280	73,447	**1996**	46,118	–	–
1988	144,701	67,934	78,788	**1997**	40,199	–	–
				Totals	**2,078,218**	**605,411**	**571,460**

Yearly totals of vehicles produced at Longbridge 1906–1999

Year	Total	Cumulative	Year		Total	Cumulative
1906	23	23	1952/53		139,694	1,943,959
1906/7	147	170	1953/54		193,810	2,137,769
1907/8	254	424	1954/55		209,575	2,347,344
1908/9	402	826	1955/56		225,642	2,572,986
1909/10	576	1,402	1956/57		166,627	2,739,613
1910/11	664	2,006	1957/58		256,883	2,996,496
1911/12	886	2,952	1958/59		236,774	3,233,270
1912/13	963	3,915	1959/60		324,127	3,557,397
1913/14	866	4,781	1960/61		319,216	3,876,613
1914/15	874	5,655	1961/62		293,106	4,169,719
1915/16	868	6,523	1962/63		336,061	4,505,780
1916/17	835	7,358	1963/64		371,979	4,877,759
1917/18	674	8,032	1964/65		376,781	5,254,540
1918/19	557	8,589	1965/66		340,556	5,595,096
1919/20	4,303	12,892	1966/67		242,484	5,837,580
1920/21	1,837	14,729	1967/68	61 wks	348,664	6,186,244
1921/22	2,559	17,288	1968/69		305,214	6,491,458
1922/23	6,417	23,705	1969/70		280,439	6,771,897
1923/24	11,880	35,585	1970/71		307,669	7,079,566
1924/25	20,377	55,962	1971/72		277,579	7,357,145
1925/26	24,920	80,882	1972/73		253,540	7,610,685
1926/27	37,565	118,447	1973/74		234,194	7,844,879
1927/28	41,936	160,383	1974/75		197,469	8,042,348
1928/29	45,918	206,301	1975/76	66 wks	231,131	8,273,479
1929/30	37,550	243,851	1977		158,196	8,431,675
1930/31	43,634	287,485	1978		145,808	8,577,483
1931/32	36,828	324,313	1979		127,687	8,705,170
1932/33	53,332	377,645	1980		132,355	8,837,525
1933/34	63,075	440,720	1981		234,982	9,072,507
1934/35	77,088	517,808	1982		239,820	9,312,327
1935/36	70,956	588,764	1983		255,668	9,567,995
1936/37	90,018	678,782	1984		221,087	9,789,082
1937/38	64,600	743,382	1985		275,484	10,064,566
1938/39	77,094	820,476	1986		255,433	10,319,999
1939/40	47,341	867,817	1987		278,758	10,598,757
1940/41	29,586	897,403	1988		277,113	10,875,870
1941/42	20,658	918,061	1989		280,308	11,156,178
1942/43	23,378	941,439	1990		313,747	11,469,925
1943/44	24,571	966,010	1991		310,293	11,780,218
1944/45	20,277	986,287	1992		296,385	12,076,603
1945/46	51,965	1,038,252	1993		280,646	12,357,249
1946/47	86,388	1,124,640	1994		297,078	12,654,327
1947/48	85,400	1,210,040	1995		293,785	12,948,112
1948/49	126,685	1,336,725	1996		321,224	13,269,336
1949/50	157,628	1,494,353	1997		343,157	13,612,493
1950/51	162,079	1,656,432	1998		281,381	13,893,874
1951/52	147,833	1,804,265	1999		173,445	14,067,319

A total of over 14,000,000 vehicles was produced at Longbridge between 1906 and the commencement of 2000. In recent years, production at Longbridge has consisted of the Mini, Metro, Rover 200 and 400 models and the MGF. The Honda Ballade (1986–89) and Honda Concerto (1989–95) were also built at Longbridge until Honda switched production to its own new plant at Swindon. The year 2000 will see the production of the new Rover 25 and 45, the Mini and MGF. From Autumn 2000 the new Mini was to be built at Longbridge but the sale of Rover by BMW means that this car will be built at Cowley and Rover 75 production moved to Longbridge.

Bibliography

Clausager, Anders, *Complete Catalogue of Austin Cars since 1945*, Bay View Books, 1992

Daniels, Jeff, *British Leyland, The Truth about the Cars,* Osprey, 1980

Edwardes, Michael, *Back from the Brink,* Collins, 1983

Georgano, N., Baldwin, N., Clausager, A., and Wood, J. *Britain's Motor Industry, The First Hundred Years*, Haynes, 1995

Golding, Rob, *Mini – Thirty Five Years On*, Osprey, 1994

Lambert, Zoe, and Wyatt R. J., *Lord Austin the Man,* Sidgwick & Jackson, 1968

Robson, Graham, *The Cars of BMC*, Motor Racing Publications, 1987

Robson, Graham, *Metro, The Book of the Car*, Patrick Stephens, 1982

Robson, Graham, *The Rover Story,* Patrick Stephens, 1988

Sharratt, Barney, *Post-War Baby Austins, A30-A35-A40,* Osprey, 1988

Turner, Graham, *The Leyland Papers*, Eyre & Spottiswoode, 1971

Whyley, David, *Austin Pedal Cars,* Arthur Southern Ltd, 1999

Wyatt, R. J., *The Austin 1905–1952,* 2nd edition Routemaster Publishing, 1995

Wyatt, R. J., *The Austin Seven*, 4th edition Routmaster Publishing, 1994

Index